Down The Dig

Down The Dig

Monmouth – An Adventure in Archaeology

Stephen Clarke

With Artwork by Jane Bray and Geoff Webb

Monmouth Archaeological Society
2008

Down The Dig
Monmouth – An Adventure in Archaeology

Copyright © Stephen Clarke 2008

Designed, typeset, originated and published by Clarke Printing,
The Town Wall, Monmouth, Gwent, Wales NP25 3DN
Printed and bound by The Cromwell Press, Trowbridge

ISBN 978-0-9558242-1-0

For Keith and Sox
who revealed another world

CONTENTS

Preface

IT IS now more than half a century since Mr A.L. Sockett, MA (Oxon), classics master at Monmouth School, organised an archaeological excavation in the orchard garden of St James' House, just inside Monmouth's eastern town wall. Mr Sockett's volunteers were members of the Monmouth & District Field Club & Antiquarian Society and included several boys who had been inspired as ten-year-olds by another teacher, Keith Kissack, at Priory Street Boys' School. Both teachers are still with us – as President and Vice-President of Monmouth Archaeological Society – in their middle nineties – and thriving. Luckily for me, I was one of the boys.

The half century of our Society can really be divided into three 'ages': the halcyon days of the first thirty years were spent mostly in tranquil excavations of rural water mills with some rescue work in front of the new A40 and on the occasional building site. The second 'age' began in September 1986, when extensive redevelopments started in Monmouth and we discovered the remains of the Norman town burgages under Monnow Street. This was soon followed by struggles with developers and the District Council which eventually led to the society winning the highest Awards in British Archaeology. Finally, after the introduction of planning guidelines to protect archaeology in the 1990s the professional wings of our Society were formed. However, our independent research and rescue work continues into the 21st century.

+ + +

When the St James' House dig came to an end in 1956 we formed the *Monmouth and District Junior Archaeological Society*. Later we dropped the *'and District Junior'* (and rescinded the rule that no girls were allowed to join) and we became the Monmouth Archaeological Society.

Over the years the group has streamlined itself to become an efficient research and rescue organisation – unencumbered by an extensive committee and inflexible rules. With a constitution geared for rapid decisions, it has become one of the leaders amongst independent archaeological organisations.

Monmouth Archaeological Society has almost a hundred metres of archive shelving (National Museum standard metre), most of which was rescued from building sites during the decades of redevelopments prior to the introduction of planning guidelines to protect archaeology. The archive includes the only complete sequences (eight of them) from the Norman houses of Monnow Street up to the time of the Black Death, together with the only material from the Roman fort. This is an outstanding archive which cries out or publication. However, writing up the huge collection requires full-time uninterrupted work and needs to be backed up with a variety of specialist studies and technological reports. When, as volunteers, we were working to retrieve the remains on the building sites of Monnow Street we were told by the Board of Celtic Studies that it couldn't help us as we were doing the work of the professionals. But the professionals could not work on the sites which we undertook as there was no funding – it was up to the amateurs to do something or to stand by and watch the destruction.

The discoveries need to be written up by the rescuers but although Cadw has provided very large sums of money for professional work in the street, together with its publication, nothing can be done for the independents. The importance of the remains has been nationally recognised but the Lottery could not help either. The Robert Kiln Trust and the Monmouth Historical and Educational Trust have made extremely generous grants towards publication and we can never repay the debt we owe to Glamorgan Investments. There has always been an excellent response from local organisations and the public but this cannot pay for the time and the specialists needed for publication and the majority of our archive will remain as archive – a very unsatisfactory state of affairs. Hopefully this book will present some of our more interesting discoveries – and tell the story – and hint at what has been and is being lost.

With the introduction of the new planning guidelines our rescue work was greatly reduced as outside professional units began to appear on the scene. However, it was not long before we found that excavations and other work was taking place in the area of which we knew nothing. It was, and still is, rare for professional archaeologists from outside Monmouth to even let the 'amateurs' know that they are in town. Unfortunately archaeological response is cost driven and workers on the ground are often under pressure to get in and out of a site as fast as possible. Sometimes this has led to unfortunate results and is, in any case, not the best way to understand the archaeological resource or enjoy the discipline.

So we formed *Monmouth Archaeology*, the first professional wing of the Society (affectionately known by some planners as the 'paramilitary wing') and began tendering for archaeological contracts. There are now two wings – Felicity Taylor and Colin Harris having formed *Church Archaeological Services*. But this is mostly a story of the amateur so there is little professional work in the book.

The exotic archaeology of other lands may be exhilarating but there is something very special about digging in one's home town. After spending most of my life (so far) working in Monmouth with some gifted and delightful people, I hope that this book will go a little way towards telling their story. It is also offered as a tribute to everyone who has supported us over the years, many of whom have themselves joined our ancestors in the great beyond. The story of archaeology in Monmouth is a continuing adventure for there are now four generations of active amateur archaeologists in town and it looks as though there will be someone 'Down The Dig' for many years to come. *Llongyfarchiadau* Keith and Sox!

At this point I intended to acknowledge all of our diggers and those who have helped in many ways to produce this book. However, after several attempts I have resorted to a long list at the end of the book while mentioning just a few of those directly involved with the publication. I realise that this is totally inadequate and I apologise for it. Two people have been essential – my wife Hazel, who has lived with bones, potsherds and my eccentricities for forty years and Jane Bray, my fellow professional, who drew all the plans, sections and maps and without whose help the book would never have been started. I am deeply indebted to Charles Boase for the Index, for proof-reading the final version and for providing invaluable advice and encouragement. Earlier drafts were read by Paul Davies and Jane Bray. David Harrison took on the impossible task of organising me and the sales side for the Society. My son Rhodri sorted the technical problems while Clive Barrett, Sue Chivers, Philomena Goodall, Lynn Harper, Colin Harris, Reg Jackson, Anne Leaver, Ron Shoesmith, John Sorrell, Sox, Felicity Taylor, Martin Tuck, and of course Geoff Webb were directly involved in the production.

The Robert Kiln Trust and *Monmouth Historical & Educational Trust* have made very generous grants towards the cost of publication while *Glamorgan Investments* allowed us to dig at 22-24 Monnow Street for an incredible ten years.

The Town Wall, Monmouth, Wales   *May 2008*

Part One

DISCOVERY

Fighting over the Ruins

IN 1965 The Council for British Archaeology designated Monmouth as one of the top ten historic towns of Britain.

For more than a year the Council had been assessing the interest and importance of over 300 towns. Only ten of them (Chester, Colchester, Conway, Edinburgh, Leith, Lincoln, Monmouth, Norwich, Stamford and York) qualified for inclusion in the list of the top fifty towns under all seven points which the Council considered.

It was suggested to the Ministry of Housing and Local Government that the responsibility for the preservation of these towns should be taken out of the hands of the local authorities. The CBA considered that the Ministry should examine all planning and development proposals for the towns. Nothing of the sort was done.

Instead, much of Monmouth was destroyed during 'slum clearances', when terraces and period houses were replaced with concrete and glass buildings of the period. Part of the town's Chippenham medieval open field and village green was surfaced as a car park – the County Council later sold it to a Waitrose supermarket. Cinderhill Street, in the Roman and medieval suburb of Overmonnow, was demolished in readiness for a new Monnow Bridge which was not to arrive for 40 years.

But the Government itself caused the disaster from which Monmouth would never recover. We became the only Wye town in 2,000 years to be cut off from its river frontage. The Ministry of Transport drove the new A40 dual carriageway through the town. The reason for the new road not being routed across the river, as it was at Ross, is the stuff of legend in Monmouth but it produced the only and most deadly set of traffic lights between here and Carlisle.

Whatever the reason for the Ministry of Transport's decision, whole streets were destroyed: Granville Street, Wyebridge Street and Chippenhamgate Street, together with riverside houses and bargemen's cottages, the last 19th century warehouse, the ornate Wye Bridge Hotel and the tree lined promenade. Little was left of The Quay, which was internationally known on the 18th century Wye Tour, where Admiral Nelson had landed on his visit to the town in 1802 and where ocean-going boats had once been built and launched.

Shortly afterwards a new 'Town Plan' to relieve traffic was produced by the County Planning Officer, Jim Keggie. A 'spine road' was to cross Chippenham and then cut through four medieval streets, demolishing at least 17 houses on its way to meet the New Dixton Road at the traffic lights. The plan was passed by Monmouth Borough Council in 1969/1973 but was not implemented for financial reasons. However, most of Cinderhill Street was demolished in readiness.

The objectors to the route of the new A40 road through the town included Percy Harris, a local antiquarian, and Keith Kissack, local historian and teacher at Priory Street Junior Boys School – an eminent figure in the history of Monmouth.

Over a quarter of a century later, property developers were offering good prices for the run-down, family owned shops in the town, especially those on the main street. Then, one day in September 1986, Keith Kissack was present on a building site when the remains of a Norman burgage were discovered beneath the floors of 75 Monnow Street. Almost two metres of stratified house floors – some of the finest archaeology seen in a small town – were exposed in the new foundation trenches and it was suddenly obvious that the street was of national importance. It was also clear that the archaeology was in imminent danger – in as great a danger as the town's upstanding archaeology had been in the early 1960s.

Keith

Sox

This time, however, also on site was a new generation of archaeologists, inspired by the two Shropshire teachers – K.E. Kissack and A.L. Sockett.

Before long, buildings were being gutted or demolished and excavations for rebuilding were taking a heavy toll of the archaeological remains. The new breed of conservationists confronted developers and an unsympathetic Monmouth District Council and were soon nearly all that stood between the archaeology and its destruction.

One day, when the destruction in Monmouth was at its height and Kwik Save plc had just illegally demolished its listed building, things were going badly for the town. At an acrimonious meeting between Gareth Griffiths, the District Council's Chief Technical Officer, and our Society, Mr Griffiths made it clear that we would get no help, indeed no quarter, from the Council. As we left, Keith Kissack turned to me and said: 'Well, now we know where we stand with them!'

Discoveries in Monnow Street

THROUGHOUT the summer of 1986 we had been watching the building of the town's first supermarket – The Oldway complex, just off the main street. It had not been a rewarding watching brief for despite the large foundation trenches and other ground disturbances there was very little evidence of the medieval town. The deep alluvial silts between Monnow Street and the River Monnow that had served as gardens for centuries produced iron slag, medieval potsherds and a few pieces of cut stone.

By late August we were beginning to think that the medieval *'Great Road to Overmonnow'* had been little more than a causeway between the high ground of the castle and the suburb of Overmonnow – over the only surviving medieval fortified bridge in Britain. It had begun to look as if the wide and magnificent Monnow Street was a late development after all; the early town was thought to have been sited on the high ground around the Castle and Priory.

Then, following the demolition of shops, rebuilding began.

5th September 1986. The shops at numbers 75-77 Monnow Street had been demolished when excavations close to the rear of the buildings exposed thick layers of iron slag and 13th century pottery. With renewed attention, we recorded the discoveries and prepared ourselves for the digging on the street frontage.

My field notebook records:
Middle section at 2m below G level. Dark clayish with charcoal/bone/pot incl cooking pot rims and decorated MVW, Furnace levels above tie in with east section. Full day watching/recording/rescue work on [the rear of] 75 Monnow Street. Great help from Andrew Helme.

The next day (Friday 5th September) the JCB machine bucket scraped and grated as it ripped out the rear wall foundation of No 75. It then cut effortlessly and almost without sound into soft earth below the shop floors. The first bucket exposed a section of dark loam, light loam, slag, clay and silt layers, like a variegated cake.

The machine driver allowed us to jump into the trench for a quick examination. Pottery and bones could be seen sticking out of what we realised were the earth floors of medieval houses.

Grabbing some of the potsherds and bones, everyone left the trench. The next few buckets revealed that there were not just three feet of earth floors but, incredibly, almost six feet of them.

The destruction of 11th, 12th, 13th and 14th century houses at 75 Monnow Street, on 8th September 1986. The first builder's foundation trenches which were dug into the medieval house floors have been archaeologically cleaned and recorded over the weekend and now, on the Monday morning, the developers are back

My notes reflect the surprise and excitement:

Section (A)

Running from cellars in the N of section through medieval levels above the 13th C layer. The levels run across the site (working section drawn) and end at a building that may be early. The layers look like earth floors inside a building. There are clay layers, occupation-like dark loam and a layer of sand; these seem to be laid and between are thin layers heavy with charcoal but very finely layered with occasional lime etc that surely could only build up on a dry floor level. We have pot from these levels – all medieval.

On the Saturday Colin Brown and a team from the Glamorgan-Gwent Archaeological Trust arrived to help draw sections and on the Sunday I noted:

Sunday 7th. Whole weekend recording 75 Monnow Street. It has turned into an incredible site with medieval levels extending almost to the street level. The floor levels in section A extend, in part to the east. The floor levels seem to have built up very quickly with thumb impressed bases in an upper level and medieval style ridge tiles just below present ground (pavement) level. It may be that the levels represent short periods and may even be seasonal with silt bands representing floods. If this is the case there is one part midway where one might read – Following the summer just after the fires of autumn had been lit there was a major flood. This was followed by a winter with one or two smaller floods ending in a spring flood (the spring melt) greater than the previous one or two but not as big as the early winter one.

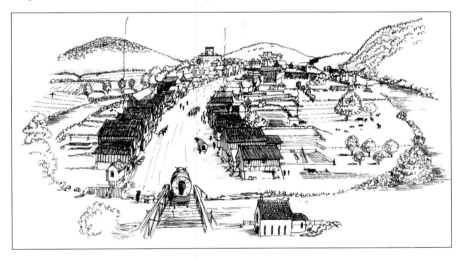

Geoff Webb's reconstruction of Monmouth from Overmonnow in 1100

So, Monmouth's late 11th century burgages of William FitzOsbern's town were revealed. The floors of other medieval houses in the area had always been remarkably clean and some were even hollow from constant sweeping. One was lucky to recover the odd potsherd from some of the house floors in the nearby medieval towns of Grosmont, Skenfrith or Trelech. But here, in Monnow Street, the layers were thick and rich in remains.

Monnow Street was built across an ancient flood plain and, although on a route that was old when the Romans arrived, the street plan which survives today dates from shortly after the Norman Conquest. The burgage settlement was laid out below the high ground chosen by the Normans for the site of their stone castle, for their Priory and for their large defended bailey.

To consolidate the invasion of the small Welsh commot or lordship of Archenfield (now southern Herefordshire), and in support of their designs further west, the Normans encouraged settlers to take up residence in Monmouth. These immigrants presumably came from France, Normandy and Brittany and probably also included 'tamed' English.

After the burgages were occupied and the first wooden houses had been constructed, the street suffered from occasional flooding. This originally seems to have been on a scale similar to that of recent times when the town was badly flooded only every quarter of a century or so. High water in the River Wye holds back the smaller River Monnow, which then floods this part of the town. The situation was exacerbated by the final meander of the Monnow which faced upstream until straightened by the 'Monnow Cutting Committee' in the 19th century. Flooding was as rare in the 20th century as it appears to have been in Norman times: three days of heavy rain are needed to bring the two rivers into flood together. It was, however, to become a more regular feature in the later Middle Ages.

The reaction of Monnow Street residents to the flooding, and to the damp floors that were not easily kept clean, was to raise the floor levels. This was sometimes done with imported soil or clay but also was often mixed with some of the domestic rubbish. The floor coverings of rushes, leaves and straw also slowly increased the levels, as did the silts that were left by the floods. The house floors of lower Monnow Street are usually undisturbed – they remain as unbroken layers, from the time that they were laid down.

Throughout history, people have been digging holes in the ground, bringing remains from previous ages to the surface. The bones, pottery or other artefacts, from earlier periods will become mixed with modern rubbish and is then known as 'residual.' In practice most finds unearthed during an excavation can be residual and therefore of less importance for various archaeological purposes than finds that date to the time of deposition. Layers are dated by the very latest finds.

Archaeologically rich, the medieval house floors of Monnow Street have proved to contain very little residual material. The vast majority of the remains in the layers were deposited, or just lost, when the floors were in use. This vastly increases their value to science.

An example of the importance of these house floors would be medieval pottery studies. Within the first six months of the discovery of the Monnow Street houses I had probably learnt more about the sequence, the dating and the origins of the region's medieval pottery than I had in thirty years.

Monnow Street, together with the medieval town green of Chippenham, lies on the alluvium of the flood plain which is composed of pebbles, sand and shale, beneath river silts. These layers are often awash with water – indeed some of Monmouth's flooding can come from underground. If a hole is dug in Monnow Street when the river is in flood and the water table is high, water will come up from below. During excavations under standing buildings at Nos 69-71, in the winter of 1988, the dig had to be evacuated on several occasions when water rose from below.

The 'archaeological record' (virtually everything on a site) of Monnow Street can be compared to a series of history books. There is a record of wooden house building technology from Norman times, followed by half-timbered structures and finally by buildings completely of stone.

Some of the first Norman houses were preserved with their hearths intact and scientifically dateable using changes in the earth's magnetic field. The dates obtained were supported by pottery and coins. We found oil lamps for lighting, including one from the top of a small posthole in the Norman house where it had been placed to keep its damaged base upright.

There was an abundance of bones, both from food refuse and as waste from cottage industries. There was occasional jewellery and some of the largest and earliest assemblages of medieval pottery to be found in Wales. There was evidence of crafts and industries including tanning, cloth working, spinning, bone working, as well as iron, non-ferrous and even precious metal working.

Some of the poignant finds were the gaming counters cut from potsherds, together with the bone dice found on one of the house floors. They were from games, probably played by the light of pottery oil lamps and tallowed rushes, during long winter nights.

The awesome thing is that these floors, like unique and irreplaceable documents, are a record of real, living people. They are also virtually the only record and they are extremely fragile.

My notebook, of September 19th, 1986:

Persuaded the builders to let us dig on the west of Section A. We have very little room – concrete blocks piled up on west and cellars on north and concrete foundations south and east To complicate things further, we have hit a wall on the west running N-S and post-med. (c.1700) on the east of our cut. Below the destruction layers, a layer of red clay on the south has ridge tile sherds (mortared).

Every available member was pulled onto the site, excavating, recording and sifting through spoil. Reg and Philomena Jackson came up from Bristol and found lodgings in the town while the local regulars worked through the evening under unsatisfactory conditions beneath the street lights. There was an air of excitement, tinged with desperation, that there was so little time to carry out a project which should have been properly planned and executed.

With the support of an experienced team led by Neil Maylan, sent from Swansea by our friend Gareth Dowdell, director of the Glamorgan-Gwent Archaeological Trust, we had managed to excavate a strip through the earth floors along the edge of a foundation trench. We had also comparatively crudely recorded parts of three burgage plots before the workers came back on the Monday to carry out more excavations and to fill the trenches with concrete.

On Sunday night, as our diggers drove away – too late for the pub – I felt a great sense of satisfaction that here, in the boot of my Mini, I had a small but probably complete sequence of the medieval history of the town.

These remains were the most important that we had ever seen and I stood under a yellow light in the gap left by the demolition of Derek Jones's Wallpaper Shop and looked up the gloomy street. After the previous frantic few days, it was strange to stop and consider. This was almost certainly just a sample of what lay under all of the buildings of the street and I wondered what we would do now that we knew that this was so. It was as if thirty years in archaeology had been a preparation for this discovery. In retrospect, it was when the second part of our adventure in archaeology really began.

Earth floors, with 14th century flood silts at the top of the section, at 83-85 Monnow Street

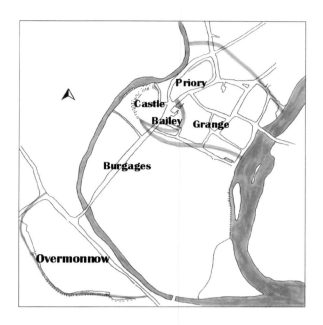

Norman Monmouth

'Cotswold Ware'

A late 11th/early 12th century cooking pot rim.
The edge has been ground to show the oolitic limestone
temper from the Vale of Gloucester
[body: 1cm thick

* Sue, Ted and Melanie Chivers, Chris Cooper, Gordon Clissold, Terry Dauncey, Ian and Stuart Donald, Tony Dunn, Joan Fleming-Yates, Audrey Tapper, Phil and Richie Grindle, Andrew Helme, Dave Jemmett, Keith Kissack, Jane, Dave and Robin Middleton, Brian Milford, Vic Powles, Dave Pritchard, Sox Sockett, Felicity Taylor, Kirstie Buckland (sorry to those I've failed to remember).

11

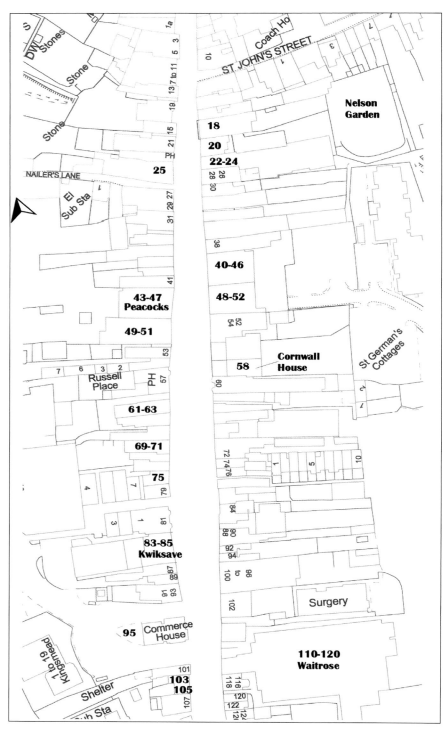

Monnow Street sites   © *Crown Copyright. All rights reserved. Licence number 10041477*

The great road west

A MAJOR overland trade and invasion route crosses the River Severn at Gloucester and the River Wye at Ross. It continues to Abergavenny, on to Brecon and Carmarthen and beyond – it is the modern A40.

Running north and west of the Wye, this route passes through the town centre of Monmouth, where it is almost surrounded by rivers and flood plains. Here, where the Monnow joins the Wye, the rising ground has attracted invaders and settlers for thousands of years. In the town, flint tools of the Stone Ages are fairly common and there is evidence of Bronze Age and Iron Age settlement alongside this ancient route in the town and at Overmonnow.

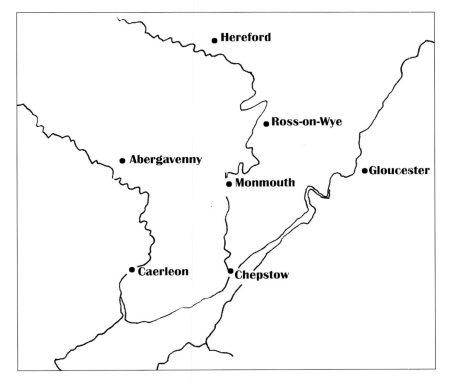

The Great Road West

'Geoffrey's Window', in Priory Street, on the site of the Benedictine Priory, looks out across the flood plain where the Battle of Monmouth was fought on St Catherine's Day in 1233. From here, with Monmouth castle rising on your left and in the distance the Graig and Garway hills standing sentinel over one of the auxiliary forts of the Monnow Valley, it becomes clear why the Welsh, the Romans, and the Normans settled on this spot.

In the middle of the first century AD, the Romans chose Monmouth as the site of one of their first forts for the invasion of Wales. They met fierce resistance and built at least one other fort overlooking the town from the west and a string of forts via the Monnow Valley into Mid Wales. The fort at Monmouth was also on the main route to the fortress at Usk and later that at Caerleon.

The Romans eventually prevailed and for several centuries Monmouth was the site of the industrial town called Blestium. A thousand years later, following an Early Medieval Welsh settlement, the Normans arrived and erected one of their earliest stone castles.

For much of the time before the Norman Conquest the border between England and Wales may have been reasonably peaceful, especially in Archenfield. Here the English and the Welsh may even have lived amicably side by side.

With the siting of the houses of the Norman town in Monnow Street, the immigrants brought new ways. Archaeologically, the most noticeable change was that the newcomers used pottery, a practice that we local Welsh, with our metal, leather and wooden vessels, were not to emulate with any enthusiasm for perhaps two centuries.

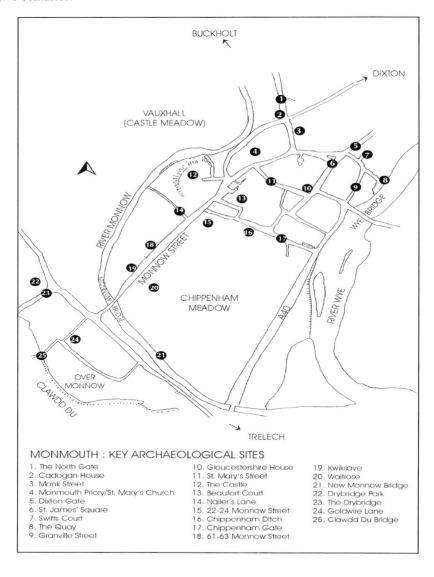

MONMOUTH : KEY ARCHAEOLOGICAL SITES

1. The North Gate
2. Cadogan House
3. Monk Street
4. Monmouth Priory/St. Mary's Church
5. Dixton Gate
6. St. James' Square
7. Swifts Court
8. The Quay
9. Granville Street
10. Gloucestershire House
11. St. Mary's Street
12. The Castle
13. Beaufort Court
14. Nailer's Lane
15. 22-24 Monnow Street
16. Chippenham Ditch
17. Chippenham Gate
18. 61-63 Monnow Street
19. Kwiksave
20. Waitrose
21. New Monnow Bridge
22. Drybridge Park
23. The Drybridge
24. Goldwire Lane
25. Clawdd Du Bridge

Flooding in
Medieval Monnow Street

Copied from a London pamphlet on the great Severn Levels flood of 1607 discussed by Joseph Bradney in his *History of Monmouthshire*, IV, 1932

WILLIAM CHESTER JORDAN, in his monumental work *The Great Famine*, writes:

> *To most observers the first major effect of the weather of 1315, 1316 and 1317 was the material devastation caused by the rains and the flooding that ensued : seedbeds sodden, crops and pastures under water, grain rotting, fish traps wrecked, dikes washed away, meadows too wet to be mown, turf too soggy to be cut, and quarries too swollen with the overflow to be worked for stone or lime . . . In many places . . . buildings, walls, and keeps were undermined.' Chroniclers record that 'the land ravaged by torrential downpours became waste and unworked and they speak of inundations as though it was THE Flood.* (Chester Jordan, 1996 p24).

BENEATH THE shop floor at 49 Monnow Street, the digging of re-development foundation trenches revealed a thick layer of silt, with the remains of a collapsed building. The house floor beneath the silts contained sherds of distinctively decorated early 14th century pottery – the same pottery that is found in the final layers of deserted villages and hamlets in the surrounding countryside.

We had found an almost identical layer at 75 Monnow Street in the autumn of 1986 when we first recognised the Norman houses and had immediately assumed that it was due to flooding. This idea was challenged by others but when more sites – fourteen to date – produced similar layers of clean silt, in the same position in the stratigraphy, it was clear that this was indeed the result of flooding. There was also the fact that the thick layers of silt near the top of the sections were always pre-dated by the same type of pottery – dated to the early 14th century.

However, there was a far easier way to convince the doubters. All floods leave sands and silts when the waters recede – sand bags do not stop water entering the

15

house, as the water goes through them – but the silting is greatly reduced. Stationary water inside the houses on the flood plain was ideal for settling out the finest silts that were held in suspension. The heavier grains had already been dropped when the river burst its banks and spread as a wide lake of slowly moving muddy water. The domination of the heavier grains close to the river and to a far lesser extent on the flood plain is increased as the finest silts tend to float away in suspension.

12th century earth floors with thin bands of flood silt at 69 Monnow Street

Silts which have settled from still muddy water inside standing or ruined buildings are easily distinguished from other flood silts by grain size while all the layers which we claimed as 14th century flood deposits were lying 'cleanly' over the floors and were never mixed with the layers below, although they had sometimes been disturbed from above.

Fourteen sites in Monnow Street have produced evidence of medieval floods, most of these occurred in the early 14th century, but some in the 12th century. The broken walls of a house on the west side of the river, near Monnow Bridge, were filled with flood silts, after the building had collapsed into the river. The silts contained large grains of sand and again were immediately pre-dated by Drybridge Park, Overmonnow, pottery – to the early 14th century *(Ominous Ceramics,* fol*).*

Sediment Analysis. We have sampled most of the sediments on the floors of the medieval houses on building sites in Monnow Street and subjected them to microscopic study. This, together with the nature and position of the sediments in the higher parts of the stratigraphy, shows that they had settled from still flood water in the early 14th century.

Dating comes from pottery in or below the silts and this is supported by archaeomagnetic dating where variations in the earth's magnetic field over time are recorded in the silts. The magnetic field in the silts aligns with magnetic north

– like a compass needle – and becomes fossilised so that the deviation can be measured and compared with that of today. The date of 1315-1345 at 60% confidence was obtained by the late Dr Tony Clark from silts at 22-24 Monnow Street.

The floods are often accompanied by evidence of the abandonment of the houses – broken roofing materials, shattered pottery and sometimes the remains of fires. It has yet to be established whether the thicker sediments had accumulated during an extended abandonment of the houses or if they were dropped in a shorter time. The former seems to be the more likely – especially as the abandonment took place at around the time of the Black Death (1348-51).

We have always believed that it was flooding which had caused the residents of medieval Monnow Street to raise their house floors, resulting in the remarkable stratification for which the street has become renowned.

There is a similar situation to that in Monmouth in the historic city of York where excavations by the York Archaeological Trust during the past thirty years have revealed nearly forty sites with evidence for flooding or past river management. The York Gazetteer contains details of all these sites and, where they exist, access to the original site records.

Andy Marvell, in his 2001 report on the Glamorgan-Gwent Archaeological Trust excavations in Monnow Street, has challenged the idea that the silts were deposited during flooding (Marvell, A.G., 2001, p123). However, his alternative suggestion that 'clean natural fills' were imported prior to rebuilding is untenable. It is untenable for several reasons, not least because the silts have retained their archaeomagnetism, but also because all the flood deposits outside the houses and on the river banks are of an entirely different nature to those inside the medieval houses.

Distinguishing flood silts. All flood deposits found on the banks of the Monmouth rivers contain coarse to medium sand while those on the medieval house floors are predominantly of silt. The larger of the sands can only be kept in suspension by fast moving water. So when the flood plains become inundated, the movement of the water slows and quickly leads to the loss of the larger grains to produce the defined levees close to the river banks.

By the time the flooding had reached the Monnow Street houses the water would have been slow moving and inside the houses it would have been almost stationary. Geoff Webb and I witnessed this in 1963 when we were landed on the Monnow Bridge by a boat from Drybridge House before catching the Army ferry service up Monnow Street to go to work. The road on the bridge was like an island surrounded by a silent sea of muddy brown water stretching away in all directions.

We have recorded flood deposits on fourteen sites in the street and samples are preserved from most of them. A list of the sites and the method of dating the flooding is given later, together with the results of microscopic examination of the samples – which shows that all were deposited from still water, inside buildings. Despite numerous samplings on river banks and on other open sites around Monmouth it has proved impossible to obtain sediments as fine as those lying in layers on the floors of the medieval houses of Monnow Street.

Flooding occurred throughout the Middle Ages and into modern times but was partially alleviated when the River Monnow was straightened at its confluence with the Wye in the 19th century and has so far been prevented from entering the

Monnow Street side of the river by the 1988 flood alleviation scheme. The earliest flood sediment sampled from the street is of late 11th or early 12th century date but this and later floods were minor affairs when compared with the 14th century ones. The earlier flood deposits, being of thinner layers, were far less likely to survive on the floors where there was unbroken domestic occupation.

There were probably many inundations of medieval Monnow Street of which there is no record. The mud left by the floods of the last 50 years was cleaned up when the water receded but in the Middle Ages they would have been trodden into the earth floors. Some medieval floods are recorded by silt filling hollows and odd corners of the house floors while others are capped with dark layers rich in charcoal which may have accumulated during the drying out of the houses. Over the years, floods would have contributed to the rising floor levels as well as being the inspiration for them.

22-24 Monnow Street flood silts (just below the centre of the section and sloping down into the hollow on the left) archaeomagnetically dated 1315-1345

It was during the 14th century that the thickest and the most impressive silt layers accumulated. These must represent prolonged flooding and probably the evacuation or even the abandonment of some houses. In modern times Monnow Street has always been flooded by the River Monnow when it has been held back by high water in the River Wye.

There are flood deposits dated to the late 11th/early 12th centuries; the early 12th century; the late 13th/early 14th centuries; the 14th century and the 16th century.

It is possible that the 13th century was relatively free of floods rather than that all the evidence has been destroyed. The 14th century silts which dominate the later archaeological record mark the beginning of the end of the rising floors. This has put them in danger of disturbance during modern times so it is perhaps surprising that so many of them have survived.

Most of the following sites contain undisturbed layers of silt with grain sizes measuring 0.02mm or less. The exceptions are at 95 Monnow Street (up to 0.2mm) which was away from the street frontage and probably inside an outhouse; 1-3 Monnow Bridge (0.5mm) which was on the river bank. At 75 Monnow Street – the first site – the silting was photographed during rescue work but no sample was taken.

22-24 Monnow Street	1315-1345 at 60% confidence
30 Monnow Street	–
35 Monnow Street	early 14th century
41 Monnow Street	–
43-47 Monnow Street	early 14th century
49 Monnow Street	early 14th century
61-63 Monnow Street	early 14th century
66-68 Monnow Street	early 14th century
69 Monnow Street	late 13th/early 14th century
	12th century
71 Monnow Street	early 12th century
	late 11th/early 12th century
75 Monnow Street	early 14th century
83-85 Monnow Street	early 14th century
95 Monnow Street	early 14th century
1-3 Monnow Bridge	early 14th century

The Samples

British Standards Metric Scale of Grades

Stones or Cobbles	>60 mm
Gravel	60–2.0 mm
Coarse Sand	2.0–0.6 mm
Medium Sand	0.6–0.2 mm
Fine Sand	0.2–0.06 mm
Coarse Silt	0.06–0.02 mm
Medium Silt	0.02–0.006 mm
Fine Silt	0.006–0.002 mm
Clay	<0.002 mm

Samples were wet sieved through standard sieves to examine larger grains and to estimate their percentage within the sample.

Control Samples:

Site	*Position*	*Grain size*
Dixton Church:	Top of river steps	many 0.5mm (some 1.0+)
	Five metres from steps	mostly 0.2mm (a few 0.5mm)
	10 metres from steps	mostly 0.2mm (a few 0.5mm)
	Inside Church porch	mostly 0.02mm (a few 0.2mm)

Monnow Bridge: Five steps up from the river:
Grains over 1.0mm not uncommon. Large percentage of 0.5mm
Less material 0.02 and below which has mostly been carried away.

Troy Meadow; Dixton Meadow; Vauxhall; Chippenham; Monmouth School playing field.
Grains over 1.0/2.0mm not uncommon. Large percentage of 0.5mm.
Less material 0.02 and below which must mostly have been carried downstream in suspension.

★ *Archive samples*

★   <u>1-3 Monnow Bridge</u>   14th century house, ruin found during evaluation.

         Grains over 1.0mm not uncommon; large percentage of 0.5mm
         Less material 0.02 and below.

<u>22-24 Monnow Street: Excavation</u>
         Dating by Archaeomagnetism, Ceramics and
         Position in column

★   Context 999   *Grain size:* mostly 0.02mm

★   Context 989   *Grain size:* coarse sand

         Date: 1315-1345 at 60% confidence level

<u>35 Monnow Street: Builders' Excavation</u>
         Dating by Ceramics/Position in column

★   Context 002   *Grain size:* mostly 0.02mm;

         Date: early 14th century   rare to 0.5mm

<u>43-47 Monnow Street: Builders' Excavation</u>
         Dating by Ceramics/Position in column

★   Context 002   *Grain size:* mostly 0.02mm;

         Date: early 14th century   rare to 0.2mm

<u>49 Monnow Street: Excavation</u>
         Dating by Ceramics/Position in column

★   Context 002   *Grain size:* mostly 0.02mm

         Date: early 14th century

<u>61-63 Monnow Street: Excavation</u>
         Dating by Ceramics/Position in column
         Context 415   No sample
         Date: 16th century
         Context 414   No sample
         Date: 14th/15th century

★   Context 418   *Grain size:* mostly 0.03mm

         Date: early 14th century

<u>66-68 Monnow Street: Builders' excavations</u>
         Dating by Ceramics/Position in column

★   Context B023   *Grain size:* mostly 0.02mm; rare 0.2mm

         Date: early 14th century

<u>69 Monnow Street: Excavation</u>
         Dating by Ceramics/Position in column

★   Context 224   *Grain size:* mostly 0.02mm; a few 0.5mm

         Date: late 13th/early 14th century

★   Context 226   *Grain size:* mostly 0.02mm; fine charcoal

         Date: late 13th/early 14th century
         Context 225   No sample
         Date: late 13th/early 14th century
         Context 236   No sample
         Date: late 13th/early 14th century
         Context 248   No sample
         Date: late 13th century

★   Context 262   *Grain size:* mostly 0.02mm

         Date: 12th century   Up to 0.2mm
         Context 264   No sample
         Date: early 13th century

Context 266   No sample
    Date: late 12th/early 13th century
Context 273/267   No sample
    Date: c.1200
Context 274   No sample
    Date: c.1200
Context 279   No sample
    Date: c.1200

71 Monnow Street: Excavation
Dating by Ceramics/Position in column
Context 115   No sample
    Date: 14th century
Context 138   No sample
    Date: late 13th/early 14th century

★   Context N170   *Grain size:* mostly 0.02mm; rare 0.2mm
    Date: early 12th century

★   Context 178   *Grain size:* mostly 0.03mm/0.02mm
    Date: late 11th/early 12th century

75 Monnow Street: Excavation
Dating by Ceramics/Position in column
Context 013   No sample
    Date: early 14th century

83-85 Monnow Street: Builders' excavations
Dating by Ceramics/Position in column

★   Context BT001   *Grain size:* mostly 0.02mm; rare 0.2mm
    Date: early 14th century

95 Monnow Street: Builders' excavations
Dating by Ceramics/Position in column

★   Context 002   *Grain size:* mostly 0.2mm or below
    Date: early 14th century
This site is to the rear of houses: Probably not still water: with fine charcoal/ calcareous fragments.

1-3 Monnow Bridge: Excavation
Undercut and collapsed house on river bank
Dating by Ceramics/Position in column

★   Context B023   *Grain size:* mostly 0.5mm; up to 1.0mm
    Date: early 14th century

Flood in Monnow Street in March 1947 (photo courtesy of Monmouth Museum)

The Earliest House

Despite the deep stratification and the early pottery found during the Society's rescue work in Monnow Street, we were the only ones convinced that the houses were Norman

A LTHOUGH most people were happy to accept that there was little evidence of a Saxon settlement in Monmouth, some were also reluctant to agree that the first houses in Monnow Street were a part of William FitzOsbern's late 11th century settlement.

An excavation at Nos 83-85 (Kwik Save) was to produce a sherd of Saxon pottery and to reveal a remarkable series of medieval floors, capped by a thick layer of silt, but inexplicably, no levels producing Norman pottery were found. The burgage was professionally sampled by the Glamorgan-Gwent Archaeological Trust team but then mostly destroyed during the redevelopment.

Dr Alan Vince had identified the late 11th and 12th century pottery discovered during the excavations on other sites and he found it exciting that the groups were so clearly separated and felt that there was a distinct possibility of identifying early Norman and other groups within the assemblages. What were needed were coins or an archaeomagnetic date from one of the early hearths.

Unfortunately, the rescue work which we had managed to carry out at Nos 75-77 and on other sites in Monnow Street, including that destroyed by the agents Bruton Knowles and developers Churn Valley Properties at 49-51, were without full medieval house plans.

Although it was obvious that we were dealing with early houses, we had no idea what the buildings looked like or much about their construction while some of our professional friends who were working in the street were critical of our dating of the lowest medieval floors.

On the 12th October 1987, we heard that there were proposals to demolish Nos 69-71 and a trial hole could be seen through the front window of the empty shop – the digging had exposed what looked like earth floors.

Fortunately, the back door was not locked and, with the assistance of a neighbour and the loan of his ladder, we scaled the garden wall and examined the excavation. The trial hole had cut through thin post-medieval earth floors and we found medieval and later pottery in the spoil.

By the 17th November, Gareth Dowdell (Glamorgan-Gwent Archaeological Trust director) had arranged a site meeting with the developers, Shop & Store Developments of Ilkley. The Trust was represented by Gareth and Paula Dixon and the developers by Mr McAlvey. Dave Jemmett and I represented Monmouth.

Diggers at 69 Monnow Street, posing in their new helmets

Society members were becoming quite aggressive after their encounter with Bruton Knowles but now things calmed down dramatically when it was agreed that the Society would be allowed to carry out excavations, first at No 69 and then at No 71. Although the dig would be at the Society's own expense the Trust would provide insurance cover and help with some equipment. Shop & Store were to bear the re-instatement costs and contribute to other expenses. This was the first excavation to be carried out under standing buildings and the first in the town where the public were allowed inside to view the work. It was an outstanding success.

Visitors were fascinated with the digging and threw money into a donations bucket; the developers were as delighted with the publicity as they were to be free of pickets.

However, the most important thing was that the excavations revealed a series of medieval houses. The earliest was a structure which had been built over plough soil containing scattered iron slag and abraded Roman pottery.

We employed the services of retired Senior Scientist to English Heritage, Tony Clark, who obtained the crucial archaeomagnetic date of 1070-1130 from one of the early hearths and this was supported by an 11th century coin and Monmouth's 'Phase One' pottery of the late 11th to early 12th century.

There would be no more questioning the early date of Monnow Street – the presence of Norman houses was confirmed and the importance of medieval Monmouth firmly established.

The plan of the earliest house at 69-71 shows that the building was based on deeply buried 'sleeper beams' – hewn timbers upon which the residents built their houses. There were other constructions: notably a small building based on posts and stakes which contained a small drain to an outside soak-away. The few finds in this first drain included a small silver finger ring – lost while washing up?

The Earliest House. The canes mark stakes for a wattle wall and there is a beam foundation slot on the left

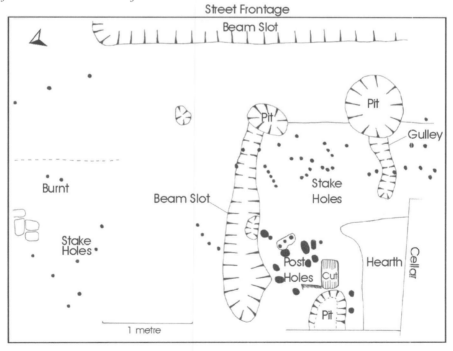

One hearth had a stone surround and, with its red-fired clay, seemed to glow under the floodlights.

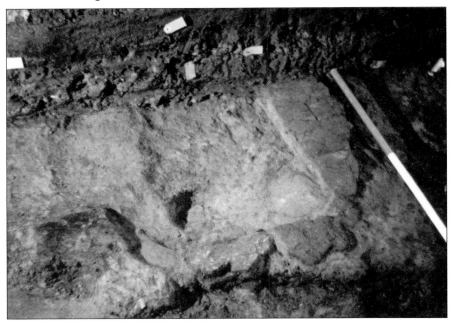

69 Monnow Street: 12th century fired clay hearth with stone surround

69 Monnow Street: 13th century pitched stone smithing surface

69-71 Monnow Street. Section through the earth floors of medieval houses

69-71 Monnow Street. Earth floors of medieval houses with stake holes

Nearby small patches and dribbles of distinctive dross was associated with sherds of thin-walled thumb crucibles of fine quartz-tempered clay. These crucibles were for precious metal working. They have been found at 22-24

Monnow Street and at The Gloucestershire House on the corner of St Mary's Street and St James' Street.

The successive small-scale industries on this site included that of smithing with a pitched stone working surface where documentary evidence gives us to believe the smiths worked on their knees. There was also a half-timbered building with evidence of its destruction by fire.

Members of the 'night shift' at 69-71 Monnow Street. Top: Tony Dunn and Dave Pritchard. Bottom: Terry Dauncey, Stuart Donald and Dave Pritchard

Then came the 14th century – with a stone house raised on iron forge dross between layers of clay – followed by an archaeological record of appalling times *(see the chapters on Prosperity and The Black Death)*.

Stone roof tiles, with sherds of the unique louver in the form of a horned devil lay on the ground – marking the end of the High Middle ages. The Monnow, backed up by the Wye, over-ran the street and the grand days of the rising floors of Monnow Street came to an end.

A little cellar or 'cool box' was cut into these remains in post-medieval times but did only slight damage. The 19th century occupation was marked by militia buttons left by the Monmouth Regiment which was billeted in the house and the 20th century by some of the frying and smoke extraction equipment of Mr Warren's fish and chip shop.

5 cms

Early 12th century turned limestone spindle whorls from Monnow Street

Prosperity

THE THIRTEENTH CENTURY – the 'High Middle Ages' – was for many a time of prosperity, when an increasing population produced large settlements such as the 'boom town' of Trelech and hamlets like that now reclaimed by the forest at English Newton overlooking Monmouth from the east.

In Monmouth, following the downfall of the Breton Lords who had ruled for two centuries, the House of Lancaster had taken over the Lordship. Under this new royal order, much of the town was rebuilt and this is evident in the archaeological record of Monnow Street.

A large part of the later town as well as modern Monmouth owes much of its character to this period of prosperity and change. Some of the early town ditches were abandoned or filled in, while new stone walls and gates were erected around parts of an expanded settlement. New buildings and roads were built over the old ditches and Monnow Street received its prestigious new fortified bridge over the River Monnow, replacing a 12th century timber bridge. Many of the town's wooden buildings were swept away and replaced with houses of stone.

Following a period of flooding, which left silts on the floors, the occupants of a half timbered building at 69-71 Monnow Street acted to improve their chances of staying dry. In a demonstration of their new prosperity, the house was demolished and the floor level raised with a thick layer of drossy slag from the iron forges, sandwiched between layers of clay. Two-wheeled handcarts left deep tracks in the clay as they were used to bring in tons of slag and dross from the local iron forges. The clay probably worked as a damp course for the substantial new house which was built. Amongst the finds from the iron forge dross was the copper-bronze pommel of a sword and the times were dated to the first half of the 14th century by sherds bearing applied clay decoration – from the Drybridge Park clamp kiln. While the 13th century demolition and re-building work was being carried out, the residents used two sets of pots to cook meals with heat produced by unslaked lime.

The stone tiled roof over this proud new building was capped with glistening green glazed ridge tiles with a unique louver in the form of a horned devil where smoke poured from a wide-open mouth. This louver seems to symbolise a flourishing age before the terrible events of the 14th century cast their shadow across Europe, bringing a revival of old superstitions and inspiring new ones which led to the witch mania and other horrors of the succeeding three centuries.

Next door to No 71, the neighbours may have shared a frivolous view of the underworld. Drink from one of the household's jugs was poured through a spout in the form of a demon which with a pair of human hands under its chin and a pair of multi-fingered hands over its ears, seems to be merrily singing its diabolical little head off.

The almost incredible prosperity of some residents in Monnow Street is shown by finds from another nearby site – Nos 61-63. Here the occupants of an impressive stone town house possessed beautiful vessels of coloured glass made in Italy, probably by Venetian craftsmen.

Medieval Venetian glass from the cesspit at 61-63 Monnow Street

Medieval glass of this type is extremely rare and this is the first record of it being found in Wales. Jewellers traded glass vessels and we are told that only royalty or the most affluent people in the land could afford such treasures. The house had a considerable amount of cut stone, a large fireplace and a stone cesspit which was situated inside the house, rather curiously right next to the well. On the roof, another Devil's Head louver fumed into the sky – but this one dwarfed that on the roof of No 71.

However, by 1316 the climate had changed and persistent rain began to fall throughout Western Europe.

The Black Death

A T the beginning of the fourteenth century the world was faced with one of the great tragedies of history. Crops failed during the relentless storms and famine spread across Europe. The suffering was so terrible that 'it would move a stone' a contemporary wrote and it was at this time that many of the houses in Monnow Street were abandoned. In 1348 the Black Death arrived in Monmouth. Of course, linking historical events with archaeological evidence is fraught with danger but the evidence of disaster from around the time of the Black Death is legion.

At Nos 61-63 Monnow Street, the lives of the prosperous residents turned to nightmare as floods swamped their prestigious new home. Some of the family's Venetian glass ended up in the cesspit, alongside finely crafted antler and bone combs as well as sherds of a bawdily decorated 14th century jug from Drybridge.

Across the road (now the frontage of Cornwall House) the owners had started work on their own scheme to build a house which would be less prone to flooding.

The street frontage at Cornwall House – the house that was never built – showing iron forge dross sandwiched between layers of clay, below later garden soils

Perhaps copying the residents of Nos 69-71, they cleared the site and put down a layer of clay and then wheeled in barrow loads of iron forge slag in readiness for a new house. But the new house was never built and the street frontage here has remained empty ever since. Centuries later, Cornwall House was built – away from the road and breaking the line of Monnow Street – like a memorial to the horrors at the time of the Black Death. The excavation here was carried out by the kind invitation of Jane Harvey and John Wheelock.

Cornwall House set behind its railings in the gap in Monnow Street – a memorial to flood and plague

At Nos 49-51 we found that deserted buildings had collapsed into the floodwaters and nearby, in the ruin of No 71, the devil's head louver lay shattered. Another, far larger devil's head louver also lay broken in the ruins at Nos 61-63 and flood silts built up inside other houses in the street where the layers had survived as unmistakable records. Time and again, we found that the sediments were pre-dated by the same 14th century pottery from the Drybridge kiln. At Nos 66-68, the same pottery mixed with flood silts beneath the fallen roof of a smith's forge.

To the rear of what were once the offices of the Monmouth bus station, a thick layer of flood silt sealed evidence of a fire which had baked the soils all around. Amongst the potsherds lying on the ground after the fire were parts of a unique 14th century jug, modelled as a woman in the fashion of the time and filled with silts *(The Lady in the Flood)*.

Higher up Monnow Street, at Nos 22-24, on the rising ground of the Norman town defences, further dramatic evidence of floods had survived. Here, above the Norman burgages, metalworkers in the 12th century had acquired the cleared area in front of the town's defences for a workshop. Throughout the Middle Ages this site may have been beyond the reach of the floods which had periodically affected the houses lower down the street, so it was a surprise to find clean silts covering the workshop floors.

There were even signs of a hasty evacuation during the flooding: when a piece of furniture with three legs, which was used in the workshop, had sunk into the ground during use and lumps of clay had stuck to the legs when they were pulled out of the flood. The lumps of clay, retaining the impressions of the furniture legs, had fallen into the silt and were then covered by further sediment. Flooding that came this high up the street must have been horrendous, for most people lived in lower Monnow Street and their houses would have been under deep water.

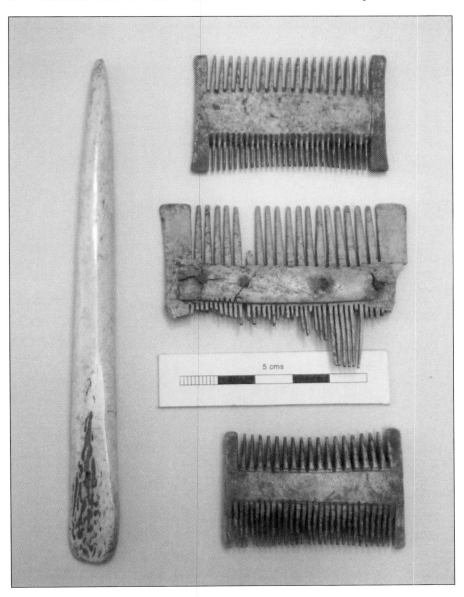

An antler tool and bone combs from medieval Monnow Street. The two perfect small combs came from the 14th century fill of the cess pit at Nos 61-63

Dr Clark used archaeomagnetism to show that the sediments had settled from floodwater at 22-24 Monnow Street and that this had happened between 1315 and 1345 *(Flooding in Medieval Monnow Street)*. A layer of coarser sand and silt which lay at the bottom of the sediments might be a record of some fast-moving water which hit the workshop in the early stages of the flooding. Although no similar deposits have been recognised on other medieval sites in the street, a torrent of floodwater was witnessed cascading out of the nearby Nailer's Lane into Monnow Street during the great flood of 1947.

An archaeological evaluation we carried out on the west bank of the river, close to Monnow Bridge, revealed a building which was pre-dated by the same Drybridge pottery as the other sites. The walls of this structure were broken on the riverside and the gaps were filled with clean flood silts.

The remains here, at Nos 1-3 Monnow Bridge, we interpreted as that of a building which had collapsed into the river after being undermined by the cutting edge of the Monnow. The shattered side of the structure was then exposed to the floods, but the silting was quite different from that on the floors of houses of similar date in Monnow Street – they are identical to those on the steps below Monnow Bridge which are often more than half a metre thick. Later, a new riverside wall was constructed.

In 1348, which was another appallingly wet year (we are told that it rained every day from Easter to Christmas), the Black Death devastated Europe and with its recurrences is estimated to have killed from a third to a half of the population. Grass was said to have been growing in the main streets of Bristol and brambles covered some of the Monmouth burgages. English Newton passed into history and, in common with other hamlets, the woods swallowed the remains. The town of Trelech entered its final decline towards becoming the pastures of the rural village that remains today.

It took some two hundred years for the population of Britain to return to thirteenth century levels but, before it did, the days of Monnow Street's rapidly rising house floors and outstanding medieval archaeological record had gone forever.

Direct Action

When the medieval sites at 61-63 Monnow Street came under threat, members took decisive action. We tendered for the building groundwork contract – and were the first amateurs in Britain to be awarded one.

The occupation of the site began with a wooden house on an early Norman burgage plot. This was succeeded by other houses, ending with a substantial stone building which was probably the home of a rich merchant. This fine house was abandoned amidst floods and famine in the disastrous fourteenth century.

D URING the total rebuilding of 61-63 Monnow Street in 1988 the building groundwork contract was awarded to Monmouth Archaeological Society. Much of the excavation work for the new foundations we carried out by hand and all machine excavations were directed by the Society. The excavations also included those for the underpinning of walls on both sides of the plot, from Monnow Street to close to the rear boundary.

A decade later, now as the professional unit *Monmouth Archaeology,* we carried out an archaeological evaluation on land to the rear of the plot in connection with an application to build a two-storey office building. Nos 61 and 63 comprised two medieval burgage plots, one of which (61) was the site of a Norman wooden house during Monmouth's earliest ceramic phase.

There was no house at 63 until after the middle of the 13th century – it seems to have been an alleyway between the burgages during the earlier history of the site. As discussed elsewhere, there are other examples of alleyways in the street which were later filled with houses. For example, further down the street, at 75, the continuous occupation of the site from Norman times up to the 14th century was not matched on the adjoining plot of 77. Here, all the early phases were missing and the empty plot was later used as a covered entrance into a supermarket and the Monmouth bus station.

The floors of the buildings at 61-63 have always, like those on other sites, kept to the original burgage and alleyway boundaries.

The 13th and 14th century occupation on the frontage of 61 culminated in a stone house which must have been the home of very wealthy residents where the fill of the cesspit reflected their affluence. The house was partly pre-dated by a wide, shallow ditch that seems to have run diagonally across the site. The pottery from the fill of the ditch is mostly of 13th century date and the house was probably built in the later part of that century or early in the following one – a date indicated by a jug sherd bearing applied clay decoration which was probably made in the kiln at Drybridge Park, Overmonnow.

More of this pottery was left on the site when the house was deserted and some of it found its way into the cesspit, supporting the date of the abandonment to the first half of the 14th century.

The ditch pre-dating the house may have been for drainage – a similar feature (but a more impressive one) was found to the rear of 83-85 Monnow Street by Neil Maylan's GGAT team and a bank set against the Chippenham Meadow was found by Dave Maynard and Dave Williams, also of GGAT, during excavations prior to the Waitrose supermarket development.

Keith Kissack has suggested that the burgage gardens on this side of Monnow Street probably extended to the riverside in the Middle Ages when there is mention of the occupants' 'river frontages'.

The Medieval Occupation

The Roman pottery which we found during the frontage excavations was all residual, so the earliest definite occupation levels found at 61 Monnow Street were the earth floors of wooden houses. They contained pottery of Monmouth's first ceramic phase – a small but securely stratified pottery assemblage on the 61 burgage plot. There was no phase one material from 63.

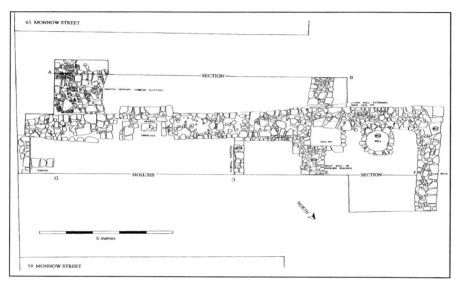

Medieval house at 61-63 Monnow Street, the cesspit (rectangular) and the well (circular) are close together on the right

Middle to late 12th century: Monmouth's first ceramic phase is thought to end before the middle of the 12th century and the second phase during the last quarter of the century. The second phase is quite well represented at 61 Monnow Street but is again absent from 63.

The late 12th to the very early 13th century (Monmouth ceramic phase 3) is again represented only at 61.

The 13th century. The thirteenth century was one of prosperity, and Monmouth did not miss out. Royalty was in residence in the town and there are remains above and below ground from the time of the House of Lancaster. There was rebuilding in stone in Monnow Street and flooding must have been the inspiration for a widespread effort to raise house floors above the occasional flood levels. Good examples are 69-71 and 61-63 where there was a similar concerted effort to raise ground levels with clay and iron forge dross (up to 25cm thick). At 63, this appears to have been carried out especially during the early 14th century, when flooding was at its worst.

Thirteenth century 61-63 Monnow Street (Geoff Webb)

The later 13th century (ceramic phase 4). Monmouth saw a revival of its fortunes in the later 13th century when the archaeological record is better preserved at No 63, where the occupation began around the middle of the century. It was some time after this that the stone house was built.

61-63 Monnow Street house floors   *14th century grindstone*

The 14th century: Flood silts were found at Nos 61-63, associated with sherds of jugs from the Drybridge kilns which included one of the distinctive 'split rod' handles found sticking up into the silt. This is the flood horizon so common in Monnow Street.

From the early 14th century, the archaeological record of Monnow Street becomes thinner and less informative and because there is less 'overburden' it is far more susceptible to damage during building developments. It is certain, however, that the cess pit, and probably the large stone house itself at No 61, were abandoned at this time. The finds from the cesspit include Drybridge pottery with iron enriched applied clay decoration, the two complete combs and the pieces of the first medieval Italian glass vessel yet found in Wales.

Vic Powles down the cess pit at No 61 Monnow Street

Europe was not to recover from the floods, famine and plague of the 14th century for some two hundred years and the disastrous century is recorded in the soils of Monnow Street.

The later medieval and post-medieval remains on the two plots are not outstanding, although one late medieval pit group contains a large sherd of a rare Saintonge ware handled vessel. In modern times, No 63 was again used as an access to the rear of the burgages, in a repeat of its earlier history.

To the rear of the burgages. As discussed, the reasons for the rising levels of lower Monnow Street are seen in the archaeological records of medieval flooding. The rivers and streams often leave impressive layers of silt after a single flood. During the construction of the Monmouth flood alleviation scheme in 1988 several inches of clean silt was left in the Watery Lane on two occasions in a single week and had to be cleared mechanically by the local authority. Flood silting along the Dixton Meadows has produced well-defined levees and near the Dixton roundabout. We found, during an evaluation in 1996, that some 1.20m of silt has been built up on the flood plain within historic times. The organic-rich humus stayed at the surface, moving upward with the plant life through worm action.

Winter floods regularly leave half a metre of silt on the steps and parapet below Monnow Bridge and slightly thinner deposits on steps near Wye Bridge – the Wye keeps moving but it holds back the Monnow. In 2002 at Dixton, in flat, open grassland, approaching 2cms of new silt was measured after high water and this increased towards the river. Along the riverbed and banks below Monnow Bridge over a metre of coarse sand, gravels and even large stones is regularly removed by the river authorities.

Throughout history, gardens or orchards covered the site – between the houses and the River Monnow. The plots were first depicted by John Speed in his Map of 1610 on the southern side of Monnow Street. Morrice's Map of Monmouth, published in Archdeacon Coxe's *Tour of Monmouthshire* in 1800, gives a similar picture of street frontage houses with gardens running behind the houses and backed by orchards.

Throughout the town, the picture provided by the map makers is of square garden plots two or more deep behind the houses with each plot covering several burgages. This is the same pattern as that shown by John Wood in his Map of Monmouth in 1835. It is unclear if these maps record the real medieval pattern or if it was simply a way of indicating garden boundaries. The plots have yet to be recognised archaeologically. However, it is noted that several large orchard areas to the rear of the square garden plots in several parts of the town, including the northern side of Monnow Street, are depicted as divided into squares thirty-five years after Morrice by John Wood in his Map of Monmouth.

By the 19th century, a large area of land between Monnow Street and the River Monnow had been developed as a tannery. This was an ancient local industry that continued into the 20th century and utilised both Monmouth rivers for transport. Later medieval/post-medieval tanning pits were found close to the street off Nailer's Lane and Paul S. Davies excavated others near the bus station in 2005. These latter ones were dated to the 17th century and had been filled with an impressive assemblage of 18th century ceramics.

Other medieval industries, crafts and occupations appear to have been confined to the frontages of the Street.

Nos 61-63 Monnow Street became the Monmouth bus depot in the 20th century until the new bus station was established lower down the street in the 1950s. Some of the upstanding remains and concrete slabs to the rear of the site were part of this depot and a large fuel tank was removed from the site during the redevelopment in 1987. Prior to the rebuilding, the frontage was used as a veterinary surgery.

The excavations for the underpinning of the boundary walls during the developments in 1988 were recorded by the Society as the groundwork contractor. These excavations, together with the removal of a large oil tank, show that the archaeological features diminish away from the street frontage. The well, cess pit and early disturbances cluster closely behind the burgage frontage inside the house. Although a variety of pits were found, most of these appear to have been dug after the Middle Ages.

Homogeneously brown coloured soils, up to 1.50m deep, were exposed during the excavations for the Oldway Development. It was the same to the rear of the burgages during most of the archaeological excavations that have been carried out on both sides of Monnow Street. Excavations for the Monmouth flood alleviation scheme revealed even deeper unchanging deposits close to the river. This suggests that there was continuous horticultural activity on the flood plain on slowly rising ground levels.

It is also apparent that most pottery and other domestic refuse which would have been incorporated into the garden soils as manure from the earliest times has not survived. This is consistent with the regular tilling of the land for it is known from fieldwork and excavations in the Monmouth area that most pottery and domestic refuse will break down and vanish from the ground where ploughing or gardening continues over a long period.

Therefore, the depth of the soils to the rear of Monnow Street must largely be due to flood silts that were deposited on garden surfaces. This may have been partly a deliberate collection and spreading of silt as manure on gardens by the occupants of the street. The value of flood silts as a manure or fertiliser is documented.

The Lady in the Flood

TO THE rear of the Monmouth's bus station offices at 95 Monnow Street, some ten feet of Roman and medieval remains were being unceremoniously ripped apart during a redevelopment. It was the 25th September 1987 and the digging was too fast and the trenches too deep for Monmouth's seething archaeologists to carry out any proper investigation. Because of the soft archaeological deposits, the trenches were around three metres deep but even so, natural subsoil was not confirmed, although the builders said that they had encountered alluvial shale at around that depth. It was established that the digging had cut clay-bonded stone structures together with bloomery iron furnace debris but the trenches were being filled with concrete soon after they were excavated for there was a constant danger of collapse. We collected Roman and medieval pottery from the spoil.

On the following day after digging had resumed our luck changed. The JCB was brought to a sudden stop by an encounter with two large fuel tanks and the top parts of one of the trenches were left open. Happily, it was then possible to get into the trench and, standing on a tank, to examine the stratification. We had no idea how long we would have to examine the site, so the exposed layers were immediately assigned numbers and the pottery and bones which were sticking out of the section were bagged. In the event, however, there was time to study and record the higher stratification, especially the layers of late flood silting.

On the removal of the two fuel tanks, the trenches were immediately concreted.

An impressive feature of the stratification was a thick layer of sand and silt lying over stone roof tiles and brown loam which itself sealed layers of burning. The position in the section suggested that this was the same fourteenth century flood deposit as we had found on other sites and the dating for this was to be supported in an unusual way – by a fashionable Monmouth lady.

A thick layer of silt was lying cleanly over a brown humus-like loam. The loam contained broken stone roof tile, 14th century pottery, charcoal, white wood ash, and burnt soil which in turn lay over sticky dark loam.

The Lady Jug. Amongst the broken pottery lying on the ground when the flooding began were parts of a highly decorated jug which was made in Drybridge Park; it contained flood silt. Other pieces of this jug were also found sticking out of the section – presumably, more was taken away on the skip.

The jug is in the form of a woman holding a small vessel which is probably an oil lamp. The figure is glazed a dark green colour and is decorated with iron free clay (white-firing) with a mixture of iron free and local iron rich clay (red or dark-firing) together with iron enriched clay where the potter had added iron in the form of hammer scale from a forge to produce a darker colour.

The flat-bottomed jug has scored vertical lines representing pleats in the woman's dress. The waist is drawn in with a studded belt which is bordered with a distinctive simple roulette. The belt is made of a mixture of iron free and local clay while the studs are formed from pellets of iron-enriched clay. A slashed strap handle is joined to the jug just below the belt.

The woman represented wears a large penannular brooch, modelled in the iron-free clay, with iron enriched clay pellets while the belt strap end hangs almost to the ground.

The Lady in the Flood: Hanging from the Lady's belt, from the left: possibly scissors; a key; a purse ('aumoniere'); the studded belt end

Three items are suspended from the belt: the first is uncertain but is probably a pair of scissors, the second is a key and the third is a purse or 'aumoniere' with three tassels, for carrying alms. All three items are in iron-free clay, the purse being of particular interest as an identical one is shown hanging from a woman's belt in the *Luttrell Psalter* which is dated to around 1343.

Penannular brooch   *Oil lamp*

Belt and jug handle   *Belt, waist and pleated dress*

The small vessel held in front of the figure is made of white-firing clay mixed with a small amount of local clay and has oxidised to an attractive orange colour with an occasional dark-grey core. The main body of the vessel, which is in local clay, is reduced to a blue-grey colour with a light brown interior skin. The external unglazed parts on the base of the jug and around the lower sides have a red-brown surface skin.

That this jug was made by the potter(s) working in Drybridge Park is shown by the style and materials used but also essentially by the rouletted borders around the woman's belt which have been produced by an identical wheel to that on pottery waste from the kiln site.

It was not possible to check if Norman remains had survived on the site but nothing from this period was recovered from the spoil. Late 11th/early 12th century material has mostly survived on the street frontages where they were 'protected' by later house floors, although Paul Davies has recently found Cotswold ware of this age in a garden immediately west of the bus station. The depth of the archaeological resource is unknown but seems likely to have approached 3 metres.

The very dark loam pre-dating the flooding is the same as that on other sites to the rear of other Monnow Street burgages and represents garden soils that have built up over centuries through cultivation and flooding. A single locally made cooking pot rim was the only definitely stratified find from the layer.

The burned sequence could have been divided into several thin contexts although they seem to represent the same event: an orange sandy layer of burnt soil, over a thin layer of white wood ash which in turn was covered by a band of charcoal and sealed by further burnt soil.

This sequence may represent bonfires rather than the destruction of a building. The brown loam which was sandwiched between the flood silt and the burnt layers is enigmatic but appeared to be humus. On site, it was felt that the layer might represent a grass grown soil with the roof tile fragments coming from the slow decay of a building to the rear of the burgage. There is considerable evidence for abandonment of houses in the street in the 14th century and the flood deposits which lie over the layer may therefore have built up over some time. It was the surface of the possible humus which produced the most interesting pottery while the jug in the form of a woman is one of the most significant relics of the period.

The Flooding. The heavy deposits of fine sands and silts on this site are similar to other thick layers inside medieval houses on the Monnow Street frontage. However, the sands and silts here are slightly different. Sand grains inside the houses almost never reach 0.5mm in size for grains of 0.02mm and below dominate them. Here at No 95, while grains of up to 0.5mm do occur, sand of 0.1mm to 0.2mm is more common although a large proportion of the context is composed of grains well below this size. The 95 Monnow Street silting is coarser than that inside the houses where in enclosed rooms only the fine silts will have remained to settle out of still, muddy water. The silting at No 95 must have come from slowly moving water for it to retain the slightly larger sands that it did. The site is comparatively close to the river and may have been inside a yard or out-building.

The site upper contexts:
(001) – Modern levels.
(002) – Flood deposit.
(003) – Brown loam.
(004) – Burnt layer.
(005) – Sticky black loam.
(006) – Very dark loam.

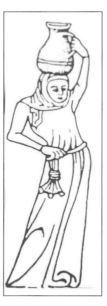

A woman with a pot and aumoniere –
the Luttrell Psalter of c.1343

Part Two

OUR TOWN

Ramparts, Walls and Ditches

After half a century of active archaeological research we realise there is still a vast amount to learn about the defences of Monmouth. Besides the ditches of at least one Roman fort and the possibility that the pre-Norman structure on the frontage at 22-24 Monnow Street was defensive, there are those of the Castle; the Castle bailey; an eastern ditch cutting off the peninsula of Monmouth and a western ditch closing the high ground from the west. There is a ditch running from the Castle 'moat' across Monnow Street and along the edge of Chippenham Meadow as well as a large and enigmatic ditch running down Monk Street. The suburb of Overmonnow is defended by the Clawdd Du. Then there are Monmouth's stone defences . . .

ARCHENFIELD was the small Celtic land originally called *Erging* which lay between the Rivers Monnow and Wye and was the first part of Wales to be over-run by the Normans following their defeat of the English at Hastings. A settlement, presumably Welsh, and the Church of St Cadog occupied the site which was to become Monmouth, at the very tip of Archenfield, it was here that William FitzOsbern, the new Lord of Hereford, and cousin of the Conqueror began the building of a castle shortly before his death in 1071.

His castle dominated the town from the highest point of the peninsula overlooking the flood plains of the two rivers. The ground on which the castle and Great Castle House stand today is suspiciously convenient in size and height and it seems probable that the Normans first threw up the mound as a motte for a timber castle.

A Motte? Service excavations in the roads and pavements around Priory Street and into Agincourt Square have over many years revealed that sterile red clay lies fairly close to the surface. This suggested that at some time the topsoil had been removed, possibly to raise a mound for the first Norman Castle – Castle Hill. However, in February 2006, we took over the County Council's excavations for a new pavement and a row of bollards in the Square. Watched over by the statue of Charles Rolls and amidst icy winds and snowstorms, the team showed that although scanty, much of the Roman, Norman and later levels were intact and had not been disturbed by the castle builders.

Assuming that any red clay in Monmouth is undisturbed natural and not re-deposited in historic times is fraught with danger. This was demonstrated during the 2002 rescue excavations at Monmouth Priory. Here, a humus of Roman date was found sealed by red clay which was overlain by another humus, this time thought to be Norman and this itself was sealed by red clay which had at first appeared to be the natural underlying the 12th century levels.

But, considering the extent of the red clay around Agincourt Square, it is almost certain that most of it is natural and this was definitely the case below the Market Hall and Museum, just off Agincourt Square, where building extension excavations in 2002 entered solid striated boulder clay just below the building's concrete floor.

The medieval ditches of Monmouth

So it is possible that Monmouth's Castle Hill is artificial, composed of scrapings from the river terrace below, probably supplemented with some of the archaeological record of Monmouth's Roman and Dark Age past. If the mound was fabricated, the red clay which we have recorded in the Castle Hill lane and on the castle parade ground must be re-deposited, although it did not seem to be.

An early motte would have been accompanied on the town side by a ditch and although no evidence of one has been found, a Castle Gate and Drawbridge is recorded. Between the Castle mound and the Market Hall (above Tibb's Bridge), the red clay lies close to the surface. Perhaps a moat was filled in when the hill was expanded as the base for the stone castle.

The Norman Bailey

During the Society's rescue work in Agincourt Square in 2006 it was found that, as elsewhere, the post-Roman humus covered the natural subsoil, although on this occasion there was also an assemblage of unabraded potsherds. Two 'sleeper beam' slots – the foundations for wooden buildings – had been cut into this old topsoil.

Keith Kissack has pointed out that the Norman bailey defences probably followed the drop in levels eastwards from St Stephen's Gate at the top of Monnow Street. This line is impressive inside The King's Head (Wetherspoon's) where one goes down the site of the rampart to the ground floor toilets. The ridge continues down Agincourt Street, swinging round to the Beaufort car park where it crosses the neck of the Glendower Street car park to the back of St Mary's Street to the castle (Keith Kissack, *The Lordship, Parish and Borough of Monmouth,* 1996).

This route fits most of the topography and is followed by property boundaries which are well shown on Wood's Map of 1835. The fall in levels fades before Church Street and there was no ditch in line with the White Swan Court beneath the Market Hall (noted during roadworks and building excavations inside the Market Hall). The building of Priory Street and the Market Hall in the 19th century would have affected this part of the bailey and probably removed any ground level trace of the defences.

However, the building opposite the Griffin Inn on the edge of St Mary's churchyard, seems to be sinking into a ditch but is it the bailey or the Priory ditch?

The Bailey Rampart. One of the most significant discoveries in this inner core of Monmouth was made early in 2002 during an archaeological evaluation in the grounds of the Beaufort Court, which overlooks the lower parts of the Glendower Street car park. Six trial areas were excavated and revealed remains dating from the Roman period up to the Second World War.

A truncated rampart was found inside and roughly in line with the wall retaining the old gardens (now Beaufort Mews) against the drop to the lower part of the car park, which was previously a small field. The rampart consisted of up-cast natural clay and alluvial shale with a lower make-up interspersed with spade sized stains of turf and topsoil cuts.

Undisturbed topsoil was preserved as a blue-black layer beneath the rampart and contained sherds of Roman pottery which were mostly small and abraded. The layer became thinner and lighter in colour beneath layers of silting against the tail of the rampart and then became fainter beyond this point. The preserved humus contained very little stone or iron slag and is seen as being the topsoil which was tilled until covered by the construction of the rampart.

A single unworn cooking pot rim sherd was securely sealed inside the rampart make-up and, proving difficult to classify, caused some excitement in that it might have been pre-Norman. However, the microscope of Alan Vince put the matter to rest when he found that it was Savernake ware of late 1st/early 2nd century date. Although there is no definitive dating for the rampart, it was constructed sometime between late Roman and Norman times. It seems most likely to be

Norman work and this is supported by it being centred on Castle Hill and by the absence of any medieval dating beneath it. However, the possibility of a Saxon settlement in the town, as suggested by Dr Paul Courtney, has not been disproved.

The reduction of the rampart seems to have taken place early – but the ditch – which has since been found in the garden of Agincourt House, was still open in the 13th century.

An east section of the rampart at the Beaufort Mews

The photograph shows the dark post-Roman 'plough soil' at the bottom which has been compressed on the right by the weight of the rampart. The truncated tail of the rampart is seen sloping down from the top right to the bottom left and contains straight edged 'fossilised' cuts of turf and clay. The left-hand side of the picture shows stratified silting lying over the tail of the rampart; this is thought to have built up rapidly during rainstorms when the rampart was being destroyed.

The only medieval pottery in any way associated with the destruction of the rampart were two sherds of hand-made cooking pottery, one of which was found just above the thick deposits of finely layered (?medieval) silt lying over the tail of the rampart. The other came from underneath the same silting in another trial trench. Rainwater would have washed silt from exposed soil as the rampart was being thrown back into the ditch – a silting process witnessed with the spring rains during the evaluation. Each storm deposited a new layer of silt over the earlier, drier one, then the whole sequence dried out and became fossilised, retaining its stratified surfaces.

If the Beaufort rampart were Norman work, the bailey to a motte, the ditch crossing Monnow Street (the Western Ditch) would have defended the larger area of higher ground above the flood plain. This might have been when the motte was enlarged to take the stone castle of FitzOsbern or of his son Roger, 'a revolting young man', who had managed to lose the earldom for the family by 1075.

If this rampart is a part of William FitzOsbern's original bailey and not a pre-Norman fortification, its abandonment could have been caused by the expansion of the town and the establishment of the Priory and the Grange inside a larger enclosure. It is therefore possible that both the Beaufort Mews rampart and the one crossing Monnow Street below Lloyds Bank (the early Western Ditch) could date to the late 11th century. The Monnow Street ditch was almost certainly sealed over on the frontage by the late 12th century although other parts were filled over a long period.

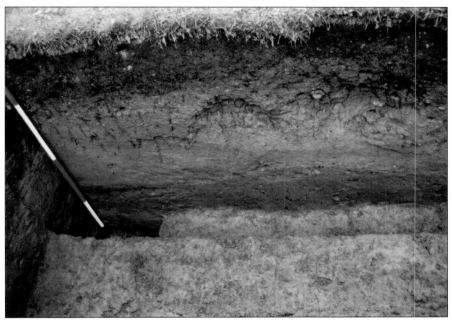

A west section of the rampart at the Beaufort Mews. The blue-black post-Roman 'plough soil' is seen lying over the natural, under the rampart

Whatever the date of the rampart, the humus that is preserved beneath it must represent the post-Roman to Norman periods. The context appears blue-black at its most intensive and is the same as the 'dark earth' or plough soil separating Roman and medieval levels in Monmouth and on the sites of many Roman towns.

With ample rich soils around the town, especially on the flood plains, it is strange to find the land inside the town used for agriculture. These areas may have been hard to work if there were urban or industrial remains surviving. However, the adjoining land now used as a public car park was pasture where sheep were grazed within the memory of the author.

The preserved topsoil contains occasional lumps of iron slag, some pebbles and the sherds of Roman pottery. The few bones and horn cores found in this layer were so rotted that they were hardly recoverable – an indication of their age. The decay of bones in the soils of Monmouth varies over time: medieval ones are often well preserved while Roman ones are rare or have left few traces. The condition of the animal remains in the 'dark earth' and the absence of medieval pottery suggest that the layer is at least as old as the late 11th century. This old 'topsoil' is noticeably 'clean', suggesting that there was an effective removal of stones while also supporting the idea that the buildings of Roman Monmouth were mostly wooden. Observation of local gardens and allotments suggest that such 'cleaning' of the topsoil took place over a long period. The tilling of the land inside the area enclosed by the Beaufort Mews rampart appears to have taken place after the construction and continued after the destruction of the rampart.

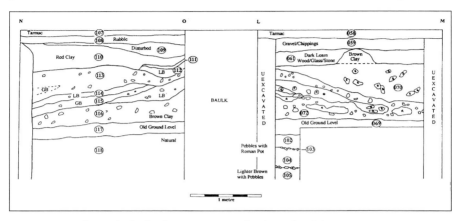

West section through the bailey rampart at the Beaufort Mews

An excavation on the southern side of the western end of the rampart was carried out in order to examine the rampart in more detail and to expose its southern slope towards the ditch. This revealed the fall to the south in both the west and the east sections of the cut. Although a baulk was left between the two sections, they give a fair idea of the rampart form and scale. Both East and West sections show tip lines and on the south the slope of the rampart towards the ditch. There is little evidence of activity in the rampart area during the High Middle Ages and the land outside may have remained pasture (or gardens) until the laying of the car park in the 1960s.

The Bailey Ditch

Keith Kissack has suggested Norman bailey defences followed the drop in levels south-eastwards from St Stephen's Gate at the top of Monnow Street. The ridge continues down Agincourt Street, swinging round to the Beaufort Mews to cross the neck of Glendower Street car park. The return to the castle is unclear.

Bailey Ditch, Site 1. In October 2004, the Society cut several trenches in the garden of Agincourt House, Agincourt Street. This was at the kind invitation of Neil Mounter of The Agincourt Group prior to the surfacing of the garden as a car park. Mr Mounter also provided the JCB machine for the excavation. The site is bounded by the Glendower Street car park on the east and is overlooked by the Beaufort car park on the north.

We entered the fill of the ditch at 2.58m below ground level which was lower here than in the Beaufort car park overlooking the site. Taking the excavation down to 3.35m, we recovered preserved wood, leather and plants, together with some later medieval pottery. The alignment of the ditch was unexpected for it was running sharply away from the Beaufort Court rampart towards the junction of Glendower Street and St John Street.

A machine-cut into the lower level of the bailey ditch at Agincourt House with preserved plants from the organic-rich deposits

Bailey Ditch, Site 2. In September 2003, we had found organic-rich soil and preserved wood in the spoil from a service trench outside the corner house at 13 Glendower Street at the junction with St John Street. The soil contained a high proportion of tiny charcoal fragments; fibrous fragments of rotted plants and bits of seed husks (not charred). The spoil was residual in that it had formed the fill of an earlier service trench which had been dug on the same site at some time in the past.

It now appeared that the ditch was heading further to the south-west than we had assumed and would need to have curved around into St John Street to cross Monnow Street at a point very close to where the eastern ditch would have crossed the street. However, the angle at the junction of Glendower Street and St John Street seemed rather sharp and it appeared possible that this ditch would have joined the eastern ditch before it reached the castle.

Bailey Ditch, Site 3 (?). An interesting complication arose during building works behind Wetherspoon's in February 2007. This site lies almost immediately below the scarp running inside the buildings against Agincourt Square and is where one would have assumed the bailey ditch to be if it were not for the alignment of the ditch established at Agincourt House. Red clay formed the upper fill of a presumed ditch and this covered a dark sticky loam containing lots of scattered charcoal and emitting the distinctive organic-rich smell of ditch fill. A few sherds of cooking pottery from this latter layer show that the backfill was medieval – possibly rampart material. It is hard to link this feature with the ditch in the garden of Agincourt House, even without the evidence from the service trench at the junction of Glendower Street and Agincourt Street. Also, the dating evidence, although conclusively medieval, is meagre, for the locally made cooking potsherds could date from the early 12th century to the 15th century. However, the pottery all appeared to be hand-made while the absence of glazed wares also probably indicates that the fill is not that late. It is worth recalling that the western ditch under Nos 18 and 22-24 Monnow Street was abandoned on the street frontage before the end of the 12th century.

The Eastern Ditch

This ditch was dug from close to the River Monnow, near the North Gate, southwards to the River Wye, near Granville Street; it enclosed the tip of the kingdom of Archenfield and closed the peninsula of Monmouth.

Who dug this ditch, or when, is unknown, but within the area covered lay the Roman, the Norman and the medieval towns. The spoil from the ditch, which was thrown up to form a rampart and, near Dixton Gate, sealed the same dark humus which separates the Roman from the medieval periods of occupation in Monmouth and is similar to that at the Beaufort Mews.

Whatever its origin, the ditch does not appear to have been cleaned out after the 12th century, and although its line was followed by the town's later stone defences, they are not always closely related. Both ditch and rampart were utilised during the Civil War.

This ditch has been exposed and examined during building developments on two occasions in modern times. It has also been entered once via a cellar by a house-owner living on top of it. The rampart has been partly explored during two rescue excavations.

Eastern Ditch, Site 1. Singleton House, 20 Monk Street, lies to the north of the traffic lights just beyond the site of the North Gate. This fine town house, on the west side of the road, is distinguished by its tilt to the north – into the ditch. There is also a dip in the road outside.

In 1982 Mr Souter, then owner of Singleton House, was digging a metre deep hole beneath the floor of his cellar when, 3 metres below ground level, he encountered a thin layer of black ash and charcoal. Beneath this was a 'clay-like' layer, about 4 metres below the street level, in which he found several medieval jug and cooking potsherds. He presented the finds to Monmouth Archaeological Society.

The largest sherd is of a Ham Green jug bearing an applied clay decoration which is almost identical to that on a well known 'Dancing Girls' jug found in Cardiff in the 19th century. The applied strip decoration is part of a leg and foot which has been impressed with a diamond shaped roulette.

Although the pottery group is small, it can be dated to between the middle of the 12th to the middle of the 13th century. With the revised dating of Ham Green ware; the accompanying A3 cooking pottery; the lack of local glazed wares and the size and unworn nature of the sherds recovered, it may be that the group was deposited in the 12th century – yet another indication that the ditch was not cleaned out after that time.

A Ham Green (Bristol) dancing girl's leg from the cellar of Singleton House and the complete example found in Cardiff in the 19th century (courtesy of Amgueddfa Genedlaethol Cymru National Museum of Wales)

Eastern Ditch, Site 2. In 1956 the first modern archaeological excavation in Monmouth was carried out in the orchard garden of St James' House, off St James' Square. Mr A.L. Sockett of the *Monmouth Field and Antiquarian Society* joined by the embryonic *(Junior) Archaeological Society* dug a section across the garden at right angles to the line of the town wall. This exposed an earth bank close to the wall which must have been a rampart of spoil from the digging of the ditch. The same bank was also revealed in 1982 when the wall replacing the town wall collapsed during a development at The Burgage, Dixton Gate. Here, the rampart had been cut back for the building of the town wall.

Eastern Ditch, Site 3. Ron Shoesmith sectioned the upper parts of the rampart, near the Old Dixton road, but was only able to examine 1.5m of the ditch fill below the level of the natural (Shoesmith, R., Excavations in Monmouth, 1973, *Monmouthshire Antiquary,* Vol. VI, 1990, 1-15).

He estimated that the approximate dimensions of the rampart were: total width – 12.0m; width at existing flat top: 6.5m; maximum existing height: 2.5m. There were traces of an eroded trench on the surface of the rampart. This, it was suggested, could have been associated with timberwork similar to that made of brushwood and thorn palings added to the rampart defence of Hereford in 1223 (Shoesmith, R., Excavations on and close to the defences, *Hereford City Excavations,* Vol. 2, CBA Research Report 46; London, 1982, 20.

Eastern Ditch, Site 4. It was also in 1982 that the remaining houses outside the town wall at Dixton Gate and The Burgage were demolished in preparation for a new housing scheme.

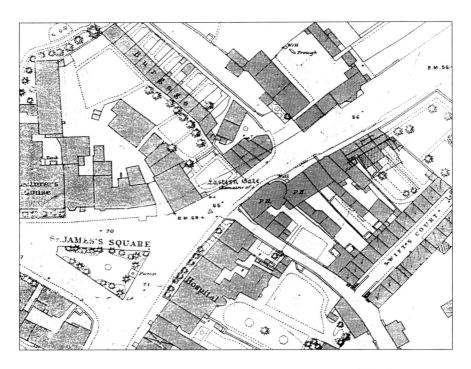

The Eastern Ditch and Town Wall centred on Dixton Gate (middle of map) on the 1880 Ordnance Survey. Excavations took place inside and outside the wall at The Burgage (north of the Gate) and at Swift's Court (lower right)

Foundation trenches, which were dug on the 2nd April (and concreted on the same day), entered the ditch at 8.4m out from the line of the town wall where natural was recorded at 1.7m below ground. At 9.3m out from the wall natural was at 2.1m and at 12m out it was over 4.0m below ground level.

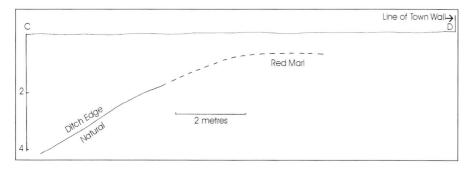

One of the three sections recorded during ground-works at The Burgage in 1982

On the 20th April, further excavations a little to the north, showed that natural, on the edge of the ditch (or the berm?) at 5m east of the wall, was only 0.50m below ground level. At 7.8m out natural was at 1.4m and at 12m out it was once again over 4m deep.

Later digging of foundation trenches (31.8.82), again further to the north, reached red clay at 0.60m to 0.70m below ground level at 5.0m out from the wall and this time an organic rich deposit, which included preserved plant remains, was overlying the red clay. This appears to be very shallow but as brown loam was recorded both above and below the organic layer there may have been disturbances here in the past.

On the 3rd September, despite flooding and collapsing trenches, it was possible to record a crude section across the site. Again, however, the true depth of the ditch was not ascertained. As the ditch at this point is closer to the wall, the two features are not in line, supporting other evidence that the two are not contemporary.

Eastern Ditch, Site 5. On the 24th August 1982, fifteen metres of the thin wall holding back the truncated rampart behind the line of the town wall collapsed. (*The Stone Defences*)

A dark layer of loam lay over the natural alluvial shale and is believed to have been the ancient topsoil; it contained Roman pottery. This humus was sealed by a layer of silt which may have been the result of flooding. The re-deposited soil and shale forming the bank must be up-cast from the digging of the ditch but as it lay directly over the Roman or post-Roman humus with no other dateable material, the origin of the ditch remains uncertain.

Eastern Ditch, Site 6. South of Dixton Gate the ditch continues towards the River Wye but its end is unknown, partially covered by the A40 dual carriageway which severs the town from the river. The ditch probably passed beneath or between two riverside warehouses and a slipway or loading bay on the edge of St George's Quay. However, no ditch was recognised during excavations for a sewerage installation there in 2003-04 although natural was not reached at over 4m.

Before the ditch reaches the new road, Swift House is the lone survivor of the south side of the 19th century cul-de-sac called 'Swift's Court'. This was a terrace of houses associated with Swift's Timber Yard on the east and which joined Granville Street on the west. The two sides of Swift's Court were built at right angles to the line of the town wall which is marked by a sharp drop down from Granville Street. Much of this terrace lay over the ditch.

The excavation of strip foundation trenches for an extension to Swift House was carried out during May 2002, and was covered by an archaeological watching brief planning condition which was undertaken by *Monmouth Archaeology*.

The groundwork extended from the rear of Swift House – some 10m from the Granville Street pavement – to 17m from the same frontage. There were also developer's trial excavations, 23m from the frontage, with a structural engineer, a geologist and archaeologists on the site.

Digging was carried out mostly by machine, as the soft infill of the ditch required very deep foundation trenches in order to reach firm ground. It was too dangerous to enter the trenches but the digging was closely monitored and, where possible, contexts were separated and recorded as they were brought to the surface. The spoil was examined as work proceeded and finds and soil samples were retrieved.

Behind the town wall at The Burgage after the collapse of its replacement in 1982

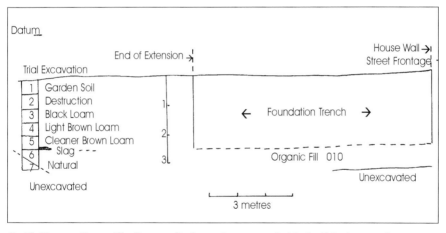

Swift House, Granville Street, ditch section recorded in builder's trench

It was estimated that the ditch was over 8.0m wide and at least 3.0m deep.

The stratification. Modern garden soil lay over the destruction debris from Swift's Court, which itself overlay a black loam at 1.0m below the ground surface. The loam changed to a brown colour at 1.40m and then to a cleaner dark brown. At around 2.0m a layer of bloomery iron slag sealed the primary fill of the ditch. The sloping edges of the ditch (cut into natural) was encountered at c.2.70m and dropped to about 3.0m on the west side of the excavation.

The finds from the upper levels show that a partly filled ditch was still discernible in the 18th century while there are documentary records of the re-use of the medieval defences in the Civil War and Leland records the ditch in the 16th century *(also discussed later)*.

Beneath the post-medieval and late medieval levels, a deposit of iron slag again sealed the primary fill lying over the natural which was sloping towards the west at around 2.30m below the modern ground level. In the trial excavation at 23m from the house frontage on to Granville Street, the primary fill was hand sorted on the surface and produced preserved timber, iron slag and a pottery assemblage.

Potsherds which were recovered from the primary fill of the ditch are mainly of hand-made cooking pots probably of 12th century date. There is no pottery definitely of Monmouth's 'phase one' period (late 11th to early 12th century) but much of the assemblage would fit the second and third phases which were established in Monnow Street and which are believed to date to some time between c.1125 and c.1175.

If the ditch is Norman, or earlier, it is likely that any very early pottery was removed during cleaning in the 12th century, after which time vegetation was allowed to accumulate. It seems that the ditch was not cleaned out after the 12th century and that the organic accumulation was sealed by the dumping of iron slag shortly afterwards. This dating confirms that the ditch is a lot older than the recorded construction of the stone town walls – perhaps two centuries older – at least.

It is perhaps surprising that the organic-rich fill of the ditch was not removed here, or from other ditches in the town, as manure was at a premium during the Middle Ages.

The Western Ditch

Contractors were constructing a new vault beneath Lloyds Bank, at 18 Monnow Street, when we saw them bringing out black bones, sticks and pieces of leather in spoil which they were dumping in a skip on the roadside.

Western Ditch, Site 1.   We asked if we could examine the excavation but found that the bank manager was reluctant to allow us to go down below his vault, which was perhaps reasonable. However, following further 'negotiations' we were allowed down into the excavations and recovered a well-preserved collection of bones, leather and other organic material, together with a group of potsherds. At the time of the discovery we thought that the deposit might be the fill of a cesspit.

The pottery was of 12th century date – mostly sherds of locally made cooking pots – but with three sherds of a tripod pitcher made near Malvern and decorated with a diamond rouletting. This ware is dateable to the second half of the century. There were 92 sherds of unglazed, externally sooted cooking pots in a local fabric, of which there were 11 rim sherds, representing at least eight pots. A single small sherd of an internally and externally glazed jug (A5 fabric) with a scratched wavy line decoration, also presumably from the ditch fill, is unexplained.

Western Ditch, Site 2.   It was on a miserably wet Saturday afternoon in December when Reg Jackson and John Perryman were digging in the second area of the excavation at 22-24 Monnow Street, under the eyes of a few bedraggled tourists. Great talkers those two, especially John, so it was a while before they realised that the rather long pit they were exploring was, in fact, the upper part of a ditch. The ditch was at least five metres wide and some 4 metres deep.

Weeks later, when the same smell as that from the Lloyds vault arose from the lower fill of the ditch it was realised that Lloyds Bank was sitting on top of the same feature. The strange thing was that this ditch was running at an angle across the site – in line with Lloyds – but breaking the alignments of the Roman, the pre-Norman and the Norman settlements. We felt that it should not have been there, or aligned that way.

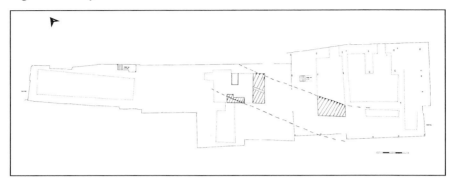

The Western ditch crossing 22-24 Monnow Street on its way to pass under Lloyds Bank. The street is on the left

The Western Ditch at 22-24 Monnow Street – Site 2

This was only one of the unexpected discoveries in our dealings with the Norman town and its defences. There were more to come.

The excavations at 22-24 Monnow Street revealed the complexity of the archaeology of the inner parts of the town and produced evidence of the Roman Invasion, the Roman town, a post-Roman structure, the Norman defences and other medieval and post-medieval remains.

The medieval ditch, crossing the site diagonally, is of special interest. It is coming from the direction of the 11th century Castle and is heading for the edge of Chippenham beside the Nelson Garden.

This is where part of a ditch which forms the boundary of Chippenham Meadow appears to join this early ditch, but this seems unlikely considering other discoveries discussed later.

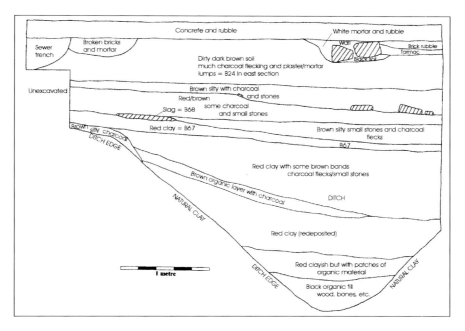

A section across the Western Ditch at 22-24 Monnow Street – Site 2

It appears that the ditch at 22-24 Monnow Street was abandoned, and possibly built over, on the street frontage in the 12th century. Why this defensive line should have been abandoned at such an early date is not clear but it is in keeping with the date of the neglect and silting of the ditch on the eastern side of the town. Away from the street frontage of 22-24, the ditch was back-filled gradually and it continued to accumulate rubbish and vegetation into the later 13th century.

Western Ditch, Site 3. During May and June of 1987, there were groundworks for the Hyam Court development at Burton Homes, beside the Police Station, off Glendower Street. On the 18th May excavations to a depth of approaching four metres below ground level entered a large ditch and revealed an 18th or 19th century brick kiln set into its side. On the 18th June, excavations to a depth of between four and five metres produced a 19th century fill with debris from the brick kiln and scraps of medieval and Roman pottery from the bottom of the ditch. On 23rd June, Bryan Walters retrieved a mortarium rim from the bottom of the ditch which he believed was about 20ft deep (c6.50m). He dated the pottery to AD50-60.

The discovery of a deep ditch at Burton Homes was something of a mystery at first. The fill produced sherds of medieval cooking pottery but if it was the medieval ditch, where it was coming from or going to was not clear. If the ditch at Hyam Court were running from near the Nelson Garden, it would have needed to cross the gardens to the rear of Glendower Street, ignoring the Chippenham boundary. This was a more likely route for the Western Ditch which crosses

Monnow Street under Lloyds Bank and which ignores all previous and later boundaries as it does. If it continues to follow a route just against the higher ground, it would pass beneath the Police Station over to the eastern side of Chippenhamgate Street. Our watching brief on engineers' trial holes behind the Police Station proved that it did not pass to the west of that building for undisturbed natural subsoil was close to the surface.

Western Ditch Site 4. A service trench at this point in Chippenhamgate Street, over the road from the Rugby Club, produced important evidence. The excavation exposed a layer of red clay which was at first thought to be natural until deeper digging revealed the now familiar organic-rich deposit found in ditches and ponds. Seeds of freshwater plants were identified by Julia Wilson amongst the remains as well as freshwater molluscs.

Western Ditch Site 5. The late Brian Evans examined the groundworks during renovations to houses belonging to Monmouth School on the east side of Chippenhamgate Street in April 1982. He found several antler tines, bones and Roman pottery in partly back-filled excavations between black soil and the natural red clay which slopes with the bank behind the houses. He noted that the antlers were sticking into both layers.

This is good evidence that this is the line of the early town defences – with a ditch dropping down from the castle, across Monnow Street and then following below the edge of the first natural terrace around to the river, passing the site of the Chippenham Gate. This would correspond with the eastern ditch from the Monnow to the Wye to enclose the higher ground.

The ditch must pass under the Glendower Street gardens from near the Nelson Garden to Hyam Court although this is only a short distance. However, there is a complication – the ditch running along the edge of Chippenham.

Below the Castle and along Chippenham

Despite a medieval reference to a castle ditch, society excavations in Dave Hancocks' orchard (in 1993) beside Monnow Mill showed that there was no moat. The orchard is situated beside the River Monnow, below the Castle. In 1994 an excavation in John Smith's garden, also off Nailer's Lane, revealed a flat bottomed, one metre deep 'pond' with freshwater snails and 13th century pottery. That this feature did not extend to the Monnow was confirmed during excavations for the Monmouth flood alleviation scheme (1988-90), when the contractors cut a trench across the lower slopes of the castle mound – inside the scheduled Ancient Monument!

The 'pond' did extend around much of the foot of the mound but excavations below the castle in Nailer's Lane have shown that there is no deep ditch in this area. Other Society excavations, continuing the search for a castle moat, revealed the stone tanks of a post-medieval tanning industry.

Mrs Bagnall-Oakeley's 1896 record of the "Town ditch recently covered up near the Priory Mill" may really have been referring to the mill leat (Bagnall-Oakeley, M.E., *'The Fortifications of Monmouth'* MCAA, 1896)

Despite this negative beginning, there are records of a ditch, crossed by a drawbridge, in Monnow Street, opposite Nailer's Lane. Parts of a ditch have been exposed on several occasions during trenching for services in the lane and the street and once during a rescue excavation.

On 23rd February 1984, developers opened the cellar at Gower's shop at 25 Monnow Street which is on the north side of Nailer's Lane. There was cut stonework in a doorway, an arch and a window light and there were old beams. The cellar was being filled with builders' rubble and was to be sealed beneath a new concrete floor so, late that night, sketch plans were drawn and measurements taken with the help of Andrew Helme, the curator of Monmouth Museum. A small rescue excavation was carried out beside the cellar on the 4th March with the help of the then owners, Mr and Mrs John Smith, in an undisturbed area between walls on the shop frontage. The dig revealed an iron-working hearth and further walling out of line with the street and the standing buildings.

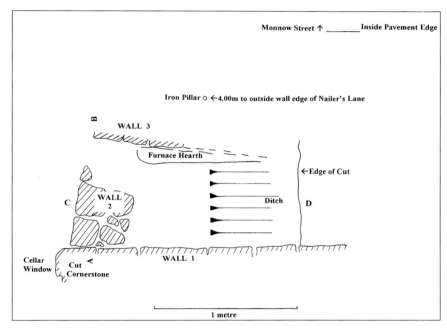

The edge of the Nailer's Lane to Chippenham ditch at 25 Monnow Street

Pre-dating these features was the edge of a ditch which was dropping down under Nailer's Lane with which it was aligned.

The iron working hearth with bloomery slag produced only a turned limestone spindle whorl, but was pre-dated by a layer (A3) containing 13th century pottery. This sealed the light brown loam of the upper fill of the ditch, which had been cut into natural red clay. A wall (Wall 2) had been built over the iron-working debris and another wall (Wall 3) had cut the hearth and the layers beneath it.

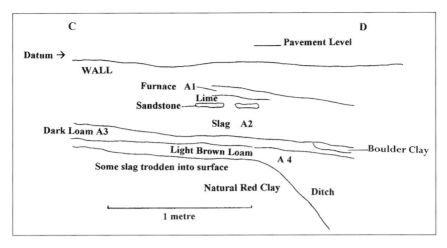

The section through the edge of the Nailer's Lane to Chippenham ditch
at 25 Monnow Street

The Nailer's Lane to Chippenham ditch in a Monnow Street service trench

The ditch was only dated by the 13th century layer above its fill but unlike the ditch along the edge of Chippenham, it seems unlikely to have been open into post-medieval times.

Considering the stratification at Gower's shop, the ditch there does not appear to have any relationship to the gate with a drawbridge at Nailer's Lane which was in use during the Civil War (Kissack, 1996, *ibid* 51). Mrs Bagnall-Oakeley wrote that 'the recent discovery of the old wall further down Monnow Street explains this gate.' (Bagnall-Oakeley, 1896).

During the autumn of 1997, service trenches were dug across Monnow Street from the entrance to Nailer's Lane, under the scrutiny of Monmouth archaeologists. The first half of the trench (at 4.50m from the southern shop-fronts) did not reach natural at 1.0m below 0.30m of iron slag. The trench on the northern side of the street was far more informative (7th Sept. 1997).

Beneath 0.50m of road levels, 0.13m of compressed red silt (in two lenses), sealed around 0.20m of bloomery iron slag. Beneath the iron slag there was a deposit of black organic rich 'ditch fill', which extended to 1.30m below the road surface and lay over what was thought to be a natural fawn coloured clay. All the lower contexts were considered to have been naturally deposited and were sloping towards Nailer's Lane (to the north-west).

The covering layers over the organic material were level while the organic layer itself was thicker to the Nailer's Lane side. It contained much bone with some iron slag. There were signs of a slow accumulation of small bones, gritty wood and fragments of leather.

The alignment of the shallow Nailer's Lane ditch with the deeper one along the edge of Chippenham is obvious and offers a straight link between the Monnow and the Wye. Perhaps this ditch was part of a long-lived medieval drainage scheme which would also keep animals grazing on Chippenham from raiding the Glendower Street gardens. This might explain why the ditch was open in recent times without drawing comment from historians or a note from cartographers.

The Nailer's Lane ditch across Monnow Street would seem to have been of little use as a defence, so the reference to a gate and drawbridge is strange. A bridge would be required over a wide, metre deep drain but a gate and drawbridge seems pointless. The Bagnall-Oakeley reference (1896) to the discovery of an old wall, lower down the street, seems to support the story of a stone gate which might not have been encountered during the 1997 service trenching as it was on the up side of the ditch. The absence of any remains of a bridge associated with the ditch also supports the idea of a drawbridge but John Speed's Map of 1610 records neither gate nor bridge.

The Chippenham Boundary ditch

A large ditch marks the eastern boundary of the Chippenham medieval field against the Glendower Street gardens. The ditch, like the Early Western Ditch, is also heading for the River Wye and its route is indicated by the gardens shown on 19th century maps as continuing in a straight line as they do today (partly obliterated by the A40).

The shallow ditch which crosses Monnow Street from Nailer's Lane and the Castle 'moat or pond' is probably a part of this feature.

Chippenham Ditch, Site 1. Monmouth Archaeology carried out an archaeological evaluation on the edge of Chippenham, to the rear of 3 Glendower Street, in December 1996. We followed this with a watching brief during the construction of three garages on the site in the spring of 1999. The edge of a ditch ran along the side of the meadow and a post-medieval brick kiln had been fired on its edge or in a hollow left in its back-fill. This was supporting other evidence that the ditch was open into early modern times.

The ground here had been raised in the past, probably to level the sloping garden and to give better views of the Monmouth Races which were held on Chippenham. In the garden, away from the ditch edge, late pottery and clay tobacco pipe stems were found at 1.50m below the surface and it was at 1.40m below this level that the first burnt clay, associated with under-fired and decayed brick, was found. The excavations only clipped the edge of the ditch, which was mainly marked by the brick clamp kiln remains, and did not enter the lower fill. Some twenty years earlier, Dr and Mrs Old had built a garage on the edge of the adjoining plot to the north, next to the Nelson Garden. Mrs Old took a series of colour photographs which show a bank of light brown coloured clay sloping towards the boundary with Chippenham. The layer was covered by a thick overburden of garden soils.

Chippenham Ditch, Site 2. It may have been the edge of the Chippenham Ditch which was exposed in two places during the building of Chippenham Court. This was in the north-east corner of Chippenham Meadow – almost opposite Dr and Mrs Old's garden. Although the lower parts of the trenches were flooded, 17th century pottery was recovered from the fill of this ditch, which, in common with sites further south, was open into the 18th or 19th centuries.

This site appears to join the Early Western Ditch to the Chippenham Boundary ditch; it is also in line with Nailer's Lane.

Chippenham Ditch, Site 3. Engineers working to the rear of the Police Station dug three trial holes (2.2.1994). The hole on the west, against the Chippenham boundary, reached the same organic deposits as the other sites along the boundary. This part of the ditch was open into the 19th century.

Chippenham Ditch, Site 4. Councillor and Mrs Tim Buckland, who live at Chippenhamgate, say that the 'Town Ditch' is mentioned in their deeds as being the boundary of their property against Chippenham. This is thought to have been in the middle of the 19th century. During excavations in the garden here 18th century and later material was found at a depth of 3m in the familiar sticky black organic deposit.

Legend. There is a remote possibility that in Chippenhamgate Street we are dealing with an inlet from the Wye, giving access for water-borne goods to Monmouth through the Chippenham Gate. There is a legend, possibly originating with the local historian Percy Harris, that there was a navigable route from the Wye to the Monnow, passing along the edge of Chippenham to Nailer's Lane and a castle moat – a route since proved not navigable, at least from Monnow Street to the castle 'moat'.

An inlet from the river at Chippenhamgate would have provided a more sheltered landing place than the Quay above the Wye Bridge where there may also have been problems getting boat masts under the bridge. If such a 'harbour' had existed, it may have been the reason for the siting of the Chippenham Gate as much as an access to and for the control of Chippenham Meadow. In 2006 a hole, some two metres deep appeared in the ground at the junction of the playground/ Chippenham and the A40; unfortunately, the council filled the hole before we were aware of its existence.

As we know that the Early Western Ditch from the castle was abandoned close to Monnow Street in the 12th century, there would have been ample time for it to be superseded at Chippenhamgate by a small landing stage and later by houses in the 18th and 19th centuries. However, the story may be destined to remain a rather charming myth, possibly scotched by the discovery of natural red clay at 0.70m below the road outside 5 Chippenhamgate Street (5.11.97). However, this would not rule out such a harbour at the A40 end of the Chippenham boundary.

Speed's Map of 1610 gives no indication of a ditch along the edge of Chippenham or any sign of quays or an inlet from the river. A break in the line of houses, of 'Wy Brid ward', where the Gate should be, is all that is shown.

Morrice's Map of 1800 does show a wavy line extending from Chippenhamgate Street to the river with 'Quay' marked beside it, but it is unlikely that the houses of the street, which are continuous on the east, might have been on a water-front.

Wood's Map of 1835 shows a two-sided feature joining the street to the river but now with a more continuous block of buildings on its west side.

It is interesting that none of the maps shows a ditch boundary to Chippenham although there is overwhelming evidence that one was open into the 19th century.

The Stone Defences

Keith Kissack discusses Monmouth's town walls in his expanded work on medieval Monmouth (*The Lordship, Parish and Borough of Monmouth*; Lapridge, 1996) which followed his *Medieval Monmouth*, 1974). Here we are but adding archaeological observations. Mr Kissack noted that the town defences were built mainly between 1250 and 1350 reflecting Monmouth's importance as a Lancastrian stronghold in the March. The King issued murage grants – authorising tolls on various imported goods – to Monmouth in 1297 and 1315. The money raised enabled the townsfolk to start work on defences in stone although it is not known if the project was ever properly finished.

John Leland records in the first half of the 16th century that the town was 'enclosed by a wall on that part which is not defended by rivers'. However, 'through age, the wall is broken and much of the defence is down. Nevertheless extensive ruins remain along with a deep ditch'.

With its two rivers, Monmouth had three fortified stone bridges: two over the Monnow and one over the Wye while there were two other medieval bridges both crossing the Clawdd Du ditch at Overmonnow. The town also had five stone gates and at least the one stretch of town wall on the east – the part not defended by rivers.

Although an earlier Wye Bridge is intact beneath its 19th century widening, the sole surviving fortified bridge in Monmouth (and Britain) is that joining the town to the suburb of Overmonnow. The Castle Bridge has left few traces while that over the Clawdd Du ditch, on the road west, survives as a scheduled Ancient Monument.

The Castle Gate. This gate stood between the Castle and the inner bailey and had its own ditch, crossed by a drawbridge, but once again there is no sign of it on the ground; in any case such a ditch may not have extended far on either side of the drawbridge.

John Speed (1610) shows the town wall coming down from the west side of the castle to the top of Monnow Street (St Stephen's Gate). This is a similar line but much higher up the hill to that of the Early Western Ditch crossing the street under Lloyds Bank, although this ditch was abandoned at least a century before the construction of the town walls.

The destruction of the town walls has been so nearly total that one cannot be certain that all the stretches were completed in the first place. The wall from the North Gate to Dixton Gate and on to the river was finished, as confirmed by Leland, and is marked mostly by a change in levels and the southern tower of the gate.

The site of the wall (and the town ditch) is marked by house boundaries from New Dixton Road to Monk Street while the foundations of the North, or Monk's gate, are still encountered and broken up in the road by service trenches, as they have been for over a century (Bagnall-Oakeley, 1896). The Gate was demolished in 1710 (Kissack, 1996). A drop in levels along garden boundaries impressively preserves the line of the wall from Singleton House towards the River Monnow but the only small portion of the line of the town wall which survives as a wall above ground is just to the south of Dixton Gate.

Dixton Gate   *The Town Wall just south of the Gate*

As mentioned, part of the thin wall holding back the truncated rampart behind the line of the town wall collapsed during the development of The Burgage in 1982. The wall had no real foundations and was composed of a mixture of various re-builds, including the walls and brick chimneys of 19th century cottages

Sue Parkinson examines the old humus below a structure behind the line of the town wall at The Burgage after the collapse of the town wall replacement in 1982

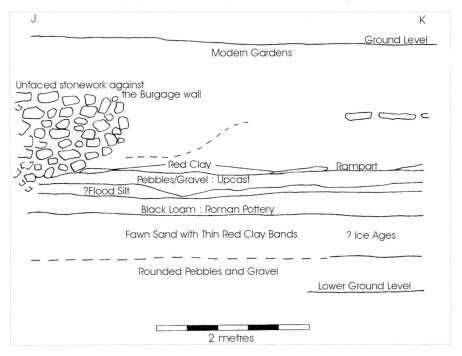

J K

Ground Level

Modern Gardens

Unfaced stonework against
the Burgage wall

Red Clay — Rampart

Pebbles/Gravel : Upcast

?Flood Silt

Black Loam : Roman Pottery

Fawn Sand with Thin Red Clay Bands ? Ice Ages

Rounded Pebbles and Gravel

Lower Ground Level

2 metres

built against it. The resulting section showed that a bank of clay, sand and pebbles had been thrown up from the ditch and lay over old humus which was clearly preserved in the section. The humus, which retained its dark colour, was some 0.25m thick and contained numerous sherds of Roman pottery. It had been covered (and sealed) with a layer which we described at the time as silt. The layer we saw to be the result of flooding from the River Wye and was similar to some of the alluvial deposits beneath the humus. If this silting was the result of flooding, it must have been quickly followed by the construction of the rampart as flood silts are soon absorbed into humus through vegetation growth and the action of earthworms. It may be that post-Roman flooding reached this level as the road near Dixton Gate was often flooded until the underpass gates were put in place.

The re-deposited shale, sand and gravels forming the bank must be up-cast from the digging of the ditch, but as it lay directly over the Roman or post-Roman humus, with no other dateable material, the origin of the ditch remains uncertain. *(East Ditch, Site 5)*.

The upper parts of the rampart were spread back from the defences when the wall was constructed at the turn of the 13th century. This is recorded in the gardens at the Town Wall off St James' Square where the tail spread seals pottery of the period.

Also in 1982, the remaining cottages at Dixton Gate and The Burgage were demolished in preparation for new houses. The re-development included the site of the northern tower of the gate and The Burgage terrace which ran northwards, partly over the town ditch where the houses had their backs to the replacement wall *(The Eastern Ditch)*.

The foundations of Dixton Gate extended 1.40m below ground level – unlike the wall behind The Burgage which seems to have had no footings.

The 'Town Wall' beside The Burgage appeared to be a thin replacement of the original medieval wall which was brought down in the quest for iron slag in the 18th century. In 1728, cinder mining reached 'the Town Wall on the Town Ditch' which was promptly pulled down so that the cinders in its foundations could be extracted (Kissack, *Monmouth, The Making of a County Town,* Phillimore, 1975, p291).

The drop in levels is very noticeable to the south of Dixton Gate and for some way north of the gate and The Burgage although here building developments have obscured the original landscape. The land outside the ditch, to the east of The Burgage to the New Dixton Road, has produced scattered Roman and medieval pottery which must have been spread during manuring Dixton Field with material from the town.

Wye Bridge Gate was, according to Speed's Map, built over the river like the Monnow Gate, but no trace has survived. Excavations in Wyebridge Street (destroyed for the A40) failed to trace walling or other defences between the Bridge and the rear boundaries of St James' Street (Clarke, *et al* and Shoesmith, R.)

Chippenham Gate does not seem to have been a part of the bailey defences but was probably more of a tollgate into Chippenham (Kissack, 1996). No structural remains of this Gate have been recognised.

St Stephen's Gate overlooked the steps at the top of Monnow Street and seems to have been on the boundary of the inner bailey. From the middle 17th century, it was known as 'the Burnt Gate', possibly because of the Civil War, and was later used as the town gaol (Kissack, 1996).

Monnow Gate has survived into the second millennium, despite double-decker buses and official attention. The stone bridge succeeded a 12th century wooden one, the foundations of which were exposed during the implementation of the flood prevention scheme.

Overmonnow

The medieval suburb of Overmonnow was protected by a wide ditch and rampart running from the Monnow to the Monnow (the Clawdd Du – the 'Black Dyke') with the Norman church of St Thomas near the middle of the enclosure. A medieval stone bridge crossed the ditch opposite Monnow Bridge carrying the road west, the predecessor of the modern A40.

On the north side of the Clawdd Du, a similar bridge to that over the centre of the ditch joined the road to the towns of Skenfrith and Grosmont to the north. The footings of this bridge lie beneath the roundabout at the junction of Drybridge Street and the Wonastow Road. They were recognised and recorded by the Society during roadworks in June 1999. Sealed beneath a layer of iron slag with an iron-panned surface a silted up abutment of the bridge was associated with 13th century pottery.

The suburb enclosed by the Clawdd Du has been occupied since pre-historic times and was an industrial centre during Roman times; this, and the important medieval industrial remains that have been recorded here, are discussed in the chapter, *Vulcans over the Monnow.*

Most of the Clawdd Du has been built over, including parts of the scheduled area, but in 1966 we cut a section across the bank before the building of the private Clawdd Du housing estate. We found the rampart to be of two phases, probably both of the 12th century, and was constructed over humus containing only Roman pottery.

Ted and Sue Chivers with Vic Powles investigate the 12th century timber bridge below the late-13th century one

Two foundation posts of the 12th century timber bridge

The Clawdd Du ditch and medieval bridge

Summary

Research into Norman and medieval Monmouth over the last half century has served to show just how complex the subject is. Some of the discoveries have been illuminating, supporting established ideas, while others have been surprising or contradictory and confusing. Hopefully the traditional inquisitiveness of Monmouth archaeologists will continue and will help to illuminate the origins and history of the town. Research in Monmouth should also help in the understanding and setting of research priorities for other nearby towns, as it has already done for Trelech, Grosmont, Abergavenny and Hay-on-Wye.

When William FitzOsbern arrived in Monmouth in 1067, he would probably have constructed an earthen motte, topped with a wooden castle together with a defended bailey. Material for raising the motte would have come especially from the scarping of the bank above the River Monnow. The rampart surrounding the bailey centred on what is now Agincourt Square was composed of spoil from the ditch running below it. This defence presumably crossed Church Street from the Castle on its route around Beaufort Mews and the upper parts of the Glendower Street car park. From here, the ditch seems to curve around the bottom of Agincourt Street to run along St John Street while another line appears to follow the rising ground around the edge of Agincourt Square along the scarp through The King's Head to the top of Monnow Street and on to the Castle.

Two major ditches enclosing higher ground between the east gate and Monnow Street are undated but may have coincided with the building of the stone castle on an expanded motte.

This would have left the early Norman burgages along Monnow Street open to Welsh assault from the west – across the fordable River Monnow. Perhaps, however, the shadow cast by the invader's stone castle was considered to be protection enough.

Clawdd Du rampart excavation, 1966
with Pat Vaughan, Alfon Williams, Diane Vaughan and the author

The Monastic Life

MONMOUTH PRIORY was founded in around 1080 by the Breton, Gwethenoc, a trusted supporter of William the Conqueror. He established his Benedictine house on an impressive plateau above a steep bank overlooking the River Monnow, just to the east of Monmouth Castle.

A few vestiges of the original Norman structure survive in the Priory Church but most of the buildings were swept away following the Dissolution under Henry VIII. A drawing by Thomas Dineley in 1684 records buildings to the south of the present church and a jumble of ruined arches and pillars joining it on the north-east. (Dineley, T. *The official progress of the first Duke of Beaufort though Wales in 1684,* 1888, London, p385)

A ditch defined the Priory precinct (or at least St Mary's churchyard). Parts of this were still open when John Speed drew his Map of Monmouth in 1610. A bridge crossed the ditch on the east, against Monk Street, and there are a few buildings and a cross shown inside the enclosure at the junction of the street with Whitecross Street. On the south, a gate tower is depicted over the ditch with another bridge a little way to the west. The northern boundary of the churchyard is shown as a wall against the land overlooking the river, but the line continues towards the castle as a ditch which stops abruptly. The south-eastern boundary of the churchyard, beside Butchers' Row (now Church Street), is obscured by buildings.

The history and upstanding archaeology of Monmouth Priory is covered by various authors in *Monmouth Priory*, edited by David Williams and Keith Kissack, a book published to mark the 900th anniversary of the dedication of the Priory Church in 1101 or 1102.

The Life of the Monks

In the summer of 2002, storm water drains were being installed around the former Priory Street School when medieval pottery was found just inches below the ground surface. We took over the excavations and exposed a midden containing a deposit of pottery and bones which formed the biggest undisturbed assemblage of 12th century material from a single layer in the town. There was also the first evidence of a high status Roman building in Monmouth.

The medieval rubbish consisted of waste from the Priory kitchens and leftovers from the meals of the monks – monks who were living in the same house and the same century as Geoffrey of Monmouth, the author of the *History of the Kings of Britain* and hero of Arthurian enthusiasts around the world.

Bones in the midden included those of various fish, of cows, sheep, pigs and goats, together with a variety of birds. Oysters and probably mussels were also on the menu. The pottery is mostly locally made unglazed cooking vessels, but these are accompanied by wares from over the English border, including two fabrics which are new to Wales. The pottery from other regions confirms the 12th century dating ascribed to the assemblage – there is a wide variety of pottery forms and rims, which, when compared with sequences found in Monnow Street, constitute an assemblage from a period after the middle of the 12th century.

The sherds of the 12th century tripod pitchers made in Malvern and the jugs brought from over the Severn and up the Wye from Bristol during the second half of the century probably reflect the monks' partiality to wine.

5 cms

Faces from the rims of late 12th century Ham Green (Bristol) jugs from Monmouth Priory. The head on the left has a circular stamp resembling the tonsured head of a monk

Residual sherds of late 11th to early 12th century cooking pots from the Vale of Gloucester which have also been found in the Norman layers in Monnow Street represent the earlier periods in the life of the Priory. A Cotswold ware cooking potsherd new to Wales was tempered with highly polished quartz and oolitic limestone and was probably made in Gloucester (Monmouth fabric D4). An example of a Hereford A2 vessel (fabric E9) was also new to Wales.

The Romans on the site

Monmouth was the site of a Roman fort during the invasion of Wales that later became the 3rd century Blestium. It seems to have been an industrial town of wooden buildings dependent on the iron industry.

The Priory rescue dig produced the first evidence, albeit residual, of a high status Roman building in the town: tesserae from a mosaic were found, complete with Roman mortar and pieces of ceramic roof tile (tegula). Considering the apparent absence of Roman stone buildings in Blestium there is a strong possibility that this is a temple site. If it was and the recorded early Celtic church of St Cadoc was near this spot it would mean that there has been religious activity on the same site for some 2,000 years.

The *Proceedings* of a 19th century meeting of the Archaeological Institute records an interesting discovery, presumably on this site, and which supports the idea that there was an important Roman building here. The note records:

'By Mr W.J. Bernard Smith. – The triangular front of an antefix of Terra-cotta, stated to have been found near Monmouth, and as supposed near the so-called

Oratory of Geoffrey of Monmouth. It measured, in perfect state, about 9 inches in width by 8 inches in height; in the centre there is a grotesque face with inflated cheeks, like an impersonation of the winds; in the upper angle is introduced a Greek cross; and below, on either side of the face, is a globular object, the whole being surrounded by a border raguly.'
Left: A similar Roman antefix found at Caerleon (courtesy of Amgueddfa Genedlaethol Cymru National Museum of Wales).

What we had thought to be the undisturbed natural ground beneath the 12th century levels turned out to be 13cm of re-deposited red clay which was lying over 6cm of brown loam – presumably the Norman humus – which contained only medieval pottery. This humus was preceded by hard and compact boulder clay which was once again assumed to be natural. But then Stuart Wilson (with his recent archaeology degree from York) followed charcoal flecks and proved it to be redeposited. The clay was only 3cm thick and laid over another humus – presumably the Roman tilled horizon. This lower humus was 18cm thick and ended at red clay which was again presumed to be natural, and probably was!

An Enigmatic Ditch

As this book was going to the printer, the discovery of two Roman ditches on a building site near Dixton Gate may be directly related to the Monk Street ditch (one of the two ditches is parallel with the Monk Street ditch and the other at right angles to it). However, I thought that it would be more interesting (and less trouble) to leave this article unchanged and to link it up with the new finds later – see *Romans Under the Floor*.

In 1982, we carried out excavations in the two front gardens of the Royal George Hotel (previously the Ivy Bank Hotel) in Monk Street. The Society and a team from Manchester Grammar School under Phil Dunlop and Martin Griffin undertook the project.

The garden had been raised above the modern road level with red clay and shale which is probably re-deposited natural material from the digging of the foundations or the cellar of the hotel during the 18th century.

The red clay covered a road surface composed of stone and iron slag which was itself overlain by a layer of brown loam. The loam may be humus which had accumulated on the road surface following its abandonment prior to the middle of the 18th century. The pottery from the upper road fabric was mainly of medieval date but there were also 18th century sherds, including German stoneware, Delftware, and a 15th century encaustic floor tile fragment. There was also a post-medieval horse shoe.

The Royal George, 1982. The Parkinsons excavate the road covering the ditch

The west side of the road was found to be sinking into a deep ditch which runs in line with Monk Street.

There were several layers of road surfacing – presumably repairs as the metalling sank into the ditch – and there were air pockets beneath the old road with a major fault above the edge of the ditch. A ranging pole could be pushed westwards through a void to hit the footings of the roadside garden wall.

The Royal George, 1982. Road surface with wheel ruts over the enigmatic ditch

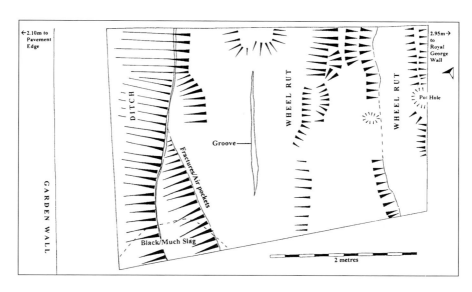

The Royal George excavations, 1982. Box A: Road surface over the ditch

The Royal George excavations, 1982. The edge of the enigmatic ditch

Ditch-fill is still being leached away; a fact which is emphasised by cracks in the brick wall requiring continual rebuilding.

The ditch, the road and the disturbances over it were similar in both front gardens. The fill contained medieval pottery, including Saintonge and Drybridge wares of the late 13th and early 14th centuries. The ditch must have been back filled during the Middle Ages or earlier – long before John Speed drew his Map of the town.

Beneath the road, and close to the edge of the ditch in both front gardens, were *in situ* iron furnace hearths. These hearths also contained 13th and 14th century pottery.

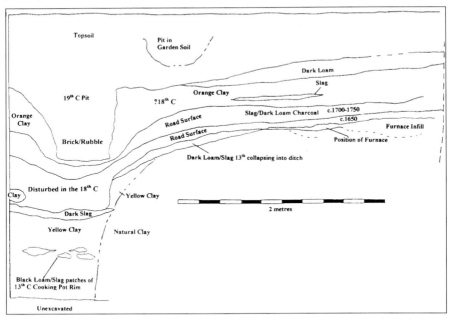

The Royal George Excavations, 1982
Box A: North Section of the ditch and furnace, showing sinkage into ditch

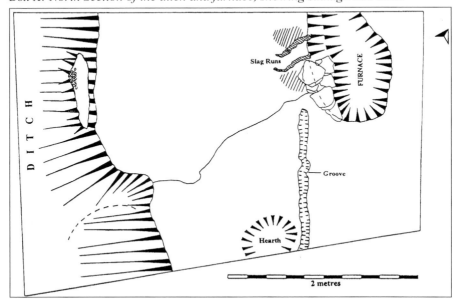

The Royal George Excavations, 1982. Box A: plan of ditch and furnace

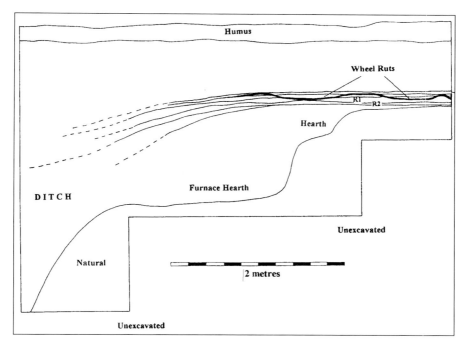

Humus

Wheel Ruts

R1
R2

Hearth

Furnace Hearth

DITCH

Unexcavated

Natural

2 metres

Unexcavated

The Royal George Excavations, 1982. Box B, north Section: ditch and furnace

It appears most unlikely that this is the ditch shown on Speed's Map of 1610 but the road almost certainly is. Observations of excavations for services in Monk Street have shown that the ditch did not reach as far as the traffic lights on the north, or as far as Whitecross House on the south. Perhaps this is an earlier Priory ditch.

The ditch itself was not dated but if it is an early Priory boundary, its digging probably coincided with the foundation of the Priory. That the ditch might be Roman has to be considered: it may be running roughly in the same alignment as the (speculated) vexillation fort. However, the Roman Army was punctilious in backfilling their defences and the leaching is strange as it was happening during the Middle Ages and appears to continue today.

A suggested sequence is:

Digging of the ditch, if Roman	?1st century
Digging of the ditch (if for the Priory)	?c.1100
Upper fill of the ditch	after c.1300
Laying of a road over the ditch	after c.1300
Repairs to the road	?c.1650
Abandonment of road (humus)	c.1700
Covering of the road with spoil	c.1750
A Priory precinct ditch was dug on	? c.1100
the west of (new?) Monk Street	c.1300
But certainly before Speed's Map of 1610	

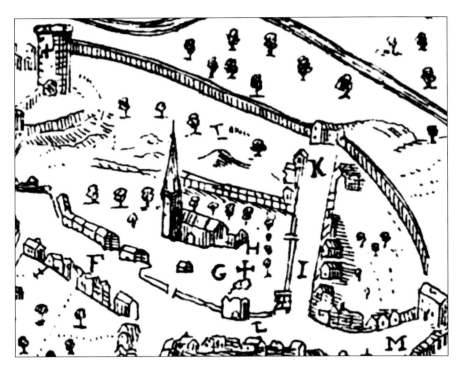

Monmouth Priory Church on John Speed's Map of Monmouth in 1610

The drawing records the Priory precinct ditch in Whitecross Street (F) and Monk Street (I) with bridges and a gatehouse
In the churchyard the White Cross is shown (usually a Plague cross) and, close by, the Castle together with the Town North Gate (K) and South Gate (M)

March 2008

Excavations for a drainage system extended to a depth of 2m in the grassed frontage of the telephone exchange in Monk Street. This is adjacent to the north side of the eastern gate of St Mary's Church and on the opposite side of the road to the home of the Baptist Church minister – well south of the Royal George.

We found that the natural red clay was reached at around 1m below the raised ground level beside the pavement. It is therefore certain that there is no Priory or other ditch at this point on this side of the street and this seems to be as shown on Speed's Map. The church boundary is marked by a wall running westward at right angles from the street (and fairly close to the church) and some way away from the town North Gate which is north of the traffic lights today. The ditch outside the Royal George continues to the north of the telephone exchange excavation providing supporting evidence that it has nothing to do with the Priory precinct which was still open in 1610.

A First Floor-Tile Kiln

THE FIRST site of a medieval floor-tile kiln to be found in South Wales was discovered in 1991 when Liz Freeman came to live in a house just north of the traffic lights in Monmouth. Her new home was Cadogan House, Monk Street, just inside the medieval town defences and to the north of Monmouth's Priory Church (Clarke, Jackson & Jackson, 1992).

Mrs Freeman had intended to dry out her cellar by building another roadside wall and found that the ground contained many pieces of encaustic floor tile. She called us in and we saw that most tiles were kiln damaged – over-fired or warped and twisted – the wasters of a Malvernian tile kiln (Vince, 1997). There were other products, including nibbed roof tiles, which were some 200 years older than any others known in the region. This kiln also produced a link between the pottery of the late Middle Ages and the early post-medieval period. (*A Missing Link*).

Some ten years earlier Alan Vince had suggested that a tile kiln of the Malvern School had been in production somewhere on the Welsh borderland. He had examined a tile from Llanthony Priory and found that, like the tiles made with Malvern moulds from Monmouth, it did not contain rock fragments from the Malvern Hills. The tiles in what he called 'Monmouth' fabric were tempered with sand from the Welsh borderland and he suggested that Malvernian tilers had set up a kiln in the region (Vince, 1980). A floor-tile kiln was discovered at Great Malvern in the 19th century (Eginton, H. 1883), but only one other kiln of the school had been found in Britain and that was in Nottinghamshire (Swinnerton, 1955).

Liz Freeman stopped her building work and we (Reg and Philomena Jackson, Chris Cooper, John Perryman, and Vic Powles) took over the excavation, which was partly carried out under halogen lights during freezing winter nights. The dig was extended to cover both of the small front garden plots and this revealed that two sides of the northern plot almost coincided with the firebox of the kiln and that this had been undisturbed since the site was abandoned.

The firebox – a square-sided pit that had been dug into the natural ground surface – was partially filled on one side by a store of clay which had been prepared for tile making. Sand had been added to the local clay and this was the same mixture as found in the kiln products and the kiln fabric. The store of clay had covered several pieces of wood which had been preserved in the damp conditions at the bottom of the firebox, but the most exciting finds were the products of the kiln itself.

Many tile wasters were decorated with the designs to be seen in the St Mary's Priory Church collection and these included the swan crest of Mary de Bohun, the mother of Henry V, while another tile is dated: AD MCCCCLVI : AD 1456.

Top left: Tile dated
    AD MCCCCLVI – *AD 1456*
Top right: Crest of Mary de Bohun
Middle left: Nibbed flat roof tile

Middle right: A quarter of a
    four-tile pattern
Bottom left: A brick with paw prints
Bottom right: A brick with tile scar

Burning on floor of the clamp kiln. One metre scale

A cloven hoof print on a roof tile and a heraldic floor tile from the Cadogan House tile kiln.

The ceramic assemblage from the Cadogan House Kiln has been donated to the National Museum of Wales.

Other medieval floor tiles found in Monmouth:

MALVERN. A Malvern encaustic floor tile in the Malvern fabric was found during field walking plough soil at Troy Meadow. Troy was one of the seats of the Dukes of Beaufort in the Middle Ages. This is the only Malvern tile in the Malvern fabric known from Monmouth. It is much abraded.

DROITWICH. A single piece of a Droitwich tile was also found during field walking plough soil at Troy Meadow. Confirmed by Dr Alan Vince.

WESSEX. Wessex tiles were used in the floors of St Mary's Church, Monmouth. They are of a different fabric to those found at Tintern Abbey in the Wye Valley which are the same as a fragment recovered during an evaluation excavation beside Llandogo Church in 2005.

WESSEX? A fragment of a tile with the distinctive Wessex School style sculpted hollow in the base was found amongst kiln waste in Drybridge Street, Monmouth. The fragment is kiln damaged, which is an enigma, as the Drybridge kiln(s) are believed to date to the early 14th century.

Cooking Without Fire

DURING EXCAVATIONS at 71 Monnow Street we removed the foundation of a large medieval wall and exposed the rim of a cooking pot. As cleaning continued, it became clear that much of the pot was intact and that it was standing upright. More pottery close by proved to be a second pot, also standing upright, but this time the rim was missing.

The two pots had been sunk into the ground to the rear of a 13th century house and although we were able to understand the circumstances of the deposition, it was only later that it was realised that this was the first archaeological evidence for 'cooking without fire'.

The two outer pots

Floods in the middle of the 13th century had left silt on the floors of the house and the residents had presumably decided to do something about it. Elsewhere in the street, other residents were also taking action. The half-timbered building was demolished and the site was covered with a thick layer of clay. Over the clay tons of dross and slag from the local iron forges was used to raise the ground level and then a second layer of clay completed the sandwich. On this 'damp course' a substantial new stone house was built and it was during the construction of this house that the two cooking pots were half buried behind the building.

The cooking pot on the left has a deposit of lime but no inner pot; the one on the right has lime with the base of an inner pot. Both pots are c.30cm across.

The careful excavation of the pots revealed that they had been used as small cooking stoves. Potsherds and small stones had been put inside the pots as a base for charcoal upon which it is presumed food was cooked or reheated. But this was only the last of three uses for the vessels which had started their working lives as cooking pots on an open fire.

When the sherds and small stones were removed, a thick white deposit was found to be lying inside both pots. In the more complete cooking pot, a smaller pot was sitting on top of this white layer. There was great interest as we assumed that we had discovered two pots of uneaten food.

After a couple of days of 'over recording', trowelling and contemplation, the pots were finally removed and were to be examined by a student at the University of Wales who was specialising in food residues in pottery. No study took place, however, as the deposit proved to be lime.

Some years before this discovery, Stephen Moorehouse had produced a booklet on the medieval kitchen and he had included documentary evidence for cooking without fire. (*The Medieval Kitchen and its Equipment*, Synopsis of papers presented to joint meeting of the Finds Research Group and the Medieval Pottery Research Group in Leeds).

An Anglo-Norman manuscript in the British Library gives instructions:

Take a small earthenware pot, with an earthenware lid which must be as wide as the pot, then take another pot of the same earthenware, with a lid like that of the first; this pot is to be deeper than the first by five fingers, and wider in circumference by three; then take pork and hens and cut into fair-sized pieces, and take fine spices and add them, and salt; take the small pot with the meat in it and place it upright in the large pot, cover it with the lid and stop it with moist, clayey earth, so that nothing may escape, then take unslaked lime, and fill the large pot with water, ensuring that no water enters the smaller pot; let it stand for the time it takes to walk between five and seven leagues and then open your pots, and you will find your food indeed cooked.

The heat produced by the chemical reaction of water on unslaked lime would be quite sufficient to cook a meal in the manner described in the manuscript.

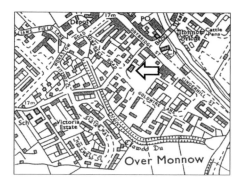

Vulcans across the Monnow

IN THE summer of 1991 the Junior Girls' School, off Goldwire Lane, Overmonnow, was demolished in preparation for the building of a block of flats – the Abbeyfield Homes. The site lay beside the lane from Monnow Bridge to the Clawdd Du Bridge, on the ancient road west.

The Society met with the developers and we were allowed a month to excavate the site, but the dig continued into January and revealed an iron working complex with what Peter Crew, a leading Welsh metallurgist, described as the most impressive medieval hearths he had seen.

The excavation covered a large area of the site so that a good picture of the industry was gained and a substantial assemblage of ceramics recovered. In consequence, a reasonable date and duration of the works was established, although this did not concur with archaeomagnetic dates obtained from the hearths.

Goldwire Lane forges. Merle Marsden and Sybil Cook beside the quenching pit

The iron working was carried out inside a wooden building which was probably open onto the Goldwire Lane. Only a single fragment of stone roof tile was found (in one of the hearths) and as there was also an absence of any other roof furniture, the building probably had a thatched or turfed roof. There were small pieces of flimsy wall foundation associated and aligned with the structure but the main building had been constructed on sleeper beams.

Goldwire Lane forges. Top: one of the hearths. Bottom: a hearth sectioned

A line of five forging hearths was found while a sixth one may have been under construction or previously abandoned.

These hearths had survived as circular bowls set on large pads of clay fired to a series of colours which varied with the distance from the hearth itself. One of the hearth bowls was taken apart (the site was to be destroyed by the subsequent building work) and its edges appeared to be composed of successive concentric layers of clay; this effect may be the result of a series of surface repairs, or, like the fired clay colours, have been produced by the variation in temperatures.

The clay settings were dug into the underlying dross and seem unlikely to have stood very far above ground level; even so, they post-dated at least some of the surrounding deposits. Hearth A8 had traces of stone flooring beside it which may mark the ground level at that time or the position of a bellows for it was very hard to identify working surfaces, as dross had been continually raising the floor levels.

Large quantities of pottery were found, scattered across the site, and it is possible that some of the cooking pots were those of neighbours who came to cook their meals against the hearths – if this were possible. However the variety of pitchers and jugs recovered were presumably for use by thirsty (? male) workers.

It seems probable that at least four of the forges had been in operation at the same time, showing that this was not a small-scale back-street business but an important and organised industry.

The forge was producing utilitarian ironwork from the blooms which presumably came from the furnaces at Overmonnow and on the banks of the Wye. Lots of iron nails were found, together with an arrowhead and a single horseshoe while other objects were unidentifiable. Examples of tuyers and base 'plugs' were also recovered.

The substantial pottery assemblage indicates that the forge was thriving during the early 13th century but that it was abandoned by the middle of the century.

The sparse material of a later date than this is no more than might

be expected from any site in Overmonnow, and in this case is unlikely to be associated with the industry. However, the magnetic date which was obtained by Dr Tony Clark from the last heating of three of the hearths was 1320-1350 at 60% confidence.

Dr Tony Clark collecting archaeomagnetic samples on a hearth

The Goldwire Lane medieval forges
Top: The water butt; presumably a large wooden tub, now rotted away, set into the ground
Bottom: Successive layers of fired clay inside a hearth

This date would be compatible with the later pottery found and it would be an apposite time for the demise of the industry – during the great decline of the early 14th century. The discrepancy in these dates is too wide and we are forced to believe that there is something wrong with the archaeomagnetic date – perhaps caused by the substantial layers of dross covering the site.

There was little difference between the pottery groups from any of the contexts across the site and there were distinctive features of the whole collection: (a) there were very few sherds of Fabric A5 jugs, especially those bearing complex rouletting which are very common in Monmouth from the middle of the 13th century; (b) there were no examples of Bristol Redcliffe Fabric C2 which also appears around the middle of the 13th century; (c) local glazed wares – jugs and a tripod pitcher – nearly all contexts were exclusively of Fabric A5b. All three features are consistent with a date in the first half of the 13th century.

Fabric A5b is the first local glazed ware to appear in Monmouth (in the early 13th century) indicating that the Goldwire Lane forges went into production at around, or later than, c.1200. The total absence of definite 12th century wares known from other sites in Monmouth (D2 Cotswold ware and B2 Malvernian early tripod pitchers etc.) also support this assumption.

Goldwire Lane forges. Tony Clark sampling, Peter Crew in the water butt and Felicity Taylor doing a 'Tony Robinson'

13th century arrowhead from the forges

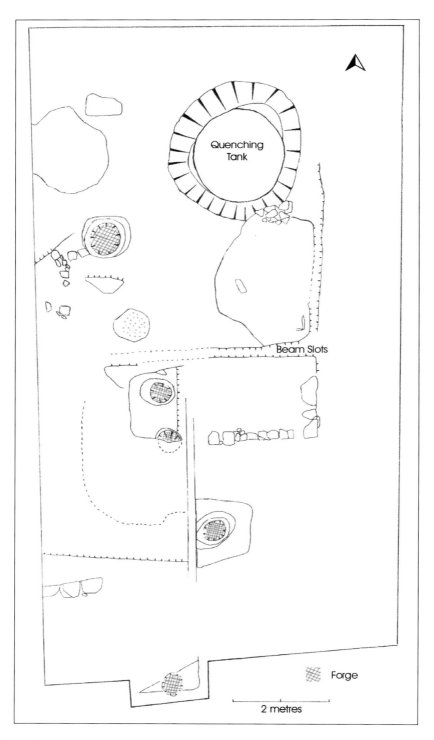

Quenching
Tank

Beam Slots

Forge

2 metres

Plan of Goldwire Lane forges

Goldwire Lane forges rescue excavations (with silver birch leaves)
looking west
The clay hearth bases are shown with the surrounding forge waste removed and
with the quenching pit in the foreground

Down the Cinder Mines

THE ROMAN and medieval iron industries of Monmouth produced prodigious amounts of waste – bloomery iron slag – which piled up around the town on empty land and especially on the banks of the two rivers where it formed islands. The medieval smelting appears to have been restricted to local urban areas whereas the Romans ranged far and wide in their exploitation of the forests and wastes, for their small bloomery furnaces are found scattered around the countryside and are easily identified by the spreads of iron slag in the plough soil. Iron working in the countryside, where dated, has always been Roman: sites often producing a few sherds of pottery, sometimes very early pottery.

In the Roman and medieval settlements at Monmouth and the medieval town of Trelech, the 'scoriae' or iron 'cinders' built up in great drifts, one of which is commemorated in Monmouth by Cinderhill Street at Overmonnow. This was a huge slag heap which had to be by-passed via Goldwire Lane.

Bloomery smelting was an inefficient method of extracting iron from the Forest of Dean ore and the resulting slag was consequently still rich in the mineral. With the introduction of blast furnaces in the seventeenth century, it was discovered that the residual iron could be extracted from the slag and that when it was added to the Forest ore it was said to produce a superior quality iron. One writer estimated that there were such huge amounts of slag lying around, both above and below the ground in Monmouth, that it could keep the furnaces supplied for centuries.

Keith Kissack mentions that although Pepys in 1662 and others had recognised the value of the cinders, Monmouth was slow off the mark and were using the resource to repair the roads ('metalling'). However, by 1700 the corporation had realised that they were sitting on what amounted to a gold mine and could think of little else. They were soon trying to claim the right to all cinders everywhere. In this, they were up against a drove of private prospectors, including the Duke of Beaufort, and were fighting a losing battle against their own enterprising tenants. There were also people like Mrs Jane Catchmayd who, in her quest for the slag, had brought down the town wall near Dixton Gate. The Council's own cinder mining was concentrated nearby on its own land near the River Wye in the Wyebridge Ward and was soon also destroying the walls and causing the Quay to subside. As Keith Kissack noted, there was intensive digging from 1716 until 1719 and sporadically for much longer. By 1767, islands in the Wye were being worked and the industry was still profitable late in the century – a re-cycling fever to make modern day councils green with envy. The cinders were sold to forges in the Wye Valley – the cradle of modern metallurgy. These included the one at Tintern, the remains of which were destroyed by the county council in 1997 when the furnace millpond was also filled in to make a car park for the George Hotel (as Ron Shoesmith and I reported in *Rescue News*).

Precisely when the market for iron slag tailed off is not clear but that it did is shown by the large *in situ* deposits remaining in the Corporation's plots along the Quayside – unless the close proximity of the Quay wall was uncharacteristically respected.

At Overmonnow, Cinderhill Street today is a perfectly level main road out of town but was, before the era of slag mining, covered by a huge swathe of waste from the Roman and medieval bloomeries. South of Monnow Bridge the road to

Trelech made a detour around the Cinderhill via what is now Goldwire Lane and was further diverted on the south when the Council cooperated with the Duke of Beaufort in order to recycle the hill. It was during this time that the workers unearthed the 'Cinderhill Treasure'. This was a hoard of unidentified coins which was promptly shared out amongst the diggers.

Excavations for the new Monnow Bridge in 2003-04 revealed just how thoroughly the Cinderhill was removed. Hardly any iron slag remained along the site of the abutments of the new bridge: only a thick layer of fine black dusk, left by the riddling of the waste. The miners had followed the slag into Roman or

An unexplained and undated feature cut into natural near the new Monnow bridge and re-excavated by slag 'miners' in the 17th century

medieval features which had been cut into the natural subsoil, totally removing the slag resource and with it much of the archaeological record. It is fortunate that there were no extensive deposits of slag under the houses of Monnow Street for the archaeological remains there might also have gone; as it is, the deep garden soils to the rear of the burgages in the street and elsewhere in the town may have been 'cleaned' during the search for cinders. The Council were continually trying to stop their tenants excavating their gardens, a practice which the tenants defiantly continued to do.

At The Barton, beside Trelech Crossroads on the southern edge of the village, a metre of black dust and charcoal (with very little slag) marks the main industrial suburb of the 13th century town. The slag was removed for smelting in the blast furnace at Woolpitch Wood a little way out of the town down the River Olwy.

We carried out excavations along Granville Street prior to the destruction of the Wyeside for the new A40 dual carriageway in the 1960s. The digging there revealed several metres of furnace waste and the first sealed evidence of Roman iron smelting in the town – a channel drain from a furnace with an *in situ* slag run.

On the Quayside near Wye Bridge deep excavations for a sewage chamber and pipeline were carried out during the winter of 2003-04 and penetrated over four metres of undisturbed iron slag without reaching natural ground. This was monitored by *Monmouth Archaeology* and published in *Archaeology in Wales* and is archived in the Sites and Monuments Record.

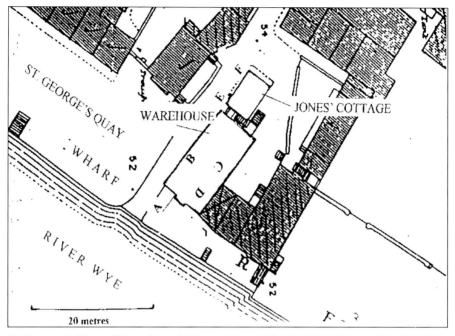

St George's Quay, Wyeside and the position of the E-F Section on the site of the 'cinder mine' beneath Jones' Cottage

The sewerage works excavations cut through the foundations of the last quayside warehouse to be standing when the Wyeside was destroyed; and the works chamber was sited directly over the adjoining 'Jones' Cottage', where my widowed grandmother lived until she was evacuated just before the arrival of the new road. The exact position of these buildings is accurately recorded in the magnificent Ordnance Survey map of the town of 1880 when even doorsteps and flowerbeds were depicted. The cottage had a stone paved floor and was regularly flooded – especially badly in 1963 – but even worse in the great flood of 1947 when the water reached to two steps from the top of the stairs before the family, including Great-Gran, was rescued by boat from the bedroom window.

The layers of compacted slag underlying the warehouse sloped downwards towards the river displaying defined tip lines. We never reached natural subsoil while Health and Safety requirements meant that no close examination of the stratification could be carried out and, just as unfortunately, very little pre-Victorian material was recovered.

When the excavations reached the cottage we found that the waste tip lines were dropping back the other way – essentially, against the riverbank slope – and now there were 18th century potsherds. The pile-driven box allowed the sampling of the various layers, together with a close visual examination of some contexts which confirmed that the incline had been reversed. In the safety of the steel-shored area inside the pile-driven box, it was possible to carry out hand digging towards the bottom of the excavation, at nearly 4 metres below ground level. Here, at the bottom of the slope, the slag was solid and fairly immovable even with a pick-axe but above that level a loose layer with black ash and charcoal produced late 17th and early 18th century pottery and black 'onion' wine bottles.

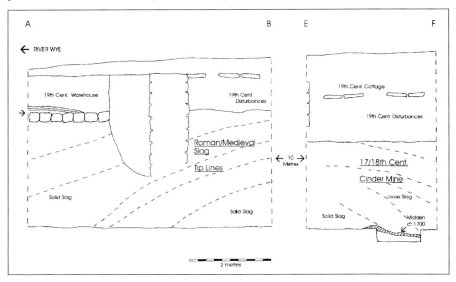

The Quay, Wyeside, Monmouth. The cinder mine, south-west section

The pottery and glass assemblage we recovered from the securely stratified lowest layers is rather earlier than what would be expected to be associated with the decline of cinder mining. However, the abandoned pit would have made an ideal rubbish tip, so its fill could include material of any date.

The pottery from the mine includes the base of a Westerwald stoneware jug or bottle dated to the late 17th/early 18th century. There are sherds of a Staffordshire moulded slipware plate which in Gloucester has been dated to 1680-90 by Carolyn Heighway but at its earliest by Ken Barton from Bristol to the 1650s. There are late 17th/18th century North Devon gravel tempered wares and a sherd of a Newent slipware plate which is also dated to the late 17th or the first half of the 18th century by Dr Vince.

It was suddenly clear that this was a 'cinder mine' – the first to be recognised in Monmouth – although they are well recorded in the town archives. For instance, in 1769 the *Cock* Alehouse in this area was offered for sale with its 'iron cinder mine'. Keith Kissack writes that the mines are sometimes referred to as 'cinder pits' and must have been rather like open-cast coal mines; they appear to have been pretty dangerous after dark as the Council, which was not renowned for its generosity or Health & Safety concerns, paid 1s 6d for the fencing of theirs in 1748.

Late 17th century pottery from the 'cinder mine: German stoneware bottle base (top), local slipware (left) and moulded slipware plate (right)

Another Hole in the Road

I DREW my first section in Monnow Street in 1958 – in a sewer service trench which exposed six feet of road levels. It was almost three decades before it really dawned on me that if the road had risen two metres since Roman times, that might also have happened to the houses on either side of the street.

Holes in the streets of Monmouth have probably been observed for longer than in most towns in the country and Society members are well known to the workmen, even though many come long distances to carry out work on sewers, the electric, and telephone, gas and water services. The photograph below, of a service excavation in Monnow Street, opposite Nailer's Lane, shows sub-contractors tolerating Society members swarming over the spoil heap.

A service excavation in Monnow Street, over-run by archaeologists

Until the last few years, excavations were backfilled with the spoil from the excavation; this made it worthwhile examining earlier backfills. However, the tendency today is to take the spoil away and fill the trench with stone hard-core. An example of redeposited spoil providing useful information occurred during the digging of a trench for a gas pipe at the junction of Glendower Street with St John Street and Agincourt Street.

Preserved wood and other plant remains in the re-deposited spoil from an earlier trench were accompanied by the distinctive smell of ditch fill. This was later tied in with the line of the defensive ditch discovered in the garden of Agincourt House which was aligned with this junction.

Several sites in Monnow Street have produced organic remains, as well as pottery – sometimes at a considerable depth. Recently, for instance, near Howell's Place, Roman pottery was found over 2.5 metres below the road surface. Further up the street a shallow ditch, probably one recorded during the Civil War, was explored during the digging of a service trench across the street. Here the nature of the ditch was examined and the organic-rich fill was sampled. The deposits outside Ron the Cobbler's was more reminiscent of ditch fill than the sort of large pothole (or cesspit?) into which Doctor Foster stepped in Gloucester.

One of the simplest but most useful results of the long-term watch on roadworks has been the compilation of a record of the depth of the undisturbed natural levels across much of the town.

The Dry Bridge

We made some exciting discoveries at Overmonnow in June 1999 when roundabouts and new road lights began sprouting across the area. Service trenching at the junction of Drybridge Street and Wonastow Road cut across the line of the Clawdd Du defensive ditch, in front of Drybridge House.

We found stonework near the bottom of the trench and the workmen were happy for us to take over the excavation.

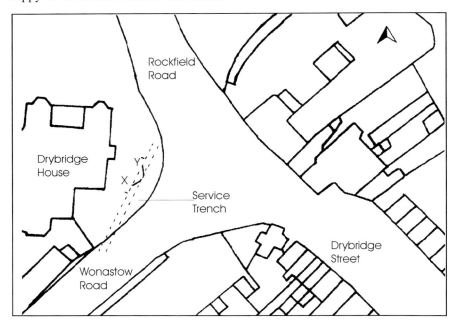

The Drybridge over the medieval Clawdd Du: the position of the service trench plan and sections X–Y

The stonework exposed in the narrow trenches was the silted-up abutment of a bridge – the 'Dry Bridge' – of Drybridge Street. Most fortuitously, we found thirteenth and fourteenth century potsherds underneath the silt which suggested that the bridge was abandoned a long time ago. Martin Tuck, an expert surveyor, and Anne Leaver, an accomplished artist, produced an accurate survey, section and plan of the discovery, reproduced here by Jane Bray.

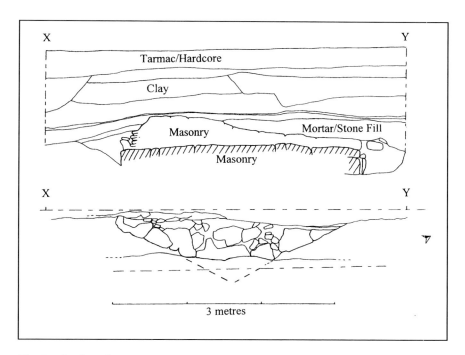

The Drybridge abutment over the medieval Clawdd Du ditch: section and X-Y plan

Archaeologists who work just five days a week must often lose out – for service trenching is regularly carried out on Sunday mornings. Some of us drive around the town from around 7.30am on the lookout for spoil heaps. When the workmen have filled in their trenches, they can go home, so the jobs are speedily carried out and we, like the early birds, have to be quick off the mark.

The Town Centre

We had never managed to dig properly on a site in Agincourt Square, in the centre of the upper town – inside the Roman Fort and inside the Norman castle bailey – and presumably inside any post-Roman settlement. We knew from various service holes in and around the square that the natural horizon of boulder clay was not far below the road level and assumed that the Normans had scraped up the surface (and any archaeological remains) to help raise their castle mound. At the end of January 2005 Monmouthshire County Council workmen began the construction of a new footpath in the road outside the cobbled forecourt of the Shire Hall in the Square. The area was fenced off, digging began, and all hell broke loose. The shopkeepers and market traders could not get deliveries and customers were discouraged from approaching stalls. The fishmonger's fresh fish sucked up the dust and fumes and the hot dog stall was debilitated, even the flower lady was in despair and a public meeting nearly ended in a riot.

The *Monmouthshire Beacon* front page for the week was headed by a huge 'CHAOS'. The rumour circulated that Cadw had stepped in as the site was in the curtilage of a Grade One Listed Building and all the work came to a stop, but the mayhem didn't. As nothing was happening (except the hostilities) we thought it was a chance to dig an exploratory hole in the road and obtained permission from the Highways section of the County Council to get inside the compound and carry out a small excavation. The rumour now quickly circulated that we had stopped the work and were delaying the conclusion of the project, so we had to spend time trying to convince the very angry stallholders and the public that this was not the case.

Our worries were compounded when problems with the telephones began around the Square and faxes and the Lottery machines failed and again the rumours spread that it was our fault. Luckily, by this time our trial excavation was about finished and we were able to escape. However, we had to be back in action on the 2nd May when, without the promised warning, machine excavations on the bollards began again. This time we managed to set up a definite warning system with the council, but the traders were not impressed with their latest exploits or by the news that another row of bollards was planned outside the newly laid low pavement which had considerably narrowed the road. The new pavement was only inches high, so drivers simply drove over it, with predictable results. Luckily, we were well away from the scene when the news broke that the council had dropped the plan for a second row of bollards and had decided to lower the whole road outside the pavement instead.

Our dig was a profitable, if risky, venture for although we only uncovered a few square metres, we were able to show that the Normans had not destroyed the post-Roman levels. The layer of ancient humus lying over the Roman natural clay surface was intact and produced eroded sherds of Roman pottery with charcoal flecks and small pieces of iron slag indicating that this was a long-cultivated soil 'cleaned' of stones.

Medieval pottery recovered from above the old humus included a sherd from a Norman cooking pot made in the Cotswold Hills – Dr Vince thought perhaps near the Cotswold Dip – of late 11th or early 12th century date. This fabric (Monmouth D5) has not previously been recognised in Wales or the borderland. However, the most exciting discovery was the foundation slot for a sleeper beam which had been cut through the Roman horizon into the natural subsoil, showing that wooden buildings had once occupied the Square.

Later, another breakdown in communications led to more destruction and a new commotion, when enlarged holes to replace the bollards were excavated with a JCB. Once again, we took over the site and with renewed help from the Council, and keeping our heads down behind very high fencing, rather despairingly salvaged what we could.

The Traffic Warden and the Medieval Shoes

CEDRIC GIBBONS, Monmouth's traffic warden, noticed black bones and timber in spoil from a service trench being dug outside 89 Monnow Street. He radioed Monmouth Police Station and one of the officers telephoned our Society headquarters in the print workshop off St James' Square. With the cooperation of the County Council workmen, we spent the evening of the 21st April 1993, recovering and recording the archaeological remains.

The trench was very deep but what we thought to be the natural subsoil was reached at around 2.05m below the road surface.

Below the road surface:

- 001 Road surfaces and make-up.
- 002 Modern Rubble.
- 003 A compacted slag layer at 0.50m extending to c.1.0m below the road surface.
- 004 An organic-rich loam and iron slag.
- 005 US from lower levels.
- 006 Natural (?) 2.05m below road surface.

The pottery recovered indicates that the main deposits were laid down in the 13th century but there was also some 12th century material and a single sherd of Roman grey-ware.

The lowest, anaerobic layers included a waterlogged deposit rich in preserved organic material including leather, plants, seeds and bones.

There were seven nearly complete leather shoe soles, most with stitching holes, a complete medieval shoe with split vamp and sole, a complete ankle boot, two vamps (uppers of shoes) and six pieces of heel, one of which retained overstitching repairs. It does appear that most of the leather was connected with shoe repair work as all the soles were well worn, with holes in heels and toes. There were large quantities of laminated off-cuts trimmed from hides ready to be worked.

Plant material from the anaerobic levels examined by Julia Wilson includes straw and bracken stems with seeds of henbane, blackberry and hemlock. Hazel nuts were also found. Pieces of bark, some cut and curled birch bark, were found, together with a stick which had been pointed at both ends.

The earliest pottery came from the lower levels but proved to be from a specific layer. A Ham Green ware jug rim and body sherd with an applied frilled decoration together with cooking potsherds were dated from the later 12th to the middle of the 13th century. The rest of the pottery is dated to the 13th century and came from the main organic-rich deposit. It contained fragments of locally made jugs and heavily sooted cooking pottery, some of which was burnt right through at the base.

The layer also produced two sherds of Worcester ware cooking pottery. One jug has fine angular sand temper with calcareous inclusions and is decorated with applied clay and stabbing. Another medieval find was a small lead spindle whorl which has small bumps on its underside.

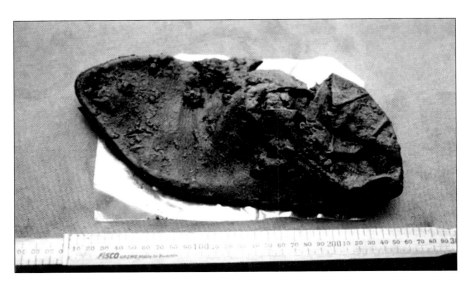

One of the medieval boots

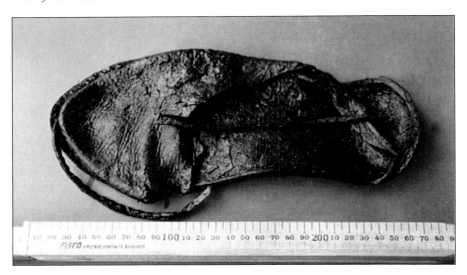

One of the medieval shoes

Felicity Taylor examined the bone assemblage and suggested that it was probably associated with the tanning industry. Post-medieval tannery pits were found during excavations by the Society along Nailer's Lane and the industry continued in operation behind Monnow Street during the 20th century.

When the story reached the local press the *The Sun* picked up the story and announced that we had found 2,000 pairs of medieval shoes. The *Western Mail* announced 'Medieval shoes turn up' and the *Fortean Times* published the 'strange coincidence' with a photograph of me (a Clarke) with shoes in the trench outside Ron the Cobbler's shop.

The Bells of St Mary's

A CCIDENTS still happen with the planning process and one of these occurred as this book was going to press – at 22 St James' Square, Monmouth.

Groundworks for an extension were underway when we checked on the site and found that the planners had imposed an ancient condition which allowed qualified (!) archaeologists to observe the work and not the normal condition for funded professional cover. Consequently, our amateur team from the Society (really made up mostly of 'professionals' of *Monmouth Archaeology* and *Church Archaeological Services*) spent a week and a weekend on the site.

Luckily, the contractors, Ian Jury and Lewis Morgan, who were working for Mr and Mrs Hilu, were amongst the most conscientious we have encountered. It was really Ian and Lewis who immediately stopped the machine and changed to hand digging when the first stones of a bell casting mould core appeared in a foundation trench. The stonework was at first thought to be a furnace with flues and filled with ash and charcoal.

However, there was further stonework at a higher level and when the trench was widened to investigate this we found that we had exposed the lower part of an 18-inch wide bell mould core with the bell-shaped clay bottom cladding remarkably well preserved. Shortly afterwards we realised that the furnace (which would have been at a higher level in any case) was in fact a 30-inch bell mould core, again with some of the clay moulding intact and four flues. It transpired that this larger bell mould core was itself sitting on the bottom stonework of a 40-inch bell mould core, again with four intact flues.

The bell mould cores in the new extension foundation trenches

Mould cores 2 & 3: 30 & 40 inches

Mould core 1: 18 inches

The mould cores from above

The mould cores 2 & 3 from above

Base of mould core 1

The flues of bell mould cores 2 & 3

112

Part Three

REMEMBER THE ALAMO!

Flying Pickets

A FEW days before Christmas 1986, I went to see the builders on site at 49-51 Monnow Street – just along the street from the discoveries of three months earlier at No 75. They had been working there for some time and were very happy for us to watch the work. There was a cellar – but it was at the back of the building, as at 75 – so I hoped that this was an indication that the frontage was archaeologically intact. The workers had removed the floor, exposing plaster and earth below, with no sign of a cellar. I was excited and talked to the builders who were happy for us to dig. I recorded in my journal for 18th December 1986:

> They have two weeks holiday from tomorrow. Contacted Trust, they have
> cleared it with the developer for us to go in. We will be under cover and there
> is electricity and a 'phone on the site. We can fix up strong lights and dig all
> hours.

On the following day, as we were getting our equipment ready, I had a telephone call from Jerry Akers of Bruton Knowles & Co, the agents for the developers, Churn Valley Properties. Mr Akers was opposed to any archaeological excavation. He said that his structural engineer agreed with him that it could cost them money. I explained that there should be no structural problems as our small excavation would be kept well away from the walls and could be filled with hardcore. I emphasised the importance of the remains that were almost certainly under the floors but to no avail, Mr Akers was not interested.

I rang Gareth Dowdell, of the Glamorgan-Gwent Archaeological Trust, which was set up by the Welsh Office as the planning authority's archaeological advisors, and he took over the negotiations. He rang me the following day. He had failed to persuade Mr Akers to change his mind and told me that the developers, Churn Valley Properties, had now also said that they did not want any archaeological excavation.

I was furious that on the whim of one man we could be denied the chance to carry out rescue work at our own expense in our own town,

I fretted throughout the day and then at 8pm rang Jerry Akers myself and asked him to give us a chance to carry out some small-scale work. I could not believe that anyone would be so heartless as to damage or destroy the site. I tried to explain how the medieval floors had been laid down and had remained undisturbed over the centuries. I said that we would not hold up the work, we would be out by the deadline; he would get good publicity; and the archaeology was of national importance.

Mr Akers was indifferent to the fate of the medieval houses and their very special remains. Eventually I gave up in frustration. I told him that if he damaged or destroyed the two burgages I would see to it that the name of Bruton Knowles stank from one end of the country to the other.

The following day Gareth Dowdell rang to say that Mr Akers had rung him to ask whether my threats had any substance. Mr Dowdell had said that he 'wouldn't like to be on the receiving end' of whatever we might do. Mr Akers, however, was still unmoved and was adamant that there would be no excavation.

Reg and Philomena came over and we held a meeting of active members where it was agreed that the archaeology was too important to lose without a fight; we would go onto the offensive. It was decided to campaign for archaeological conditions to be imposed by Monmouth District Council on planning consents in Monnow Street.

We hoped that at the same time we would cause embarrassment to Bruton Knowles and Churn Valley Properties as an example to other unsympathetic developers.

I worked into the night casting hot-metal type on my Intertype machine and printing leaflets explaining the importance of the archaeological remains of Monnow Street and appealing to the people of Monmouth to support us by writing to the Planning Department of Monmouth District Council. Further leaflets were printed to be handed to customers outside Bruton Knowles agencies in Gloucester, Cheltenham, Tewkesbury and Cirencester. Press statements were prepared and a meeting was held with Monmouth Action Group. The Group, led by Richard Evans, Sue Chivers and Jane Middleton, immediately volunteered support: if pickets, leafleters or simply extra diggers were required, Monmouth Action Group responded with unwavering support.

On my way to the site I met Charles Boase of Monmouth Civic Society, who was also a printer. He was taking leaflets that he had produced to distribute in Monnow Street.

The campaign was underway when Mr Dowdell rang to say that Mr Akers wanted a meeting. I asked if he had he changed his mind? 'No!' Was there any chance of him changing his mind? 'I doubt it!' He wanted to explain why he didn't want an excavation. I asked, 'Is there any chance at all of him allowing a dig?' The answer – 'Very unlikely.'

We had started our campaign and I felt that Mr Akers was trying a delaying tactic. When the builders returned from holiday, the excuse would be that any dig would hold up the work. I refused to meet him. In retrospect, this was a mistake – not because Mr Akers would have relented but because of what happened next.

Mr Dowdell decided to send a representative to meet Mr Akers on behalf of GGAT. The representative was an archaeologist but unfortunately a specialist in Roman studies – apparently with no experience of the narrow burgages of a medieval town. Strangely, Mr Dowdell also seems to have left him unaware of the deep urban remains which lay beneath the shops of Monnow Street. As it was to prove, this was a very silly mistake. At the site meeting with Jerry Akers he agreed that the planned excavation on one of the two threatened burgage plots was not worth carrying out. He agreed with the developer that the plots were too small to produce anything useful and Mr Akers maintained that the archaeology was not threatened in any case as the site was to be 'rafted' – a concrete floor was to be laid over the remains, leaving them undisturbed.

When I was informed that GGAT had withdrawn its support for us I was amazed and bitterly disappointed. Considering that Mr Dowdell himself had seen the remains a few doors away, the agreement was incredible.

Later in the day I called Reg and Philomena and they shared my very angry mood. It now seemed that only the amateurs recognised the true historical value of Monnow Street. That evening, two days before Christmas, I realised that we stood alone between the town's archaeological resource and its destruction.

With Monmouth Action Group, we started our campaign by handing out leaflets outside Nos 49-51 and with a table for signatures to a petition in Agincourt Square. The response was overwhelming and many people, including visitors, wrote to the planning department or signed the petition. The people were coming to our aid and scores of cars were now displaying fluorescent *'Protect Ancient Monmouth'* stickers.

On Christmas Eve our 'Flying Pickets,' with freshly printed leaflets, were launched on Bruton Knowles' agencies in three counties and the press and local radio stations loved it.

Archaeologists
Banned

Although there would have been no delay or cost to the development, professional and part-time archaeologists have been banned at the last minute from an agreed excavation of the potentially important site at No. 49 Monnow Street, Monmouth.

Monmouth Archaeological Society therefore

APPEAL TO THE
PEOPLE
OF CIRENCESTER

*for support in the fight to
Save Monmouth's Heritage*

TO THE PEOPLE OF CIRENCESTER

MONMOUTH Archaeological Society is asking for your support in their efforts to record the history of our very special town. We are not opposing building developments. We are simply asking that we, or others, be allowed to investigate unique archaeological remains and record them for the town and for future generations.

The removal of floors at No. 49 Monnow Street indicates that there may be similar deposits to that unearthed at No. 75 Monnow Street when the earth floors of medieval houses were found to contain a record of the town going back nearly two thousand years.

A formal agreement was reached with the developers of No. 49 Monnow Street (Churn Valley Properties Ltd., of Cowley, Nr. Cheltenham) that Monmouth Archaeological Society with The Glamorgan-Gwent Archaeological Trust Ltd., should excavate a part of the soft dirt levels below the shop floor. These levels may be replaced with concrete. The Work would have been carried out over the Christmas holiday, at no expense or delay to the developers.

As the Society was about to move in, a representative of Bruton Knowles & Co., Cirencester, Agent for the developers intervened and objected to the investigation.

After two days of negotiations with The Trust and Monmouth Archaeological Society, the representative informed The Trust that the developers had changed their minds and were now also against any excavation.

No satisfactory explanation has been given and there is now little we can do to make a proper record of the site.

In other areas of Gwent an archaeology clause is inserted when planning consent is given. Monmouth District Council, unlike authorities across Britain does not do this, despite the fact that Monmouth was designated one of the 'Top Ten Towns' in Britain worthy of special treatment by the Council for British Archaeology.

It would be of considerable help if members of the public would write expressing concern to :
The Chief Executive, Monmouth District Council, Mamhilad, Pontypool, Gwent.

Stephen Clarke
Chairman, Monmouth Archaeological Society

One of our Christmas Eve campaign picket leaflets

The campaign received even more impetus on the 28th January 1987 when the builders dug their first trench inside the shop frontage at No 49 and exposed nine earth floors in the first metre of digging. I got in over the back wall and took photographs which I sent to the Heritage Officer, Gus Astley, of the District Council. I also sent a copy to Mr Dowdell, who seems to have been on leave. In his absence, his deputy, Henry Owen-John, agreed in writing that serious damage had been caused to the archaeological remains on the site. At least some members of the Trust now appeared to be back in our camp. Our friend Bryan Walters, a leading but now late lamented Forest of Dean archaeologist who was temporarily working for Monmouth Museum, was helped by the builders to quietly record the exposed sections. We also managed to clandestinely 'preserve by record' other threatened parts of the site.

Although we had sent Mr Astley copies of the photographs and drawings of the exposed floor levels he still denied that any damage had been caused to the site. We then produced a leaflet with a photograph of the damage, together with drawings and a copy of Mr Astley's statement, which he was still repeating in letters to anyone who wrote to the Council:

> *It is important to note that the decision not to excavate is not the archaeological disaster which the leaflet campaign implies. Considerable areas have been left undisturbed, sealed below a concrete raft foundation.*

Our leaflets noted that *'At the time of going to press there is still no sign of a concrete foundation – quite the opposite – further trenching is about to take place.'*

Only the *Monmouthshire Beacon,* our own local newspaper, appeared to see the viewpoint of the developer and of Monmouth District Council. The *Beacon* printed the District Council's statements in full while ignoring our press releases. Later, and following my complaint to the editor, our response was published.

The campaign was now well underway. But Bruton Knowles and Jerry Akers were about to be let off the hook by dramatic events further down the street.

A Geoff Webb cartoon drawn in the Robin Hood Inn during the troubles in 1987

Storm Clouds

A NEW THREAT to the town and its history had now appeared in the form of plans for the re-development of Nos 83 and 85 Monnow Street: the Georgian home of the Kwik Save supermarket. The proposals were added to the Society campaign leaflet on *The Destruction of Medieval Monmouth* and the public was asked to object.

On 3rd February I spoke to Mr Astley on the telephone and noted in my journal that he seemed to think that it was a foregone conclusion that the buildings would be demolished, despite the fact that 83-85 were listed buildings. I noted that there was nothing of this on the Monmouth District Council planning agenda for that night, although Sue Chivers, the secretary of the Action Group, had been told by Mr Astley that the building was unsafe. She had then asked him why, if that was so, the public were still being allowed to use the store.

A lot seemed to be happening around the town. Foundation trenches were being marked out at the rear of the Bus Station at 95-97 Monnow Street; there was more destructive digging at 49; and we were collecting Roman and medieval remains from spoil produced by large scale excavations at the Overmonnow Girls' School, which was now a building site.

A campaign leaflet

On the 6th February I stayed at work late, printing leaflets and letters appealing for support, to be ready for the afternoon meeting of the county society, the Monmouthshire Antiquarian Association, that was to take place at Caerleon on the following day.

I drove home through the silent town in the early hours: Monnow Street was deserted; there were no revellers, no policeman and the chip papers were lying quietly in the gutters.

However, it was to be the calm before the storm.

A Geoff Webb cartoon, drawn in the Robin Hood Inn, 14th February 1987

'Let History Judge'

Sir,

In September, following the demolition of 75 Monnow Street (in a Conservation Area), professional and independent archaeologists had a matter of hours to record some of the most important medieval archaeology ever discovered in Wales. Three medieval house sites were almost totally destroyed.

At Christmas another developer refused permission for an excavation at 49 Monnow Street where two more medieval house sites are now being seriously damaged. The builders on the site are doing their very best to help by putting finds on one side but the sight of archaeologists scrambling in skips and over chuck-heaps is pathetic.

Last week a third company demolished a Grade II listed building without Listed Building Consent.

Let history judge the reaction of the people of Monmouth.

STEPHEN CLARKE
Gibraltar Drive, Monmouth

+ + +

AT ten past four on the afternoon of Friday 6th February 1987, Monmouth Police received a telephone call informing them that cracks had appeared in the Kwik Save supermarket building, 83-85 Monnow Street. Stones were said to be falling from the frontage and the building would have to be evacuated.

Two police officers went to the store; one of them was the Monmouth station Inspector. They found shoppers going in and out as usual. There were no stones fallen from the frontage, no noticeable cracks in the walls and the shop was trading as normal. The two policemen walked around the store and returned to the police station, assuming that the telephone call had been a hoax.

On checking, retired Police Sergeant Bill Harris (a District Councillor himself), found that the telephone call had come from Cwmbran and was recorded as being made by an employee of Tarmac – the contractors who later carried out the demolition. No explanation for this strange incident has ever come to light.

An hour later, the Police were at the store again – following another telephone call – but this time they met an un-named engineer. He told them that the building must be evacuated immediately as it had become dangerous.

Mrs Margaret White of Monmouth and her daughter Sharon were the last customers to be served, at precisely 5.25pm. The Police then complied with the engineer's request and evacuated and cordoned off the store.

During the evening, Monmouth District Council officers visited the store and entered the building.

+ + +

Driving up Monnow Street just before 8am the following morning I saw scaffolding being unloaded from a lorry outside Kwik Save but at the time did not see the significance of this – being unaware of the events of the previous evening. The scaffolding must have been ordered some time before the building was declared unsafe but when this was suggested, we were told that it had been ordered earlier to shore up the building. This explanation was strange as the Society was told by a professional scaffolder that shoring scaffolding was quite different from demolition scaffolding and that this was demolition scaffolding.

Demolition workers suddenly appeared and began erecting the scaffolding. When I returned from the county antiquarian meeting later in the afternoon I was told of the day's events and went early the next morning to look at the building and compare it with photographs taken earlier. I considered that there was absolutely no difference whatsoever in the frontage. Things had begun to look very suspicious, especially as notices had been displayed in Kwik Save saying that the store would be *'Closed for repairs from Saturday, 7th February, 1987'*.

I rang Reg and Philomena Jackson in Bristol – two figures at the centre of the story – and told them that I had telephoned Mr Astley, the Council Heritage Officer, and that he had admitted that the impending demolition was 'unauthorised' but had told me that 'That will be put right tomorrow.'

We decided to go on the offensive.

I opened my printing workshop and within an hour had overprinted hundreds of the latest leaflets with the question *'Is This Breaking the Law?'* I rang Sue Chivers and she organised a team of Monmouth Action Group members which then picketed the store handing out leaflets until after dark.

Journal extract, Monday 9th February:

> *A rather eventful day. Picketing Kwiksave from 8am. A telephone call to the Welsh Office revealed that they knew nothing about the affair, except that there were protesters in the street. We made sure that Cadw and Monmouth District Council were well aware of what was happening. Instead of the reaction I expected from the Council office staff, there was some confusion and work on the site seemed to falter.*

> *A Cadw spokeswoman said that they were trying to find out what was happening but if the Council did agree to the demolition they would have to prove that the building had been unsafe. She couldn't see how they could do that if the building had been demolished.*

> *The Heritage Officer's deputy told the secretary of the Action Group, Sue Chivers, that he was trying to get an injunction to stop the demolition. He was unaware that his boss, the Chief Technical Officer Mr Gareth Griffith, had investigated the dangerous structure claim. A Welsh Office official told Charles Boase that they had put a stop to the demolition. A spokesman for Monmouth District Council said that there would be a statement following a meeting then in progress.*

Realising there was some sort of mess and confusion we went all out with our campaign. We increased the numbers on the picket outside Kwik Save and by lunchtime had brought in the television, radio and the press.

Preparations for the demolition continued.

I was told by a local sub-contractor that he had been working at Kwik Save on the 23rd January. This was two weeks before the building was declared unsafe, and he found that a meeting was taking place. He said that people from away were at the meeting discussing the building. He alleged that he was told shortly afterwards that the building was to be demolished in two weeks' time and that Tarmac would be carrying out the contract. If this were true, it would explain the telephone call to the Police at 4pm, an hour before the store was actually declared unsafe. My informant gave me a signed statement which I agreed to use only if it was necessary. Another Monmouth man also gave me a signed statement: he was in the Punch House, Agincourt Square, on the Tuesday evening before the demolition, talking to two men. One of them told him that they were in Monmouth to demolish Kwik Save at the weekend.

The store continued trading after the Tarmac phone call until 5.25pm. The public were therefore allowed to continue shopping for over an hour in a building said to be so 'dangerous' that immediate demolition was necessary.

The demolition went ahead.

There has never been a structural engineer's report to justify the demolition and Listed Building Consent was never granted for the demolition.

Monmouth Archaeological Society carried out its own investigation, paying for public notices in the press asking for information and taking statements. The Society engaged solicitors and a barrister in the fight to protect the archaeology and to investigate the strange circumstances surrounding the demolition. A thousand signatures protesting to the council were collected in Agincourt Square on the following Saturday; Monmouth Civic Society joined the protest and a Monmouth Association was formed with Philomena Jackson as secretary.

When correspondents to the *Monmouthshire Beacon* complained that their letters were not being published, the editor of the paper publicly admitted that he had received more letters on the Kwik Save demolition than any other subject in his memory.

Dafydd Wigley, a Plaid Cymru MP, asked a question in the House of Commons about the destruction of the listed building and the satirical magazine *Private Eye* published an article in its 'Piloti' column on 'the oldest trick in the book', with a photograph of the demolition, and asking:

> *'Is Monmouth District Council going to prosecute Kwik Save for damaging a listed building? Of course not. But many local people would like to know why their Council actively abetted Kwik Save in this vandalism.'*

Cadw-Welsh Historic Monuments funded a partial excavation of the site by the contracts wing of the Glamorgan-Gwent Archaeological Trust, the archaeological advisors to the District Council. I was told that the cost of the contract was £70,000. The excavation, which consisted mostly of a single trench, showed that the plot contained some of the finest stratified medieval remains in the country and a sherd of Saxon Chester ware was the earliest medieval pottery ever found in South Wales.

When the building foundation groundworks began, the surviving archaeological remains on the site were effectively destroyed.

Confrontation : A Geoff Webb cartoon drawn in the Robin Hood Inn, with characters suspiciously resembling two Monmouth District Council officers

Over the following weeks hundreds of fluorescent posters urging *'Prosecute Kwik Save'* appeared around Monmouth. The District Council designated one of its employees to investigate this illegal activity and council workmen went around the county removing the offending notices, only to find on their return journey that they had been replaced with new ones. More notices appeared inviting people to 'Boycott Kwik Save' or in cars with a single 'Kwik Save' below a skull and crossbones.

The Society bought shares in Kwik Save and turned up at a shareholders' meeting to ask if there was a company policy on Listed Buildings. When the chairman asked the questioner (Philomena Jackson) if she had any particular building in mind, she replied 'Yes – one in Monmouth!' She was applauded by other shareholders. The story was spreading well beyond the town.

On the 2nd September protesters filled the District Council chamber and the Kwik Save plans were rejected by a majority of 17-15, throwing the officers into something of a panic. The Chief Planning Officer, who had made an impassioned plea for the Council to pass the application, stood up and asked the Council what he was to do and the leader, Councillor John Parker, replied, 'That's your problem.' However, Mr Parker wrote to his party members, including the retired Police Sergeant, Bill Harris, asking them to support the application. We thought that there would now be an appeal and a public inquiry or even a prosecution.

Mr Harris, who was also a District Councillor, had carried out his own investigation. During the very heated council meeting on the 2nd September he accused the Council officers, in open Council, of supporting the illegal demolition of the Listed Building. Councillor Harris later apologised to the Council officers, following legal advice. A highly popular and respected figure in the community, he died in 1997.

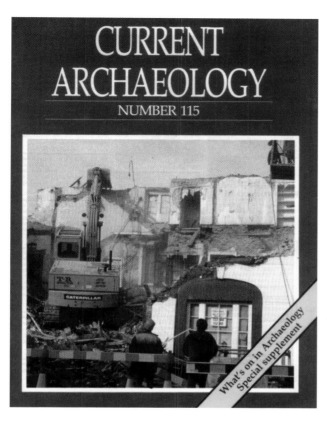

Full colour pictures of the demolition appeared in the national magazines *Current Archaeology* and in *British Archaeology* with headings such as 'Archaeological Disaster at Monmouth'. The press (with the exception of the *Monmouthshire Beacon*) also gave extensive coverage.

Report by REG JACKSON

British Archaeology, No1

125

Builders at work in previously undisturbed medieval levels on the Kwik Save site

Replacing the Kwik Save Grade II Listed Georgian House

Although ostracised by some of his fellow councillors because of his investigation and stance on the Kwik Save demolition, Bill Harris was widely respected in Monmouth and there was even a suggestion that a small plaque be placed on the new Kwik Save building in his memory.

There were problems, however: Conservation Area Consent would have been required from the District Council – and Kwik Save owned the new building

Former Police Sergeant Bill Harris (28th Jan. 1917 – 23rd Dec. 1997), when Mayor of Monmouth

The Councillors caused further consternation amongst the officers on the 7th October when they voted out the Kwik Save application for the second time.

Some members (like Councillor Margaret Coates) kept up the pressure for a while but eventually the District Council decided that there would be no Public Inquiry or prosecution for the illegal demolition and gave planning permission to Kwik Save to replace the four-storey building.

Three years after the demolition the store was rebuilt. The majority of the archaeological resource had been destroyed and the demolition remained illegal – as it does to this day. The upstairs floors were never installed and in 2005 Kwik Save closed (it was merged with another supermarket chain) and the building was sold. Today, this replica of a fine town house remains an empty shell – a memorial to the 1987 Monmouth District Council's guardianship of its Listed Buildings and of its Conservation Area.

+ + +

On the 19th March 1987, developers dug trenches into the archaeological levels of the frontages of 79-81 Monnow Street – next door to Kwik Save – while no archaeologists were around.

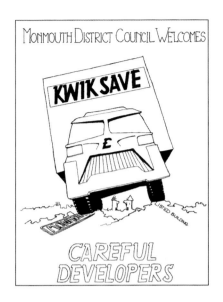

Anonymous cartoons, February 1987

A Kwik Save demolition anniversary leaflet – 1988

'Town full of Concrete Wagons'

WHILE THE Kwik Save mêlée was at its height, redevelopment work began at No 50 – the former *Monmouthshire Beacon* newspaper offices – on the southern side of the street. On the 29th August the builders began taking up the floor of the cellar (6ft 3in below the pavement level) and exposed loam and iron slag; however, when we managed to examine the work while the workers had the afternoon off, we found that the construction of the cellar had removed all of the archaeological resource. On the 2nd September, coinciding with the councillors' rejection of the Kwik Save plans, we began a daily check on this site and on the adjoining No 48. Two days later, this cellar and a smaller one to the rear of No 48 were filled with hardcore and concrete. Two trial holes had been dug in the front room of No 48, exposing undisturbed medieval house floors – we salvaged medieval pottery – unstratified from the spoil.

Things were becoming hectic, with large drainage trenches cut between Chippenham and the rear of the street; service trenching next to the scheduled field in Trelech and Roman remains ploughed up at Raglan. On the evening of the 17th of September, my visit to No 48 left me appalled at what had taken place during the day.

Journal, 17th Sept. 1987:
Daily check tonight reveals disaster at No 48. Builders have cut a yard wide trench across the room (shop front) of Keeling's and gone down 4ft into medieval floors/hearths, etc. Denis Loffhagen rallied to help me and we spent a couple of hours photographing the section which is very impressive. The trench runs across the room (in line with Monnow Street) and goes under both walls and across the Beacon (tunnel) access. The whole section contains clear floor levels, hearths and other features and I don't know where the spoil has gone. Pegs are in for concrete. Rang Ron Shoesmith and Jeremy Knight, etc. Later: we have the weekend to sort the trench out, although the men will be working Saturday.

The Council officers were aware of the destruction that was taking place but explained that they had no power to stop it while the Council's archaeological advisors were quite understandably keeping their heads down during our public protests.

The amount of rescue work which can be carried out in a builder's trench is very limited. A section is useful, however damaging to the remains, but understanding the occupation and the dating is limited to what can be pulled out of the trench edge, which is not a lot without running the risk of a collapsing trench or of getting oneself kicked off the site. A lot of the trenching now was concerned with under-pinning and reinforcing the shop frontages. This caused serious damage to the archaeological remains but provided a section all along the frontages of Nos 46-50. The section revealed that all of the burgages damaged had been occupied at an early date and this was later found to also be the case at No 44.

We obtained pottery of Monmouth's late 11th/early 12th century phase from the lowest floors together with a sandstone spindle whorl and part of a second one which had been cut from a sherd of a Cotswold ware cooking pot.

The next burgage to be damaged was the adjoining No 52 – The Wool Shop. Here a wide trench was dug across the front room at right angles to the street and again the digging cut through a series of medieval house floors. The devastation was beginning to dishearten us; we seemed powerless to stem the tide. Journal:

22nd Sept.: Rear of No 52 – 4ft deep trenching.
No 48: Concreting trenches as they are dug.
Nos 93-95: Three metre deep trenches.

Builder's trench cutting medieval floors and hearths at 52 Monnow Street

The Council's eccentric preservation and conservation of the façade was only matched by the abandonment of everything else. There were timber-framed structures behind the early 20th century frontages of Nos 46-50 and during the destruction of these the workers showed us 17th century coins they had found in the floors. We dated the façade saved by the Council with an 1871 penny we found in the rubble make-up of the integral floor and during underpinning there was a clay marble inside the mortar of the wall foundation of No 48. These 100-year-old frontages were practically the only parts of the buildings to be preserved.

Journal:

28th Sept.: Missed trenches immediately behind Beacon Office – part concreted as soon as dug. How the hell can we cope with this sort of thing? Bus Station builders at 10ft.

29th Sept. Town full of concrete wagons.

The section through Nos 44-50 confirmed that the modern shop boundaries coincide with the earliest burgage plots. The building at No 46 is very narrow; at one time it displayed the notice 'The Smallest Shop in Britain' and is shown on the 1880 Ordnance Survey as an alleyway between the houses.

There were no medieval house floors on this narrow piece, although they were intact beneath the floors on either side. The early earth floors in the section of No 48 could be seen dropping down beneath the dividing wall with No 46 – perhaps as a feature of the burgage boundary.

'The Smallest Shop in Britain' (No 46), filling an 11th/12th century alleyway

It appears that No 46 was always an alleyway to the rear of the street from the very beginnings of Norman Monmouth.

The shape, width and property boundaries of modern Monnow Street are probably the same as those of their earliest Norman antecedents; this is not surprising but is fascinating all the same. Evidence to show that some Monnow Street houses were later turned around to have their gable ends to the street has been found by Neil Maylan but this may be limited to the part of the street covered by his study (Maylan N. in Marvell A., 2001).

On the October 7th Monmouth District Council members rejected the Kwik Save plans for the second time and on the 8th building work began inside the town defences at the Royal George in Monk Street.

The Heritage Officer, Mr Astley, told me that planning conditions to protect archaeology might be challenged in the courts by developers, so there could be no protection for the remains.

On the 12th October we found that developers had dug holes in the floors of Nos 69-71 and we heard that these buildings were now proposed for demolition.

Investigating medieval house floors by torchlight in a builder's trench

A selection of campaign stickers and leaflets

Geoff Webb's cartoon of the Waitrose 'ticket only' public meeting

Waitrose comes to town

IT WAS to be the first Welsh Waitrose, but the plan was to build it beside lower Monnow Street, close to Monnow Bridge – the only surviving fortified medieval bridge in Britain – in the Conservation Area and probably over some of the town's most sensitive archaeological remains.

The flood alleviation scheme was now in place, protecting Monnow Street (and the proposed Waitrose site) but, as predicted by sceptics, increasing the flooding across the river in Overmonnow.

Waitrose also wanted the public car park, which had been built on Chippenham, the 'Village Green' which had been partly given to the town by the local gentry and partly purchased by the townspeople.

The new planning guidelines (PPG16) to protect archaeological remains had recently been brought into operation so it was assumed that there would be an archaeological evaluation of the site prior to the Council's consideration of the planning application. But Waitrose did not want an evaluation; they proposed that if their plans were approved they would provide a 'six-figure sum' to cover the archaeology. We pointed out that if a major excavation was required on such a large and complex site, £100,000 might not be nearly enough. For example, we had been told that one trench on the Kwik Save site had cost Cadw £70,000.

However, we were ignominiously defeated when Mr Gareth Dowdell, of the Council's archaeological advisors, Glamorgan-Gwent Archaeological Trust, wrote to the Council congratulating Waitrose on its proposals for dealing with the archaeology. The contracts wing of the Trust carried out an evaluation of the site and later a watching brief.

Monmouth Action Group and Monmouth Archaeological Society were prominent in the opposition to this intrusion into the Conservation area and were just as strongly opposed to the planned sale to Waitrose of most of the

Chippenham car park which covered part of the town green. Waitrose held a public meeting to put their case to the public but admission was by ticket only.

I printed 5,000 two-colour A4 leaflets, partly copying the *Monmouthshire Beacon*'s front page report of September 1971. The report had concerned the public outcry when eleven mature trees were felled for the construction of the car park . . .

'Workmen moved into Chippenham on Monday to start work on the new car park amid strong protests from many local people opposed to the destruction of the trees,' said the report. The county planners had asked that Monmouth Borough Council reconsider its proposals but the Council had stuck to its original decision, felled the trees and laid out the car park.

However, we decided to withdraw the leaflets when the editor of the *Monmouthshire Beacon* intriguingly threatened me with legal action for breach of copyright.

Waitrose held their ticket only 'public meeting' and then went through a series of planning applications: the first proposal was for a 16,000 sq ft supermarket, but they ended up with a 24,000 sq ft superstore.

There was a Public Inquiry, when it was shown that the original boundaries to be registered as the village green on the definitive map had been altered (with a different pen) to exclude the area of the car park. No one knew who had altered the map, but it meant that the car park was not registered as a part of the village green, although of course, it should have been.

When work got underway Monmouth archaeologists were not admitted to the site which was surrounded by high fencing. However, Ron Shoesmith and I watched the work from the fire escapes of sympathetic shops and businesses which overlooked the development.

Frontage area of the Waitrose builder's excavations seen from a neighbour's fire escape

An unauthorised photograph of the Waitrose excavations
taken from a builder's trench

The store was being built on a 'raft' – a concrete slab supported upon piles sunk deep into the flood plain. This type of construction can help preserve archaeological remains *in situ*, although excavations around the piles and for the edges of the slab can cause considerable destruction and this appeared to be happening here.

In frustration, I put on a fluorescent jacket and wearing a hard hat, walked onto the building site. Nodding to the workmen and muttering absentmindedly, I signed the site admission book with a flourish and headed for the trenches.

Everyone soon got used to me being around and for nearly three days I was able to come and go, scrape the sections, take photographs, and make measurements at will.

And then, on the third day, someone realised who I was.

+   +   +

Today, we have our new bridge over the River Monnow – built to the dictates of the Environment Agency and consequently one of the least attractive structures. It was originally planned to cross the river close to the medieval bridge – almost directly in line with the Waitrose entrance – but thanks to the late John Edwards and Monmouth Action Group it was moved further downstream. John, who was an outstanding architect, took on Monmouthshire County Council and produced his own plans and statistics which eventually saved the day for Monmouth. Tragically, John and his wife were killed in a horrific road accident in 2005 which justifiably produced the newspaper front page headline 'Death of a Local Hero'.

Crossing the New Monnow Bridge one has a wide view of the town, dominated by the spire of St Mary's Church and Great Castle House – above a shining sea of metal – once part of Monmouth's Village Green – now the Waitrose car park.

In the Monmouth Conservation Area: Monnow Bridge and (right) Waitrose

Part Four

HISTORY AND LEGEND

Abandoned to the Woods

IN APRIL 1976, I was recording post-medieval cottage sites with Tony and Margaret Ginman in woodland on Newton Court Hill when we noticed a levelled area close to a recently re-cut forest track. There was a lot of stone under bramble and ivy-covered hawthorn; scratching the surface we found two sherds and a slashed round-sectioned handle of a green glazed jug – Drybridge ware – although we didn't know it as such at the time.

In July, we used the annual visit of Manchester Grammar School students under Phil Dunlop, with some of our society under Dave Jemmett, to explore the site when we enjoyed the enthusiastic support of the landowner, Charles Griffin.

With the removal of the leaf mould, the stone footings of a building were revealed, together with cooking pottery and more jug sherds. Later, a second building was discovered. This seems likely to have been the medieval settlement of English Newton which was set on the poor uplands while Welsh Newton flourished on the richer soils of the valley below.

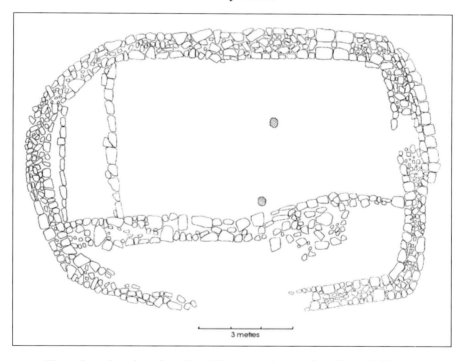

Plan of an abandoned medieval house in the woods at English Newton

The occupation of English Newton was centred on the 13th century (dated by jugs bearing complex rouletting) and ended (with the Drybridge pottery) in the 14th century. The house consisted of two rooms, one of which seemed little more than a cupboard but with a dividing wall. Opposite the main door there was a second door into the smaller room while a platform at the end of the main room was probably the base for a bed. The house must have been roofed with thatch or turf. A key was found inside the main room – perhaps to a chest – as the house appears unlikely to have been lockable. There was also a Neolithic axe – presumably a curio picked up in the fields.

Over the years other settlements have been found on the hillsides around Monmouth – most established in the 13th century but abandoned in the 14th. It appears that the pressures caused by the expanding population in the High Middle Ages was the motivation for the clearance of areas of woodland and waste outside the town (assarting). With the dramatic drop in the population in the first half of the 14th century the demand for new land also fell away and any survivors left on the hills would have abandoned their hovels and the thin soils to move down into the valley. Scrub, followed by woodland would soon have spread over the ruins of the deserted 'new towns'.

The discovery of subsistence settlements in the woods is usually a matter of chance – the remains of the English Newton house were comparatively substantial, with stone foundations, whereas other houses may have been exclusively of timber.

One of these small settlements was situated along the edge of Middle Warfield at Great Warfield, just to the east of Monmouth, on the land of the late Major Patrick Waller. The site was discovered following ploughing and at the time consisted of a pottery scatter and dark soil over an area of around 20 metres by 10 metres. Reg Jackson noted that the presumed occupation site was situated on a more level area between the steeply dropping field and the sharp bank below the hedge above Great Warfield Cottage (SO 5278 1351). There was some indication of stonework just below the plough while the pottery assemblage consists of 54 coarse ware and 7 glazed sherds. Two of the glazed sherds are probably parts of roof tile. Also on this side of the town we have recovered medieval cooking pottery from around Conegre Barn.

Another site revealed during ploughing is at Lower Buckholt Farm (the late Mr and Mrs George Davies) to the north of Monmouth. This is believed to be 'Maynestowe' which was recorded by Richard le Messager in his 1432 description of the borough boundary. The site was situated on Pear Tree Banks and extended some 25 metres into the field from the southern hedge. The centre of the pottery scatter was along and especially below a ridge halfway up the field. Some stone is evident above the ridge but less pottery. Also on this side of town but just over the border at Parkside, Welsh Newton, we have recovered medieval ridge tile and 14th century jug sherds.

A settlement near the edge of Orles Wood on the White Hill, overlooking Monmouth on the west, is marked by a scatter of medieval pottery. Also on White Hill a site with stonework and medieval ridge tile was recorded during forestry maintenance work in 1980 near the junction of White Hill Wood and Long Hill Wood. There may have been a more substantial building here which was occupied into a later period as two fragments of pale green window glass were also found. To the north of the exposed stonework an area of iron slag extended some metres along the bank of the forest road ditch. The site is close to a change in the borough boundary and (like 'Maynestowe') could be one mentioned by le Messager in the 14th century.

Large parts of the countryside were reclaimed from the woodlands during the 20th century, especially in the Second World War, and ploughing will have removed much of the evidence of any medieval houses.

It was not only medieval and earlier homesteads which were left to their fate around the hills and quiet valleys of Monmouth. House sites abandoned in the 18th century can sometimes be traced in the woods – an excellent example being one in the Buckholt Wood where the house plan, outhouse, garden and the stone surround of the spring water supply are evident in the undergrowth; the site is marked by clumps of snowdrops. Snowdrops also grow in profusion on the numerous ruins of 'squatters' cottages along the lanes, often accompanied by a yew tree or some other surviving 'clue' garden plants.

Numerous farmsteads were abandoned during the 20th century, especially following the two World Wars; on the White Hill – immediately to the west of Monmouth – the Berry Farm; Thorn Farm; the Upper Bailey Pit and the Old Bailey Pit all lie ruined beneath the brambles.

Before History

THE deep soils of northern Gwent and Herefordshire are turned red in the spring and autumn when the ploughs come out. But it's not only the seagulls who will follow the plough, for archaeologists too find the exposed ground of interest – especially after it has been broken by rain and frost.

Field walking is an exciting way to explore the past and we in Monmouth have found two Roman forts, a Roman villa, and numerous Roman industrial sites together with medieval and later settlements by walking ploughed fields. But field walking is mostly associated with prehistory and although this book is generally concerned with later times it would be incomplete without at least a brief look at that part of the adventure.

Little has survived of the very distant past – before the last glaciations to periods over 200,000 years ago – for we are told that the melting of the ice sheets would have washed most remnants of Neanderthal man and his camp sites out to sea. The ice sheets of the last glaciations were close by, running from Abergavenny to Hereford, but land above 500 feet may have been above the melt outwash. This must have been the case where Bob Flynn chanced upon a Lower Palaeolithic ovate Acheulean hand-axe while working in a potato field near Pembridge Castle at Welsh Newton in 1971 (SO 4923 1905). This hand axe would have been owned by a Neanderthal – one of the first humans to live in Wales – or at least one of the first visitors. It led Bob to become a dedicated enquirer into Stone Age life and he found many later Stone Age implements.

Bob Flynn's Lower Palaeolithic hand axe from a potato field at Welsh Newton

King Arthur's Cave on the Great Doward was occupied during Upper Palaeolithic times and similar flints have been found at Blackbrook, Skenfrith (Lydia Buckland, SO 433 210); Hadnock (Steve Clarke, SO 5280 1355); Newton Court Farm, Dixton (Dave Pritchard, SO5175 1544) and Llanishen (Julia Wilson). However, many worked flints (outside caves) are notoriously difficult to date and we are only on safer ground after the most recent retreat of the ice sheets.

Late Mesolithic/early Neolithic style blades and Microlithic barbs of the Middle and New Stone Ages are not uncommon finds in Monmouth and the surrounding countryside. There is a 5.5cm x 8mm blade that came from Wyebridge Street and various microliths (flint barbs) from other sites – those at 22-24 and 66-68 Monnow Street being the most productive. The impression is of hunter-gatherers exploiting the fauna along the banks of the two rivers.

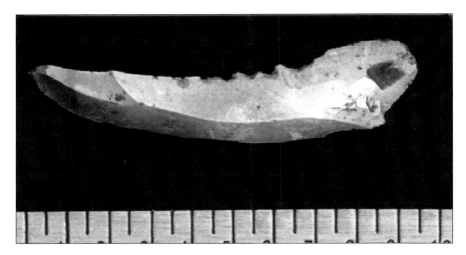

Upper Palaeolithic Chedderian backed blade from Llanishen (Julia Wilson)

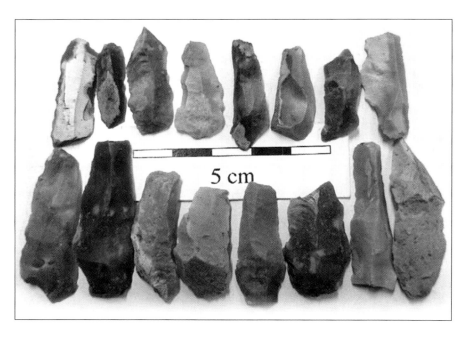

Some of Dave Pritchard's Mesolithic style flints from Troy Meadow, Monmouth

Naturally, most sites of this period are marked by flint scatters in the topsoil and it follows that any traces of camp sites on arable land are likely to have been destroyed by ploughing. So sites in woodland or moorland are likely to be more intact but with little broken ground they are of course far less likely to be discovered. An interesting woodland site of this period at the Buckholt, with wide views overlooking Monmouth from the north, has produced microliths and a substantial scatter of waste flakes in the leaf mould.

Most of the flints from the town and the surrounding countryside are attributable to the New Stone Age (the Neolithic) and axes or reworked fragments of axes from a variety of sources have been discovered by members of the Society including three by Bob Flynn. The sources of these axes include East Anglia, Cornwall, Langdale/Scafell Pike (Group VI) and Scandinavia. A Group VI axe was found inside a medieval house which had been abandoned in the 14th century in woods at English Newton Common.

Arrowheads are also frequently recovered and include both wide and narrow leaf-shaped examples together with oblique or single barbed ones. A beautiful leaf-shaped arrowhead 5.7cm x 2.3cm was found by Phil Parkinson at Penallt.

A Neolithic or Bronze Age Saddle Quern found in a builder's trench at Clawdd Du, Monmouth

Flint knives also feature in the Society collections and include one in off-white flint polished on both faces with a re-touched notch end. This piece was found by Reg Clarke on Chippenham Mead during the construction of the A40 dual carriageway (SO 509 124) and is similar to a knife from West Kennett Long Barrow.

About a dozen Beaker barbed and tanged arrowheads have been found in and around Monmouth. Of those recovered during excavations in the town is one from ancient river sands and gravels at 22-24 Monnow Street which is highly polished, as if water-worn, and this may be an indication of the water level and the position of the Monmouth rivers during the Bronze Age.

In 1980, the excavation of a pipe trench a few metres from the hedge south of the Clawdd Du ditch at Overmonnow was covered by a Society watching brief when Roman and medieval remains were recovered. However, during a final check of the backfilled trench, I found a saddle quern stone of Neolithic or Bronze Age date sitting on top of the spoil heap.

An Iron Age glass bead and a cooking pot rim were found near the Gaer earthwork at Hygga Farm, Trelech, and a similar bead at Parkside, Welsh Newton, by Sue Powles. Single Iron Age gold staters were found on two farms near Trelech by John Bray while detecting and another of these coins came from Dingestow.

We have recently found small sherds of Iron Age pottery in exposed soil on the sides of a track in the Buckholt Woods just to the north of Monmouth. One sherd is of a shell-tempered ware and the other is Malvernian (both kindly identified by Dr Vince). These sherds are probably related to the earthwork (now scheduled) which was discovered by the Society and surveyed by Barry James and the Woolwich Polytechnic over thirty years ago.

Neolithic flint knife from Paul Davies' excavation at 100 Monnow Street

The Legend of a Lost Town

During a major uprising in 1296 the Welsh attacked the border town of Trelech. Black smoke would have drifted across the Wye Valley as more than a hundred houses were burned.

On a summer's day, over seven hundred years later, a young Monmouth archaeologist raises potsherds from the remains of a medieval house. The sherds he is finding came from pots which had been so severely burned that they had melted, and the surfaces of stones in the house had turned to glass.

He is digging a quarter of a mile outside the village of Trelech – along a quiet country lane – where, contrary to received wisdom, legend put the lost town.

TRELECH lies above the Wye Valley on the heavily wooded plateau of eastern Gwent. During the High Middle Ages the settlement was a thriving industrial centre, one of the biggest towns in Wales. However, following famine, the Black Death, attacks by the supporters of Madog ap Llewelyn in 1296 and by Owain Glyndwr in the early 15th century, together with economic problems, the settlement fades from history to become a legendary lost town.

The documented thirteenth century iron-working and agricultural town of Trelech was naturally assumed to have been the same place as modern Trelech – centred on its imposing church and small earth and timber castle – in a classic planned grid pattern.

However, when we were first digging in the village in the early 1970s I was told by an elderly resident that Trelech was once 'up the Catbrook Road'. As the Trelech wayside Cross was along this road, exactly a mile from the church, I assumed that was the origin of the legend. Another story was that Trelech once had seven churches and that the three standing stones beside the village were thrown from Garway Hill during a stone throwing contest between the Devil and the Welsh magician Sion Cent (Jack o' Kent). Even so, perhaps we should have taken more notice.

As the years passed, we could not understand why so many areas inside the village were devoid of remains when it was estimated that there were nearly 400 burgages there in the 13th century. On site after site, the thin topsoil came cleanly off the natural subsoil producing only a few handfuls of eroded medieval potsherds.

We were eventually to carry out excavations and watching briefs on some thirty sites, covering over 20,000 square metres of land inside the village, without a single 13th century burgage coming to light. The only 13th century stone buildings in the village were the Church and the large stone structures in Church Field West – we really were looking for a lost town. When we discovered it, every building was of stone – in fields, gardens and on the roadsides – but this was well away from the village and its 'planned town grid'.

During the 1960s and 70s there had been occasional ground disturbances in and around Trelech. There was usually 'Trelech Treacle' – the iron slag from bloomery furnaces – and small amounts of medieval pottery, but otherwise nothing that one would expect inside a medieval town.

By 1980, the field to the north-west of Trelech churchyard was scheduled as an Ancient Monument. Here it was that Joseph Bradney had detected building foundations and an ancient road which he recorded in his great work on the history of Monmouthshire, published at the beginning of the 20th century.

Shortly after the scheduling, a driveway to one of the houses was cut through the field, against the churchyard wall, and was followed by a rescue excavation. The three of us who carried out the excavation represented the three archaeological interests in the area: one from the Ministry of Works, one from the Glamorgan-Gwent Archaeological Trust and one from Monmouth Archaeological Society. A note was published in *The Monmouthshire Antiquary* (IV, 1981/82) which seems to have been the first publication of archaeological work in Trelech since Bradney's in 1914.

In the 1980s developments inside the village increased but the absence of anything that looked like burgages was unexplained. Topsoil stripping of large areas around the Babbington Centre and the new Trelech School on the north side of the village produced occasional sherds of eroded pottery but showed that there were no other remains in this area.

In the autumn of 1987, a deep service trench was dug across the unscheduled part of Church Field – between the scheduled area and the Castle (Plot 63 south on the 1880 Ordnance Survey map). My field notebook records:

There is about a foot of clean topsoil upon natural. The more I see inside the village the more I'm sure that it was never properly filled.

In the middle of the village, deep excavations – both inside and around the Crown Inn (later the Village Green) – failed to produce any evidence of the medieval town. The only discovery here was a large 19th century well, which was filled with stone and rubbish in the 20th century (Plot 72).

In 1993, Harry Evans stripped the topsoil from some 400 square metres of his field immediately to the west of the castle mound at Court Farm (Plot 64). These excavations were for a silage clamp and other foundations and although Dr Ray Howell found a sherd of Roman Samian-ware, we could find no other archaeological remains except for a few sherds of medieval pottery and some modern stonework beside the field gate. Nearby, other watching briefs had shown that Plots 66/68 and 70-72 were also empty.

By now, Dr Howell, with teams from the University of Wales Newport, was on the scene and his enthusiastic excavations have been a feature of research into medieval Trelech ever since.

In 1995, Felicity Taylor was carrying out rescue excavations inside St Nicholas's Church, sympathetically moving the skeletons which were buried there amongst earlier skeletons. It was at that time that the somewhat dismal picture of Trelech's archaeology suddenly changed. Deep foundation trenches for an extension behind the Ebenezer Chapel, brought up black organic-rich vestiges from two metres below ground (Plot 86). The spoil heaps contained a wide variety of medieval and post-medieval pottery and animal and plant remains, together with parts of leather shoes and a wooden bowl. The wet, dark and airless conditions had preserved a remarkable picture of life during the hey-day of the medieval town. Underneath the sticky black deposits, a solid layer of bloomery iron slag lay upon the waterlogged natural. However, this was outside the town 'grid plan'. The foundations of the new extension had to be re-designed and the remains now lie under a concrete raft.

With the introduction of the planning guidelines to protect archaeological remains, further developments in and around Trelech came under scrutiny. The planning authority required an archaeological evaluation in the car park of The Lion Inn before considering a planning application in 1995. *Monmouth Archaeology*, the Society's professional wing, was awarded the contract but the digging showed that it was another empty plot (74 north).

In 1999 Ed Rogers of Trelech Farm applied for planning permission to develop a large area of his land inside the supposed 'town grid'. Again, the planning authority asked for an archaeological evaluation before considering the application and Mr Rogers also employed *Monmouth Archaeology* (Plot 76).

Part of 12,000 square metres of the supposed 'town grid' but devoid of remains

We dug six two-metre wide trenches around the site, four of them twenty metres long. All of these showed that the undisturbed natural ground surface lay immediately beneath the thin humus. A scanty group of abraded potsherds came from the topsoil – spread with medieval manure. When planning permission was granted, we carried out a programme of archaeological recording when work began. The developers stripped the topsoil from the entire site, proving conclusively that the burgages of industrial Trelech were not inside the village – or at least not inside this extensive plot of over 12,000 square metres.

We were now convinced that something was seriously amiss if such extensive areas of the largest medieval town were empty during the 13th century. However, a new theory was now thrown into the ring – an idea which was to change everything.

Inside the 'town grid' at Trelech Farm, 1999, showing complete absence of archaeological remains

+ + +

One day in 1997, Julia Wilson, the Society's treasurer, brought a paper which she had written – *'Trelech: A new location for the old town'*.

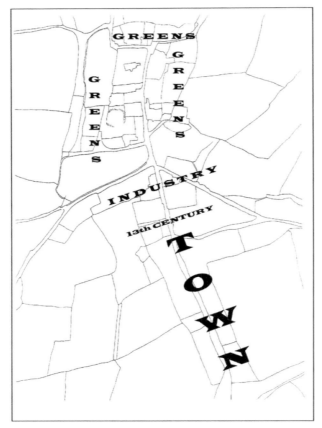

The archaeological evidence for 13th century Trelech (drawing by Jane Bray)

Mrs Wilson suggested that the burgages of the 13th century town of Trelech lay to the south, outside the present village – along the Catbrook Road. As I read it, I recalled Thomas Huxley's *'How stupid of me not to have thought of that'* on reading Darwin's *Origin of Species*; and I also remembered the legend.

Julia submitted her paper to an appropriate journal but the editor, apparently considering it too innovative and requiring more research, turned it down, so I sent it to the *Council for British Archaeology Wales/Cymru* which published it in *Archaeology in Wales,* 38, 1998.

It was very fortunate that Julian Wilson's article was published at that time for her priority would almost certainly have been lost, as information on the whereabouts of 13th century Trelech then rapidly increased.

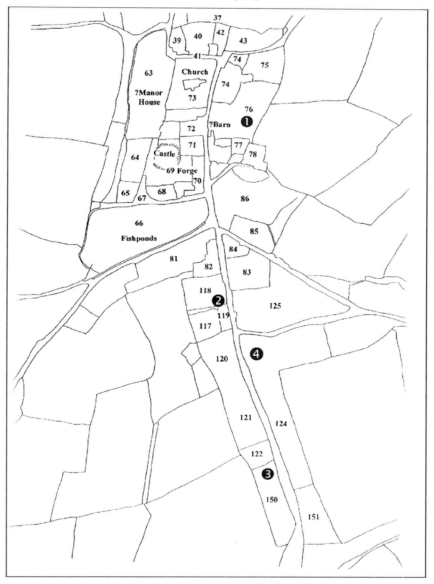

Trelech, the 1880 Ordnance Survey (drawing by Jane Bray)

Opinions Diverge

Supporting evidence quickly came from a site allocated for housing between the Catbrook and Tintern Roads (Plot 125). Trial excavations by *Thames Valley Archaeological Unit* revealed medieval stone buildings in all the trenches excavated beside the Catbrook Road and *Cadw-Welsh Historic Monuments* intervened and scheduled the site as an Ancient Monument. The excavators considered that the buildings were burgages of the 13th century town (Hull, 1998). However, Dr Mike Hamilton and Dr Howell, of the University of Wales Newport, who had been working alongside us for many years, challenged this conclusion and criticised the nature of the excavation and its recording.

Following their own geophysical survey, they decided that the structures were not burgages at all but were the remains of a medieval farm (Hamilton and Howell, 2000).

The University geophysical surveys elsewhere were confusing, for Dr Hamilton, who directed them, was claiming to have found burgages on all the sites he surveyed inside the village while, wherever we dug in the village, the sites were empty.

Dr Hamilton claimed that all his surveys within Trelech had found clear evidence of divisions, usually 10m-wide plots, while none outside the village had produced similar evidence (Hamilton, *ibid*, 145). However, Dr Hamilton recognised that if the burgages were on 10m-wide plots, only half of those recorded in 1288 would fit into the town. He suggested that if the plots were divided in half, all 378 burgages could be accommodated. Over more than thirty years, we have found no evidence that such divisions exist.

University excavations in the village, following Dr Hamilton's surveys, never revealed medieval stone buildings – only structures which relied on occasional stone 'post pads' and shallow beam slots – remains which were open to different interpretations, especially that of field drains filled with broken stone. Later articles in *Archaeology in Wales* highlighted the dangers of publishing interpretations of geophysical surveys in the village prior to excavations.

+   +   +

By 2005 Dr Hamilton was reporting burgages on all the sites that he surveyed inside the village (Hamilton, 2002, 142-3) and, in dismissing our evidence, was claiming that there were none outside the village centre (Hamilton, *ibid,* 145). Dr Howell also contested Julia Wilson's theory and described the lack of remains as 'areas of apparent vacant possession which have exercised minds in the Monmouth Archaeological Society for several years' (Howell, 2005, 48). He suggested that caution is always prudent in cases of 'negative evidence'. Both sides agreed that Trelech had been one of the largest towns of medieval Wales but there the agreement ended, as we ourselves felt that we had proved beyond reasonable doubt that the 'evidence of absence' in the village was overwhelming.

We had shown that there were no archaeological remains in any of the fields surrounding the plot to the rear of The Lion Inn (Plot 75). However, following his geophysical survey, Dr Hamilton claimed in *Archaeology in Wales* (2002) that the field contained many archaeological features. These included clear walls (possibly with some industrial function), banks, ditches, linear features, hard standing or floors and up to 44 burgages. If this was true, such remains would not have existed in isolation – we must have missed scores of sites in the surrounding fields. I decided to write a paper drawing together evidence from over forty sites both inside and outside the village and submitted it to our county journal, *The Monmouthshire Antiquary*.

It was published in Volume XXII (2006).

In August 2006, *Cotswold Archaeology* carried out an archaeological evaluation in the field behind the Lion and five 20m trenches were excavated down to natural. None of the features described by Dr Hamilton were found.

+   +   +

Inside The Village

Today, there is irrefutable evidence that Trelech Village was not the site of the extensive 13th century industrial settlement.

During the summer of 2003, Dr Howell led a University of Wales excavation on the large buildings in Plot 63 – Church Field West (Howell, 2005, p46). These structures are isolated and unique inside the village; Dr Howell identified them as the remains of a hospice or an inn. Whatever the buildings were, most of the field in which they were built was empty throughout the Middle Ages, as can be seen in the contour survey by Dr Neil Phillips (Howell, 2005, 58). We carried out rescue work in this field in 1980 (Clarke, *et al*, 1981-82). On the south of Plot 63 Dr Howell excavated the robbed remains of a 14th century long house but much of the evidence had been destroyed by a post-medieval agricultural building (Howell, 1993).

We have shown that there is no significant archaeological resource in any of the plots to the north of the Church (Plots 37 and 39-43). The wide ditch behind the Babington Centre deserves exploration but no corresponding defensive work is apparent and there have been extensive groundworks across the whole area. Most of these parts were stripped down to the natural subsoil and trenched during developments: at the Babington centre (Plots 39-42); during the construction of the new school (Plot 37); and during the building of several houses in Plot 43. A building under the patio of The Lion Inn (Plot 74) was built over the old humus and was pre-dated by 14th century pottery, so it could not be claimed to be a part of the 13th century town.

Monmouth Archaeology carried out another large archaeological evaluation inside the 'grid' at Court Farm during the summer of 2005. The work was in relation to a planning application for housing and five trenches were excavated in Plots 65/66 and part of 69, covering around 120 square metres of the 4,000 square metre plot in and around the farm buildings. No archaeological features were discovered and the natural boulder clay and bedrock were proved to lie directly below the topsoil. Single sherds of a medieval jug and of a medieval ridge tile were recovered. We are carrying out another archaeological evaluation – this time adjoining the scheduled castle mound on the east – as we go to press (May, 2008).

+   +   +

A Medieval Iron Forge. In 1997 we carried out an archaeological evaluation at Court Farm Bungalow in the north of plot 70 which is to the south of the Church, overlooking the main road through the village. Immediately beneath the thin garden topsoil, we uncovered the remains of a medieval iron forge which, in common with so much of the town and countryside, had been abandoned in the 14th century. These remains had then lain undisturbed for over six centuries. The planning authority asked for preservation by record, and the unit were contracted to totally excavate the footprint of the new extension – we were to destroy it, instead of the developer.

Apart from the salvaging of some building materials, including the unbroken ridge tiles, the remains lay relatively intact as the site was untilled during medieval and later times and appears to have been used as a paddock or an orchard until the construction of the adjoining Court Farm Bungalow.

The total excavation of the site revealed that there was an early, undated occupation, followed by a middle 13th century iron forge. The site may then have lain dormant for some years until the occupation which produced most pottery and which seems to have been of a short duration in the early 14th century. The industry was established in a sturdy half-timbered building

Phase One: The primary occupation was of ironworking; it is undated and consisted of a series of stake holes probably associated with a hearth which was damaged during the next phase.

Phase Two: This was the earlier of the two 13th century phases on the site and consisted of a structure based on sleeper beams. This building was also concerned with the iron industry and was pre-dated by the hearth of the first phase which was cut by the trench for one of the sleeper beams.

Phase Three: This was the main 13th century occupation made up of a hearth, two hollows or shallow pits and a post-hole. The pottery dating Phases Two and Three were the same and include Bristol Ham Green ware (12th to middle 13th century) and Monnow Valley ware jug sherds bearing developed diamond and fleurs-de-lis complex rouletting and cooking pots, both dated to around the middle of the 13th century. Other pots of the period were tripod pitchers from North Wiltshire – Minety ware. This securely stratified 13th century phase is best attributed to the second quarter of the century when Trelech town would have been thriving.

It may be illusory but there seems to be a gap in pottery dating, perhaps for as long as half a century, between the 13th century phase and that of the 14th century.

Phases Four and Five. The main surviving evidence for the occupation of the site is dated to the first half of the 14th century when Trelech had probably already started its decline. The two phases cover the stone foundation for the workshop, the drain fill, paving and hearths.

The forge was probably working blooms produced in the nearby Trelech iron furnaces. The different amounts of iron slag inside and outside the village shows that primary iron smelting was not usually practised inside the modern village. There is little difference between the pottery assemblages from the contexts of the 14th century occupation – ample Bristol Redcliffe pottery which post-dates Ham Green ware (from the middle 13th century) together with the ubiquitous early 14th century Drybridge Park ware.

The industry was carried out inside a paved workshop which was situated on a levelled platform. A University of Wales archaeomagnetic date on the site points to the 13th century but does not rule out a date in the early 14th century and the latter seems certain considering the wealth of dating evidence for Drybridge ware from elsewhere.

The impression gained from the remains was that the workshop consisted of a sturdy wooden building, probably open on one side, and roofed with sandstone tiles, capped with ceramic ridge tiles. It appears that the workshop was limited to the platform cut into the slope on the western part of the site and that the structure was based on sleeper beams set on a stone base near ground level with a rectangular post as an extra internal support.

Phase Six covers the dismantling, abandonment and decay of the building. Although documentary sources suggest that Trelech suffered a long slow decline, the occupation of this and other sites in the town ended suddenly in the early 14th century. Before the site was abandoned the roof seems to have been dismantled and most of the tiles were taken away for re-use elsewhere. The upper stones of the wall footings were removed and parts of the sandstone paving robbed. It may have been that the roof timbers and other woodwork were also removed when the building was demolished although they could have rotted on the site. There is no evidence of the burning of old timbers or for a destructive fire ending the life of the workshop.

After the workshop became a ruin, probably of rotting timbers covered with brambles, there was a slow build-up of humus across the site. The remains survived relatively undisturbed, perhaps because the eventual clearance of the scrub was achieved by animal grazing, possibly goats.

Another aspect of the ruin was that much of the paved area remained intact. Although there had been some stone robbing, the floor must have been essentially as it was when the building was occupied. That only a single, almost complete ceramic roof ridge tile remained and that intact stone roof tiles were lying where they had been stacked shows that there was careful dismantlement and salvaging of materials for re-use.

A large sherd of a Drybridge Park jug with the distinctive applied clay decoration had slid down the drain close to the end of the life in the workshop. This jug must have been broken during the final phase of occupation.

Summary: The Medieval Sequence:

Earliest, undated occupation
Middle 13th century occupation
Late 13th/early 14th century break in occupation?
Early 14th century: main occupation
End of the occupation ?before the middle 14th century
Garden, pasture or orchard until 20th century

+ + +

Further professional contracts under planning conditions imposed by the local authority failed to reveal more archaeological remains inside the village. These included the watching briefs on groundworks for barn construction at Court Farm and a programme of archaeological investigation on building work at the village stores. There was also a further fruitless watching brief in the grounds of The Lion Inn.

A Tithe Barn? The monitoring of excavations during the re-development of the barns alongside the main road at Trelech Farm, opposite the Village Green restaurant, suggests that the southern barn may have been built on medieval foundations. The barn footings were set in a foundation trench filled with clean soil. The layers above the foundation trench contained a lot of iron slag with some medieval pottery but none of this had got into the back-fill of the foundation trench. It could be that the foundations, predating the iron slag, were the first things on the site.

The other barns were of post-medieval date, built over the undisturbed humus and bedrock with no trace of the medieval town even though the floors were lowered well into the bedrock.

The Fish Ponds. In April 2002, Monmouthshire County Council began a flood alleviation scheme along the Olway, on the south side of Trelech village. The County Council had not obtained archaeological cover for the work so volunteers from Monmouth Archaeological Society and its professional units, *Monmouth Archaeology* and *Church Archaeological Services*, together with the University of Wales, Newport, carried out rescue work when well-preserved organic remains were found in the spoil heaps (*Archaeology in Wales*, 2002). Medieval remains, including pottery, bones, wood, plants and leather shoes were recovered, together with a timber trackway dated to 1226-27 by Nigel Nayling from the tree rings of a plank (financed by the County Council).

Rescue work on a 13th century wooden track way in Trelech Fishponds

Since that time, continuing investigations along the Catbrook Road are revealing the character and extent of the 13th century settlement. All the house foundations discovered are of stone – unlike any of the sites claimed as burgages within the village, except for the plots occupied by the substantial buildings in Church Field West.

A site on the west of the Catbrook Road (Plot 118) was destroyed in 1999 before the planning authority could intervene, but permission for a new building was withheld until *Monmouth Archaeology* had carried out an archaeological

Trelech Cross – exactly one mile from the Church – along the Catbrook Road

evaluation on what was left. There was a medieval well, walling and medieval pottery, showing that this was the site of a 13th century house with stone foundations which was abandoned during the 14th century. The well is preserved as a feature in front of the new house.

In May 2006, an application to build a house to the north of Plot 119 required an archaeological evaluation under planning legislation. The contract again went to *Monmouth Archaeology* and excavations revealed that there were substantial structures in the front garden. One of the walls of two buildings was found to be four feet thick (1.20m). Although there had been the domestic occupation on the adjoining plot to the north, this building may be a very large barn as household pottery was sparse. There were five different sources of ridge tile – two types were the products of local kilns, another came from North Devon; there were others from Malvern and yet another from an unknown source. We interpret this as evidence for the re-roofing of a large agricultural building over some centuries where domestic pottery would be uncommon. As with some of the remains on Stuart Wilson's site (which lies along the east of Catbrook Road), a heavy deposit of bloomery iron slag predated the structure. When building work began another large building was revealed on the south side of the first one.

Firestorm. Earlier Stuart had sampled another plot almost at random at Mr Badham's, The Hostry, further along the Catbrook Road, in 2003-04. This time the site lay a quarter of a mile outside the village – at the northern end of Plot 150. The remains of two medieval houses were found, each represented by several phases of robbed walling with one phase ending dramatically in the late 13th or early 14th century with a terrible fire. Pottery melted and some stone surfaces turned to glass. It could be that this is evidence for the Welsh attack of 1296 when a hundred houses are said to have been burnt (Wilson, S, 2002).

Excavations at The Hostry, Catbrook Road – a quarter of a mile from the village centre (Plot 150)

The Boy who bought a Field

When a local newspaper referred to the uncovering of the buildings at the Hostry as the discovery of a 'Lost City', press and television coverage became frenetic. The media had an even greater field day when Stuart bought at auction (for £34,000) the field over the road and immediately showed that there were substantial stone buildings wherever he dug (Plot 124).

The meadow bought by Stuart Wilson. Such long narrow fields survive on both sides of the Catbrook Road and contain the underground remains of the lost town

Stuart Wilson (left) before his Radio Four interview with Francis Prior (right)

The Trelech Town excavation in 2007

There is now no room for debate on the whereabouts of the 13th century town since Stuart Wilson's excavations started on his Plot 124. The exposure of extensive stone foundations of houses in every trial excavation along a 70m stretch of the field (see photograph) is evidence enough. Although at least one of these buildings was occupied into the 17th century, they are probably all medieval – 13th century pottery and roof furniture being widespread in and around the ruins.

Medieval stone buildings, mostly houses, have now been found during every excavation on both sides of the Catbrook Road.

Part of the Trelech excavation in 2007 – the burgages on the street frontage

Elsewhere in this field, buildings have shown up as parch-marks in the 1970s. The farmer had tried to plough the field in the 1940s, but had given up along the roadside because of the stonework and instead planted potatoes by hand. Moles, raising black soil and medieval pottery in other parts of the field, avoid the roadside stretches, presumably because of the amount of stone beneath the surface. Interestingly there are also indications of a road running to the rear of the house sites. As this book goes to press the latest discoveries include a substantial house to the rear of the burgages with a well and an enigmatic stone-roofed circular structure together with outbuildings; also, the frontage 'burgages' continue wherever the team digs. Stuart has taken up the *Lost 'City' of Trelech* appellation with enthusiasm, regardless of counsel from my generation; even so we have to admit that it has increased media hype for his dig.

Summary

Twelfth-century Trelech lies under the modern village and is similar to other small settlements in the area which were centred on a motte and a church. Dr Neil Phillips has shown that there was a wooden bridge on the church side of the motte and he suggests that this is evidence for a bailey in that area of the early town (Phillips, 2002, 143-145). Although the extent of a bailey has yet to be established, it would presumably have enclosed the forge at Court Farm Bungalow. If other buildings in the area between the castle and the church were constructed of wood, it is possible that they have not been detected although there have been watching briefs on a number of building works in these plots.

Whatever the nature and extent of the settlement inside the village, it is now irrefutable that most, if not all, of the large 13th industrial town lay to the south of the River Olwy, along the Catbrook Road, as an entirely separate development. Early Trelech, inside the present village, must have consisted of a castle (and any buildings inside a bailey), a church and an iron forge. At least by the 13th century the large buildings in Church Field West had appeared – possibly with a tithe barn near Trelech Farm and of course the industrial suburb over the river. The main iron smelting area was also over the Olwy – with the major slag heaps paradoxically centred where very little slag is found today.

The claims for the existence of burgage plots inside the village rely on geophysical interpretations while the archaeological evidence is that the core of the settlement was surrounded by large greens.

Iron working in Trelech

Paradoxically, the evidence for the centre of Trelech's primary iron industry and its greatest slag-heap comes from a site which now produces clear evidence but very little iron slag. An extension to The Barton, close to Cross Hands just on the Tintern Road, in December 2004, revealed a metre of black dusty, charcoal-rich loam which was the residue from the riddling of the slag. This deposit is identical to that in parts of Cinderhill Street in Monmouth where the Council and the Duke of Beaufort removed a huge 'cinder hill' for recycling in the 18th century (*Down the Cinder Mines*).

Although there is documentary evidence for post-medieval slag recycling at Trelech it is not known how much existed or was taken away but the evidence from the Barton is that it was substantial. In Monmouth, it is clear that thousands of tons of slag had remained in great drifts from Roman and medieval times and the 17th and 18th century 'mining' of slag became a major industry. The transport problem would have been far greater at Trelech than at Monmouth where slag was dug on the riverbanks and taken directly to the Tintern furnaces by barge. The slag from Trelech was recycled at the nearby blast furnace at Woolpitch Wood (the Trelech Furnace) which must have been built especially to exploit the resource in the village. One can confidently assume that vast amounts of iron slag existed in the industrial suburb between the old town in the village and the 13th century industrial town along the Catbrook Road as it did in Monmouth where over four metres remain on the banks of the River Wye at The Quay.

Evidence of iron working from inside the modern village is sparse compared with that from around and beyond the junction of the Whitebrook, Catbrook and Chepstow roads. Besides the workshop excavation at Court Farm and a heavy slag fringe on the east of Plot 76, there is little evidence for iron working to the east of the church. On the west of the Church Dr Howell has explored slag areas in the southern part of Plot 63 while iron working remains were recorded during rescue and research excavations just outside the churchyard in the northern part of the same plot. Dr Howell's work on the large buildings in Church Field has revealed slag overlying parts of the structure which post-dated the main occupation. Other areas inside the modern village have produced iron smelting waste but only occasional evidence of hearths. It is likely that all iron working in the village, excepting the forge at Court Farm Bungalow, is of late medieval date.

As mentioned, the areas producing most evidence of iron working are outside the village, especially over the River Olway – to the south-east, towards the Virtuous Well and to the south-west, on the village side of the medieval fish ponds. Heavy concentrations of bloomery iron slag were recorded to a depth of 1.5m just to the west of Cross Hands and similar deposits were revealed during drainage works beneath the junction of the Chepstow and Catbrook roads where it may have been harder to recover for recycling. To the south-east of Trelech Pound slag concentrations were found in the meadows beside the stream towards the Virtuous Well in 1999 and during later excavations by Dr Howell. Similar extensive slag deposits were recorded in the field beyond the Virtuous Well – no doubt producing the waters that are prized by pilgrims to the chalybeate well. A major deposit of iron slag was also found to the east of the Virtuous Well (Cross Hands Farm) when the farmer was attempting an excavation for a pond in 1982.

The iron industry is evident along the Catbrook Road south of Cross Hands and is listed with other evidence that this was part of the documented 13th century town. Large deposits of bloomery iron slag were recorded under the buildings at The Paddocks (Plot 119) and there is also evidence of iron working predating the large building set back from the burgages on Stuart Wilson's site.

A deposit of non-ferrous metal working slag was found associated with structural remains during the *Thames Valley Unit*'s trial excavations between the lower Catbrook Road and the Whitebrook Road.

A Farmer's Tale. Mr Rogers Senior, of Trelech Farm, a lifelong resident of the village, told me an interesting story about Trelech Bog, a story that may be very ancient. He tells that his grandfather told him the story which his grandfather had told him . . . "Long ago a mule was lost in the bog" . . . Workers were using split tree trunks as a trackway for ponies over the marshes when one day a mule lost its footing and sank into the bog. The mule and the ponies were fitted with side panniers – wicker baskets made for transporting something they were

Large wall foundations at The Paddocks, Catbrook Road (Plot 119)

collecting from the marshes – and the weight must have helped push the animal to its death. The main point of the story was that the bog was deep and dangerous; a fact he said was recently confirmed when a telegraph pole was erected in one of the fields and was found the next morning to have sunk to half its length. Mr Rogers wasn't sure what was being brought from the marshes, for the point of the story was the nature of the bog and the loss of the mule, but he thought that it was a mineral and was being taken to Tintern (or could it have been to the Woolpitch Wood blast furnace?). If this is a true story, and there is little reason to doubt it, it must surely be one of slag recovery, a folk memory, perhaps going back three centuries.

Some of the rescue team during the Trelech flood scheme excavations. Left to right: Jane Bray (Monmouth Archaeology/Monmouth Archaeological Society); Nigel Nayling (Dendrochronologist); Ray Howell and David Howell (University of Wales, Newport); Felicity Taylor (Church Archaeological Services and Monmouth Archaeological Society)

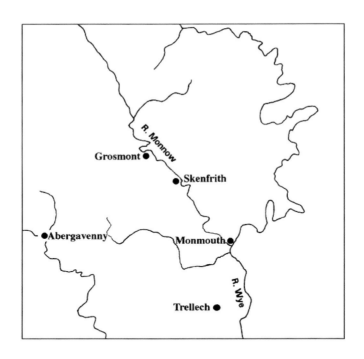

Grosmont –
Another Lost Town ?

GROSMONT was built on a hillside overlooking the Monnow Valley. It is an impressive sight from the south during winter but is practically unseen when approached from the north, east and west. The village has changed little in recent centuries and even today has been saved from large-scale development by its remoteness and narrow, winding lanes. It has retained an air of rural tranquillity into the twenty-first century with its Angel public house, small shop and nearby coffee house and it is one of the few villages of Gwent which has public toilets – a facility shared with the public house and kept in pristine condition by the County Council. It also has a Town Hall.

Grosmont from Hill House on the Graig Hill

The Church of St Nicholas appears big from outside but inside seems vast, especially for that of a rather sleepy village. It is, like St Nicholas's at Trelech, an echo of former glory and in this case there is a place in significant events in the long struggle between Welsh and English.

Although not on the scale of medieval Trelech, Grosmont was once a substantial settlement and Ian Soulsby has estimated that the town would have contained some 160 burgage plots during its 13th century heyday. The whereabouts of many of these houses is something of a mystery although the remains of some should lie beneath the houses of the modern village. Despite numerous archaeological evaluations and watching briefs, only a few well-preserved medieval stone-based house sites have been found. A few other sites, with far less substantial remains, were also discovered, and these may provide a clue to the nature and fate of others.

The first medieval house to be excavated in Grosmont was unearthed by Neil Maylan of the Glamorgan-Gwent Archaeological Trust in 1989 during an evaluation for a housing development at Well Farm on the north-west side of the village. Survey and trial excavations, followed by watching briefs, covered some 5,700 square metres of the field. Only in the south-east corner of the development site – that closest to the village centre – was there any sign of the medieval town. An area of 400 square metres was cleared to expose the foundations of a substantial house which had been occupied in the 13th or 14th century. The size of the building – of several phases, together with its surrounding yards – indicated to the excavators that this was a farmstead. The pottery from the site shows that it did not survive the fourteenth century.

Later discoveries at Well Farm by Monmouth archaeologists were far more transient and made as much by luck during the digging of foundation trenches for new buildings. On the southern part of the development site a small area of burnt ground had survived below the plough soil and contained a few stones with a group of jug and cooking potsherds. This was at first thought to be the remains of a pottery clamp kiln *(Pottery Kiln or House Fire)* but it is now realised that it was the site of a house fire. The cooking pottery associated with the fire had melted and blistered in a distinctive way – identically to pots at Trelech and Oldcastle but here few signs of a building remained.

It is strange that so much of Neil Maylan's building had survived while in the same area the remains of another house had been almost totally destroyed. However, it is very likely that a peasant's home would have been built of timber, which would leave few traces for subsequent ploughing to destroy. This theory received support during later developments further up the Well Farm field in 2002. Several thin courses of a stone wall were found built into the bedrock, which in Grosmont tends to lie on a horizontal plane looking deceptively like walling or paving. These layers of Devonian sandstone may have been the origin of some of Archdeacon Coxe's 'causeways' which he recorded as being like Roman roads leading out of Grosmont in several directions (Coxe, 1801). The Well Farm stonework, however, was confirmed as walling by the presence of stone roof-tiles (with nail holes) leaning against it where they had landed after sliding down the roof of the building or had been stacked during dismantling – not such a flimsy structure after all. This building was probably associated with a large sherd of a Drybridge type jug of 14th century date which was found by a neighbour in her garden. The position of the wall – built into the bedrock – had preserved some of its footings, together with score marks left by the plough; the rest of the building was probably of wood. Timber structures which were capable of supporting a stone tiled roof are known from other sites in the district and there are many still standing over the border in Herefordshire. So it may be that few of Grosmont's medieval houses were built in stone and consequently have left little structural evidence in the archaeological record.

Even so, sites nearer to the village centre, explored during watching briefs, at Avalon, Bank House, Homefield, Onaway and along Poorscript Lane, have shown that there was no occupation here during the Middle Ages.

In 2006, Mike Ponsford's team from Bristol discovered a medieval house and some small-scale metalworking in the field across the road from Well Farm. However, the building was isolated and the field was otherwise empty.

Development excavations at Town Farm, Grosmont, showing absence of archaeological remains

Town Farm is situated beside the churchyard where one would have expected to find many of the medieval houses that are recorded in the town. But when *Monmouth Archaeology* carried out large-scale evaluations in two of the fields on the farm, no structures or other features were unearthed. Only a handful of abraded medieval potsherds were found and they were probably distributed over the field during the spreading of manure (Clarke & Bray, Oct. 2000).

We really were wondering where the burgages had got to, when a medieval house came to light at the very southern edge of the village, beside the road to Monmouth – at Tan-y-Lan. During a watching brief on the digging of foundation trenches for a garage, a single celled building was revealed and preserved by record by *Monmouth Archaeology*.

The house was occupied during the thirteenth century and despite a fire had survived through the fourteenth century into early post-medieval times. There was an enigmatic, well-preserved, shallow stone tank which was floored with stone roof tiles. This building is shown as a small black and white house on the remarkable Duchy of Lancaster map of 1588 which depicts half-timbered buildings dotted around the landscape and centred on Grosmont with its church and castle. The map was first recognised amongst the Badminton papers by Philip Morgan of Grosmont who has carried out much research on the town. Amongst the pottery was a face-mask from a jug.

This is believed to be of Scarborough ware – a face apparently contorted by toothache.

One might conjecture how this jug came to Grosmont – the furthest west the fabric has been found; Might it have ended up amongst rubbish from the royal household in the castle and taken home as a curio or child's toy?

The 13th century face mask from a jug thought to be Scarborough ware

The garage foundations were redesigned and some of the building has now been preserved *in situ* (Clarke & Bray, July 2001).

Parch marks. During the exceptionally dry spring and summer of 1984 a variety of structures were revealed as parch marks to the north west of Grosmont Castle. The late Dr Stephen Pickford, who lived in the nearby house, 'Castle Acre', recorded the marks and an article was published in 'Monmouth Archaeology', the 1989 Newsletter of *Monmouth Archaeological Society* (Pickford, S., 1989) and in *Hidden Grosmont* – a series of articles published in 2001. During redevelopments following the sale of Castle Acre in 2002, we found areas of bloomery iron slag and some medieval pottery in the garden ('Monmouth Archaeology').

But still, where are the rest of the 160 medieval houses? Are Ian Soulsby's calculations that wrong or do scores of homesteads remain to be discovered, as did the 13th century town of Trelech?

Another unexpected discovery was a medieval house which we unearthed during groundworks for the conversion of a barn beside the churchyard at Town Farm. This substantial building of several phases appears to have been abandoned (once again) in the first half of the 14th century. Parts of the remains are preserved *in situ* beside the drive to the converted barn and two new houses.

A Pottery Kiln? The Grosmont Tithe Map of 1840 shows a 'Kiln Field' near the end of Poorscript Lane. The field has not been ploughed for many years but a thorough search of hedgerows, banks and ditches over several years has produced no evidence of a pottery kiln; there is no limestone, seemingly ruling out a limekiln. During *Monmouth Archaeology's* watching brief on housing groundworks at Town Farm Meadow in 2005 we picked up a small piece of a post-medieval pot which had melted – a fairly definite fragment of a kiln waster. In 2006, we collected a small assemblage of 17th century pottery, some kiln damaged, from a stony area on the west of the field above the end of Poorscript Lane. The site may be that of a post-medieval wooden house and the pottery which is mostly 'seconds', but it is the next to the 'Kiln Field'.

Hill House. Overlooking Grosmont from the north-western side of the Graig Syfyrddin is Hill House – an ancient farmhouse with impressive views to the mountains – and, in local lore, the oldest house in the parish. During redevelopments in 2004, trenches were dug for new drainage from the north-east and north-west corners of the house to a large soak away in the garden. A substantial building was encountered with walling 2ft 6in wide (0.75m) which must have been demolished when the existing house was built in the ?17th century. Pottery of this date was sealed in the abandonment layers of the building ('Monmouth Archaeology').

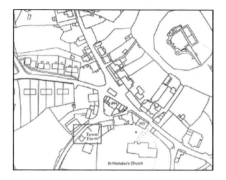 

Town Farm, Grosmont, rescue excavation on medieval house

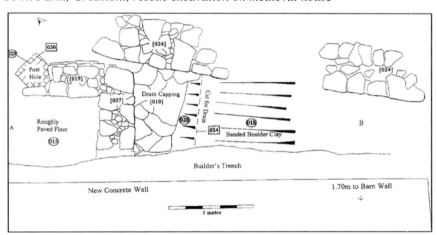

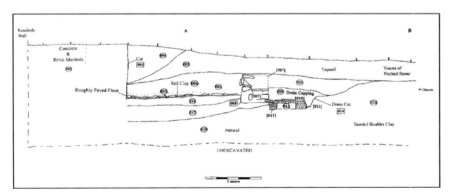

Town Farm, Grosmont, rescue excavation: plan and section of medieval house

169

Town Farm Barn, Grosmont, 2007
Builder's trenches cutting through the remains of a medieval house and into
natural boulder clay

Mysterious Dixton

D IXTON CHURCH – the eighth century Celtic Llan Tydwg – stands beside the River Wye, a mile or so above Monmouth. Even though the charming Vicarage next door has been spoiled by the private school flood banks and that the modern A40 provides a constant thunder, this is still, somehow, a peaceful corner of the world.

Today, Dixton cannot be called a village for although the parish is larger than Monmouth it is mostly under grass and trees. The remains of the 15th century homestead of 'Chattrescroft' now lies beneath the nearby A40 dual carriageway roundabout and the medieval houses which would have clustered around the Church have long vanished, although there are some interesting features in the fields.

There are the sites of two ancient water mills: the eleventh century Dixton Mill and thirteenth century Newton Mill; they were powered by the leisurely little Mally Brook and both were working for many centuries. Dixton Mill, which was mentioned in the Domesday Survey of 1080, rose again after being left a ruin by the supporters of the great Welsh leader Owain Glyndwr in 1404 and its remains are now used as a cowshed visible from the A40. A little further up the brook, Newton Mill was partially excavated over five years in the 1950s by our embryonic *Monmouth and District Junior Archaeological Society*. This site is overgrown with trees but in winter and spring the remains, which were abandoned around the time of the Civil War, can still be traced.

Back on the Wye – upstream – at the ancient crossing of the river on the 'Royal Way' from the Forest of Dean, was Chapel Farm, the site of the medieval Hospital of St Michael. Perhaps founded by John of Monmouth as a leper hospital, this site also now lies under the dual carriageway. Over the river is Hadnock – the Saxon 'Hodenac' – another enigmatic settlement which was exchanged for three Monmouth iron forges in around 1170 and later swopped for Skipton Castle in Yorkshire.

But Dixton has other secrets. Over the road from the Church and the Vicarage lies the 'Hall of the Lord of Dixton' – a low moated mound. This scheduled Ancient Monument has been the cause of much speculation, for archaeologists cannot agree whether it was a motte, a manor house or perhaps even a Roman or Saxon burial site. Archaeological interest in the mound is first recorded in the middle of the nineteenth century when several clerics dug a hole into it, rather like taking a slice out of a cake. Their report, in the *Gentlemen's Monthly Magazine* for 1849, recalls the first archaeological excavation to be carried out in Monmouth. The finds included a bone handled knife, an antler pick and a fragmentary bone comb. The clergymen also describe pottery which they thought was Samian ware. This latter discovery we thought unlikely until Stuart Wilson found scraps of first century South Gaulish Samian ware eroded from the bank of the stream beside the mound. This find supports Mr Sockett's suggestion that the Dixton would have been the ideal site for a marching camp during the Roman Invasion.

'The Hall of the Lord of Dixton'

The other surprise from the mud of the stream was the discovery of small sherds of oolitic limestone-tempered pottery from the Vale of Gloucester – the late 11th to early 12th century cooking pots which followed the Norman invaders into Wales.

So the Dixton mound has produced some of the earliest Roman pottery from Wales as well as some of the earliest Norman pottery while Keith Kissack has also drawn attention to the eleventh century herringbone masonry exposed in the north wall of the church. He wondered if it may date from a rebuilding of the church after the devastation of Archenfield in 1056 by a mixed army of Welsh, English and Vikings, under the 'formidable' Welsh leader, Gruffydd ap Llewelyn.

Also, I wonder what it would mean if the three archaeological vicars were right when they identified the bone comb that they had found in the 'Hall of the Lord of Dixton' as Saxon?

Invasion

Silurum gens non atrocitate, non clementia mutabatur, quin bellum exerceret castrisque legionum premenda foret.

'The tribe of the Silures was turned neither by brutality nor by clemency from pursuing war and requiring encampments of legions to keep it down.'

Tacitus: *The Annals* (XII, 32)

MONMOUTH was the site of one of the earliest Roman forts in Wales – one which George Boon of the National Museum of Wales believed was probably of vexillation size, and may have housed two thousand troops.

Monmouth Town. First century pottery was occasionally found on the higher ground of Monmouth prior to the more definitive discoveries in upper Monnow Street. Bryan Walters had discovered an early Flavian period primary smithing hearth during rescue excavations at Glendower Street School in 1988 and other early pottery came from the old Ebley Tyres site in Glendower Street. At 22-24 Monnow Street, timber building slots, Roman cremations and a drainage ditch were associated with early pottery but both had been truncated by post-Roman ploughing.

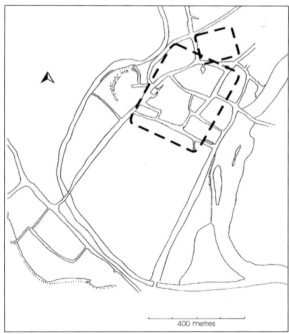

The probable site of Monmouth's pre-Flavian Roman fort (as suggested by George Boon) with the possible position of a later fortlet indicated by discoveries near the Dixton Gate

Then Phil and Rich Grindle, doing their own thing in Mr Badman the Jeweller's garden next-door (No 20), found themselves in a ditch. Positively sealed in the backfill of the ditch was a group of potsherds including a piece of a Dragendorf 15/17 Samian 'saucer' of pre-Flavian date. This discovery confirmed Monmouth's place in the first Roman Invasion of Wales – as a fort as early as the fortress at Usk.

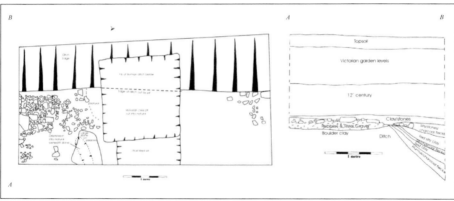

The edge of the pre-Flavian ditch at 20 Monnow Street

Mr Boon suggested that the ditch at Monmouth was part of a pre-Flavian vexillation-sized fort which would have supported the Roman advance to the west and north and he sketched the area that the site may have covered. Since that time, further first century pottery, including pre-Flavian Samian ware, has been found in other parts suggested by Mr Boon.

In 2004 we carried out an excavation in the garden of Agincourt House, Agincourt Street and revealed a ditch and slots backfilled with clean soil at 2 metres below ground level while another slot on the site produced early pottery. In 2005 a watching brief during renovations at 19 St Mary's Street also revealed a metre deep ditch with a fill which produced a few lumps of iron slag and the base of a pottery flask.

Geoff Webb's reconstruction of Monmouth in the first century

These ruler-straight ditches were running roughly in line with the suggested orientation of the fort and may have been features inside the early fort where most of the archaeological record has been disturbed and ploughed away.

The fort at Monmouth was a focal point on the route between the fortresses of Gloucester and Usk and therefore important in the invasion of southern Wales. It was also at a nodal point for the attack on Mid-Wales up the Monnow Valley.

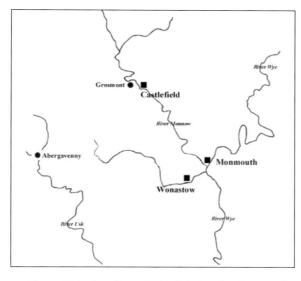

The pre-Flavian Roman forts at Monmouth and Castlefield (Kentchurch) with the fort at Wonastow

Once Ostorius Scapula had determined upon the invasion of Wales, some of the first guerrilla country which his army would have faced was that of the hills and river valleys along the borderland.

Avoiding the high ground of the Forest of Dean, a Roman advance against the Silures would have arrived overland from the fortress at Gloucester. It would have followed the line of the modern A40, to break through the low hills on the east and north of Monmouth – the modern boundary between England and Wales – and into the lowlands of central Gwent.

A Roman spearhead fond in a ploughed field 'plate' at Croft-y-Bwla farm, Rockfield Road, Monmouth

A sherd of a first century Samian (Drag. 18) from 20 Monnow Street

A Roman cremation at 22-24 Monnow Street

The advance to middle Wales probably passed through Monmouth on a route via the auxiliary forts at Kentchurch and Abbeydore (and probably Peterchurch) in the Monnow Valley and the Golden Valley to Clyro.

Another line of advance may have been along the coast, crossing the Wye at Chepstow. However, the locals did not take kindly to the invasion and it took the Romans thirty years to finally subdue the land of the Silures. Eventually the Celts were conquered (but perhaps not defeated!) and there remained three Roman fortresses in Britain – two of them on the Welsh border.

176

Wonastow Roman fort (around the barn just right of centre), looking north-west from Lydart on the road to Trelech

Court Farm, Wonastow

Just to the west of Monmouth, at Wonastow, another fort overlooks the town and the route of the Roman Invasion. The fort here, at Court Farm, would have been ideally situated for signalling across the lowlands of Gwent to the fortress of Usk and to the Black Mountains. It is also in sight of the Buckstone at Staunton which is said to be the highest point in the Forest of Dean. We discovered the site during walking the ploughed fields but then found that the landowner, the late Mr Richard Wheelock, and his family of Treowen manor house had found it first and had gathered a fine collection of pottery and coins.

The first archaeological excavations at Wonastow were carried out by our Society and *Monmouth School Archaeological Society* while more recently *Monmouth Archaeology* carried out an evaluation in connection with an application to construct an agricultural building. Both the Society excavations and those by *Monmouth Archaeology* revealed the remains of Roman wooden buildings both sides of the lane.

In the early summer of 2006 John Sorrell photographed crop marks on the western side of the site which appear to be those of the round corner of a fort. Also in 2006, following the construction of an extension to the barn, an excavation by *Monmouth Archaeology* revealed the rampart and double ditched defences of a fort. However this was clearly not the same fort as discovered by John Sorrell so there appear to be two enclosures (shown on John Sorrell's photograph). However, in 2006 it was finally established that Wonastow was the site of one, and possibly two, Roman forts.

John Sorrell's photograph of Court Farm, Wonastow, 2006.
The alignment of the proven defences are marked in front of the barn and the
unrelated crop marks on the right. The photograph is looking to the south-east

The majority of the pottery and coins found at Wonastow show that the occupation was of first century date but that at least part of the occupation was of the Flavian period, probably contemporary with the founding of Caerleon, rather than pre-Flavian like Usk and Monmouth.

If the site is as large as it appears to be from the spread of pottery and industrial refuse, it would be more in keeping with the pre-Flavian Invasion, when, it has been suggested, vexillation forts may have been the norm.

Nearby, a farmstead, which was long ago abandoned to the thorn-trees, was called 'Berry Farm' – perhaps, like Castlefield, indicating some tradition that the site was known as a fort (Bury). However, all structures and ditches must surely have gone by the end of the Roman occupation so Keith Kissack suggests that the name was originally 'Borough Farm.'

Rescue excavations at the Wonastow Roman fort in 2006. The truncated rampart lies in the centre of the photograph with the section being dug at right angles across the ditches

A timber building beam slot inside the rampart of the Wonastow fort in 2006

Castlefield, Kentchurch

Dave Pritchard and I stumbled on the fort at Kentchurch in March 1984 when we found pre-Flavian pottery and coins on Mr Renshaw's Castlefield Farm in the Monnow Valley. To the north of Monmouth, this auxiliary site lies on the vital route to Mid-Wales and overlooks the River Monnow where the valley narrows between the Graig Syfyrddin on the Welsh bank and Garway Hill on the English – both rising to over twelve hundred feet.

Trial excavation on the Castlefield Roman fort

As we drove Graham Webster to see the site in 1984, he described it as the most classic situation for a Roman fort that he had ever seen. A small exploratory excavation on this significantly named site was carried out by Monmouth Archaeological Society, pupils from Manchester Grammar School and friends from Garway and Herefordshire, when it was confirmed as pre-Flavian. Subsequent air photographs have shown the extent of the fort, together with a smaller and presumably later enclosure inside.

Perhaps Castlefield is named after discoveries made on the fort site rather than the name being a folk memory of the Roman Invasion.

Blestium –
Roman Monmouth

Geoff Webb's reconstruction of Monmouth in the third century

THE ROMAN TROOPS which were stationed in the fort on the site of the future Monmouth may have been withdrawn when the fortress at Usk was established. However, we cannot be sure if the Silurian territory between the two rivers was totally abandoned by the Romans or if some form of police post remained. Just as this book was ready for printing, we discovered the right-angled corner of another Roman feature at The Town Wall off St James' Square. This may be the first evidence that there was a military presence here for many years after the establishment of Caerleon, let alone Usk.

As was Roman practice, the defensive and drainage ditches were methodically backfilled – conveniently with dateable pottery in the ditch at 20 Monnow Street but unfortunately there was no such luck with the drainage ditches in St Mary's Street or in the garden of Agincourt House.

Whatever the nature of the military withdrawal, a settlement later appeared – probably during the second century – an industrial centre which thrived until at least the end of the 4th century. The town is recorded as Blestium in the 3rd century Roman road book, The *Antonine Itinerary,* and was eleven Roman miles from Burrium (Usk) and eleven miles from Ariconium (near Ross).

Blestium was a town of iron workers, built on three things – Forest of Dean ore, local timber and the two rivers. It appears to have been a town of wooden buildings with furnaces clustered on the banks of the Wye and at Overmonnow. Along the Wyeside, close to Wye Bridge, the remains of the industry are to be found on the higher ground between the flood plains of the Dixton Meadows and of Chippenham Mead. At Overmonnow, furnaces were mostly sited in the area since enclosed by the Clawdd Du ditch which is slightly higher than Chippenham although they did extend into Fitzroy Close near the Clawdd Du medieval bridge. Huge amounts of iron slag from the Roman and medieval smelting built up in the two areas, providing the raw material for the recycling industries of the 17th and 18th centuries.

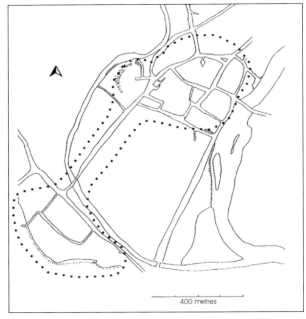

Left: The areas of Monmouth producing Roman pottery and coins

400 metres

Foundation slots of a Roman wooden building at 22-24 Monnow Street

The only firm evidence for a Roman stone building in Monmouth comes in the form of tesserae and tile fragments from the site of Monmouth Priory. The standing remains of the Priory include numerous blocks of tufa – prized by the Romans – which seem likely to have been re-used from earlier times. The site of the Priory lies in a commanding position above the Roman industrial areas and overlooks the River Monnow and the Vauxhall flood plain. The building may have been a shrine for the ironworkers of the settlement (how about Vulcan!) while the management may have lived outside the town – perhaps in villas at Osbaston or Hadnock.

In the surrounding countryside, small iron smelting industries are not uncommon and are usually discovered in ploughed fields (which were probably forest in Roman times) although they are occasionally recognised in woodland. These rural sites are normally marked by a scatter of slag, perhaps ten or twenty metres across, and where dateable are early, suggesting that they were the work of the Roman army and not connected with Blestium.

Although the Monmouth area is not thought of as 'villa country' some did exist and the first to be discovered by the Society was in a field above the eastern bank of the Wye at Hadnock. Here, on the edge of the forest a small exploratory excavation revealed stone buildings, tesserae and tegula and the site was scheduled as an Ancient Monument. The long sloping meadow was at one time two fields, the lower one named Barn Close, after the 'Black Barn', and the upper one 'Green's House.' The Black Barn must have acquired its name through the areas of iron slag surrounding it, but Green's House is unexplained, as there has never been a house anywhere near it. Could the name refer to the Roman Villa? One might recall that green is the colour of elementals (the Green Man, etc) so did the local folk know of the villa remains and associate it with the spirit world? Coincidentally, this remote site figures in *'Ghosts and Legends of Monmouth'* (1965 – one of my early and now somewhat embarrassing publications) where the figure of a ghostly faceless lady was recorded – years before we found the villa site with some human remains. Sadly this villa, although scheduled, has fared badly over the years. Cultivation has led to heavy erosion with metre-deep runnels cutting across the site and down the field.

Meadows at Osbaston, just north of Monmouth, are also likely to be long lost 'villa country', for Stuart Wilson has found tesserae and worn sherds of Severn Valley ware there when following the plough.

An abraded sherd of Roman pottery from an annually ploughed field at Lower Monkton, St Weonards, led me to check the plough there over many years, without result. However, one spring the plough cut deeply into the hedge bank showing that its slope continued down into a shallow ditch. I recovered representative sherds of several Roman pots, including an almost complete black-burnished cooking pot. This group must have come from a nearby occupation site – one that has been totally destroyed over millennia – for surely the shallow ditch and the hedge boundary must have been there in Roman times.

The top of a Roman Spanish amphora from The Malthouse, St Mary's Street, Monmouth. The rim is 16.5cm across. Kindly donated by Brent Watkins.

Romans under the floor

MANY years ago I bought a builder's workshop and yard near Dixton Gate, on the east side of Monmouth. Pulling down large galvanised iron sheds. We built our printing works on part of the site and called it 'The Town Wall' as it was on top of the town wall. We left a tumbledown old building which, according to the 1880 Ordnance Survey was once the site of a forge; it then was used as Manns' Garage and later Croudace's builder's workshop. We used it to store sacks of post-medieval pottery kiln waste.

During the foundation excavations for the printing works we exposed a layer of sand and shale spreading back from the town wall. This we interpreted as ancient alluvial deposits thrown up to form a rampart during the digging of the ditch from the River Monnow to the River Wye. The shales had been scattered when the stone defences were built in around 1300 and everything under the layer dated to the early 14th century or before. The foundation trench, at a metre or so, was too shallow to reveal what lay below.

By 2007, the old building with no foundations was collapsing so we obtained planning permission to remove it and build a small bungalow on the site. The builders had started digging the foundation trenches, accompanied by a programme of archaeological work imposed by the planners, when they dug part of the trench deeper because the ground was soft. The building inspector was concerned, so we employed a structural engineer who, while producing a solution to the problem, was happy for us to dig down deeper. By now we had recorded the layers predating the rampart spread and the trench was producing Roman pottery. Ground worker ('Digger') Dave Dodds had found a coin of Constantine II (324-337) and it now seemed likely that the earth was slumping into a pit or a ditch. The backfill here was unlike the fill of the military ditches which we had previously encountered; those ditches contained mostly redeposited natural clay from the ramparts which was practically indistinguishable from the undisturbed ground into which the ditch had been dug. This was so deceiving at the Kentchurch Roman fort that we eventually gave up trying to find a second ditch believing that there had been only one; this was later disproved by crop marks seen from the air. At the Town Wall the ditches contained mixed and slightly darker soils which made it easy to trace the edge of the cut. Whether this was caused because the ditches formed the corner of the fort, accumulating more topsoil, or because the fortifications had been in use for many years when re-digging or refurbishments had produced a slightly more organically-rich rampart mixture is unclear.

The sharp angle of the cut looked very much like a military ditch and we eventually took the excavation down nearly three metres below ground level on the northern side, recovering an assemblage of Roman pottery and convincing ourselves that we had found the ditch of a Roman fort. The alignment of the ditch edge was sharp and clear, so I paint-sprayed it on the tarmac of the yard and we then set about digging deeper in the opposite foundation trench. The foundation trench here had reached 'hard ground' – the undisturbed natural below the 14th century rampart spread – we did not give up easily but eventually were satisfied that it was natural and that there was no ditch there.

Back in soft ground – this time in the western trench – around the corner from the first ditch – we found another sharp cut. Things were now becoming unsafe and we could not reach more than about a metre into the ditch (again some three metres below the yard surface) but ditch it certainly was and with a similar sharp angled cut and distinctive fill. Lining up two ranging poles on the ditch edge, I again sprayed the alignment on to the yard tarmac; that showed that not only were the ditch edges converging but that they formed a perfect right-angle.

We had uncovered the outer edges of two ditches which were converging at right-angles; these ditches contained only Roman pottery and looked convincingly military.

However, now we were facing the danger of three metre deep trenches collapsing and we had held up the development for several days and considerably raised the cost of foundation concrete. I had also convinced the builders that archaeologists were raving mad – something, I gather, that they had already suspected from watching Channel 4's *Time Team* programme.

Putting the alignment onto a large-scale Ordnance Survey map was not difficult and then easily checked when several ranging poles lined up with distinctive parts of neighbouring buildings. It was then immediately apparent that the ditches we had found were not connected with the ditch which had produced the pre-Flavian pottery at 20 Monnow Street – this was an entirely separate feature.

The alignment from the Town Wall ditch corner ran westwards through St James' House and the Library towards Pitman's Corner. Suddenly I realised that a right-angled turn outside Pitman's Court would go straight up Monk Street exactly along the line of the ditch which we had found but could not date in 1982. But that was not all, for this time we knew something about the nature and depth of the Monk street ditch, together with its northern and southern limits.

In 1982, with Phil Dunlop, Martin Griffin and students from Manchester Grammar School, we had carried out excavations in the front gardens of the Royal George Hotel in Monk Street. Here we unearthed a medieval road which had been sinking into a deep ditch since at least the 13th century. The road, which is shown on John Speed's Map of Monmouth in 1610, was abandoned in the 18th century – around the time that the Royal George was built.

A layer of humus (abandonment?) on the road surface had been covered with redeposited natural red clay and shales probably spoil from the digging of the house cellars. However, the ground over the ditch had continued to sink, as it still does today, leaving large air gaps under the old road and causing visible damage to the roadside walls.

We could not ascertain the depth of the ditch as it went under the modern road and pavement but we took the first box down almost three metres below ground level and the second one well over that without reaching the bottom.

There was some Roman pottery amongst the medieval pottery on the edge of the ditch and a worn Roman coin came from amongst the medieval pottery which had sunk into the ditch. George Boon identified the coin as probably of Gallienus (sole reign 260-268).

Although the origins of the ditch were not established at the time, it was clearly not the medieval Priory precinct ditch which surrounded parts of St Mary's churchyard. That ditch was on the other side of the road and was still open, with bridges and a gatehouse, when John Speed drew his Map in 1610, so it must now lie partly under the west side of modern Monk Street or under the edge of the churchyard; also it should have turned west before reaching the Royal George. Neither, except for the fill, did the Royal George ditch seem likely to have been medieval at all, for most of the defences of that period were well known. This is even truer today.

Crucially, later excavations and roadworks proved beyond doubt that the ditch did not extend as far north as the traffic lights or beyond Whitecross House on the south. There have been excavations behind Whitecross House, in St James' Mews, under and around Pitman's Court together with service excavations in the roads; there have also been service excavations proving natural ground around the traffic lights and at Lancaster House and all of these have shown that both ends of the ditch must have turned sharply somewhere else – east or west. This distance matches that from the Town Wall site to Pitman's Court and when joined with the suggested eastern and northern alignments creates a conveniently rectangular shape – the imagined small fort. A recent archaeological evaluation (October 2007) at the Clinic off New Dixton Road and east of the Royal George failed to produce evidence of any Roman ditches.

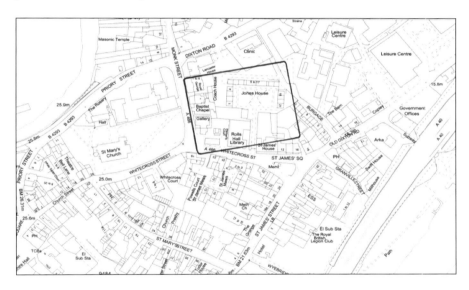

The possible location of a later Roman fortlet in the north-east of Monmouth

If this is a new Roman fort, it is small – around 120 metres long – and a lot later than that of the Monnow Street pre-Flavian ditch, the limits of which are unknown. It covers an area bounded by Monk Street, St James' Square, and The Burgage and just to the south of the New Dixton Road. It is tempting to speculate just how late such a fort might be. The pottery from the ditch fill covers a wide date range and has the appearance of 'sweepings up', as our president Sox put it. However, it does suggest that the 'fort' was not abandoned until the early fourth century or, of course, later. This makes the 'fortifications' a potentially exciting source of information about the later Roman occupation of south-eastern Wales.

New bungalow groundworks at The Town Wall near Dixton Gate

The alignments and the junction of the two Roman ditches are marked on the left of the excavations with ranging poles and yellow lines. The houses in the background (The Burgage) are built over the eastern town ditch and are overlooked on this side by the replacement town wall. The printing works is on the left of the picture. It was built over the rampart behind the town wall.

In and out of the Dark

Monmouth commemorates the birth, in Monmouth Castle, of Henry V with a statue on the Shire Hall that Keith Kissack has called 'rather deplorable'.

Geoffrey of Monmouth, of world renown for his links with the story of Arthur, King of the Britons, has no memorial, deplorable or otherwise.

WITH the withdrawal of the Roman army from Wales in around AD380, the great fortress at Caerleon and the city of Caerwent appear to have fallen into rapid decline and with them the Roman industrial town of Monmouth also enters the shadowy age of myth and legend. Lamentably for archaeologists, the era is devoid of pottery and coins. However, at this time – towards the end of the 4th century – Blestium of the *Antonine Itinerary* appears to have been thriving as a Roman industrial town.

Throughout much of post-Roman Britain life may have continued normally for a while, at least until the Saxons in the east began the long struggle to overrun the country. Monmouth was situated at the southern tip of the small Celtic commot, or kingdom, of Erging (later Archenfield) set between the Rivers Monnow and Wye, and should have been isolated from the early overland incursions. The Saxon invasion was stemmed for an age through the efforts of a shadowy 'Arthurian' leader so that it took some two centuries to reach the Severn and another two centuries to reach the Wye. Monmouth and Archenfield were, however, open to penetration up the Wye, which might sometimes have been worse, perhaps inspiring the abandonment of much of the town to agriculture in the first centuries of the Early Middle Ages. But if the inhabitants did move out, where did they go? There is increasing evidence for the re-use of hill forts, so should we be looking towards The Buckholt and other Gaers?

The evidence for the desertion of at least parts of Roman Monmouth comes from the many excavations carried out in the town over the past half century. But exactly when the hiatus began – or even if there was one – has yet to be established, if it ever can be. The settlement was certainly flourishing during the 3rd and 4th centuries and some of the pottery, the parchment ware for instance, could have been in use for a generation after the departure of the military. However, with the replacement of imperial coinage with a barter system, combined with the collapse of the state into smaller independent communities, pottery also soon became a thing of the past.

The most common Roman coins from Monmouth are of Constantine, which suggests to Jeremy Knight that there is 'something' going on at Monmouth. The latest coin, an important one, came from the Society's excavations at 22-24 Monnow Street – a coin of Magnentius – the Emperor who withdrew the troops from Wales (380-383).

One of the problems associated with our understanding of the end of Roman Monmouth is the nature of the settlement itself. This was an industrialised centre, based on working Forest of Dean iron ore and which was situated at a nodal point for overland and riverine trade. However, the buildings of the Roman settlement seem to have been almost exclusively of wood, the one exception being a structure with ceramic roof tiles and a mosaic, which incorporated tufa in its fabric, on the site of Monmouth Priory. This may have been the home of an administrator, but it is just as likely to have been a shrine or a temple, for surely the smoke and fumes from the iron working in town would have driven any aristocratic type to move out and build a villa in the suburbs.

As mentioned, the natural subsoil under much of Monmouth is covered by a layer of humus which produces abraded sherds of Roman pottery and which is presumed to be post-Roman plough soil. This layer, which covers truncated Roman features, underlies the Norman and later remains of the town (in Monnow Street and on the higher ground). The layer in the town centre is also believed to be post-Roman cultivated ground but perhaps in this case it should be thought of as the equivalent of the 'dark earth', which is well known, but not that well understood, in other Romano-British towns.

Roman tesserae from Monmouth Priory. They are mostly 2cm across

Exactly when digging or ploughing first began to destroy the upper Roman remains is unknown but it was certainly before the arrival of the Normans – probably a long time before. This post-Roman 'plough soil' may have been augmented with material from outside or from ditch digging and was probably 'stone picked', leaving just small pieces of iron slag and eroded potsherds in its make-up. How long the layer took to accumulate is also unknown although at 22-24 Monnow Street the pre-Norman structure had been cut through it. Why the gardeners or farmers did not use a 'greenfield' site instead of one in the ruins of a town is strange.

Whatever its origins, it separates Roman Blestium from Norman and pre-Norman Monmouth. Sadly, the sherds of Dark Age pottery from Monmouth and Goodrich recorded over 45 years ago have proved to be misidentifications (*Goodrich, North African Slipware:* Bridgewater, N.P., 1960 and *Monmouth, 'G' ware sherd:* Thomas, C., 1959, 110). I have examined the Goodrich sherd, which is now in Hereford Museum, and it has a late medieval/early post-medieval Malvernian fabric (fabric B4). The Monmouth sherd, which I found near

Overmonnow in 1959, was published by Norman Bridgewater but is still in the Society collection and is an eroded rim sherd of Roman Severn Valley ware.

Although the presence of the 'plough soil' may indicate a break in the residential occupation of Monmouth, perhaps in the fifth or the sixth centuries, this need not necessarily be total abandonment. Someone was close by to build up and till the humus and by the seventh century there was probably a small Welsh settlement here which was associated with the church of St Cadoc. Although towns seem to be unknown in Wales at this time, Wendy Davies has suggested that Monmouth was one of the more likely sites for an early medieval nucleated Celtic settlement, while its position at the tip of Archenfield, between Saxon Dean and Welsh Gwent, was paramount (Kissack, 1974, 9).

The west wall of the post-Roman/pre-Norman structure on the frontage at 22-24 Monnow Street, showing post sequences including a square post hole cutting a round one (round edge marked by white card)

The most dramatic evidence for pre-Norman occupation in Monmouth was revealed during the Society's excavations at 22-24 Monnow Street. A structure based on very large posts had stood on the frontage in line with the street and had covered the remains of a simple post and wattle building. The structure was erected over the post-Roman 'plough soil' and had been rebuilt on more than one occasion so that it must have been old when it was destroyed, probably by the Normans during clearances of the area in front of their ditch and rampart defences. Although there was no datable material associated with the building – which is of course, consistent with a pre-Norman date – its situation, its construction and its position in the archaeological record is indicative of it being an important element of early medieval Monmouth.

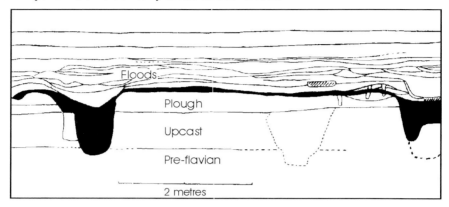

22-24 Monnow Street, west section of frontage with pre-Norman structure

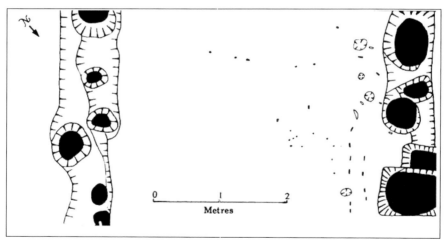

22-24 Monnow Street, plan of frontage with pre-Norman structure

Other features which appear to prove the existence of a pre-Norman settlement at Monmouth were also discovered at 22-24 Monnow Street. A medieval defensive ditch, assumed to be Norman, was found to be running diagonally across the site, en route for the castle, via Lloyds Bank. So in an attempt to obtain dating for the rampart, excavations were carried out close to the ditch. A pit had been dug outside the ditch to remove a large post and the backfill, mostly of natural red clay, contained a few sherds of the earliest Norman pottery (Cotswold ware) and, right at the bottom of the post-hole, an uncrushed goat horn-core. The interpretation is that the post had been removed at around the time

192

that the ditch was dug. The resulting hole was filled with spoil from the digging of the ditch and the few potsherds and the horn-core had fallen in when the post was removed, providing further evidence of the Norman razing of earlier structures. Nearby the ditch had cut through a stone drain, which, if not Roman, might also be pre-Norman.

Another pit, larger than the previous one, was found further along the site and again it had been filled with natural red clay but this time there were defined tip lines interspersed with layers of charcoal and some pottery – again of Monmouth's Norman phase. No reason for the pit could be suggested but there was some evidence that it might have been wood-lined before it was abandoned.

A final exciting discovery, made through the flawless skills of diggers Anne Leaver and Martin Tuck before the excavation ended in 1999, was that of a grave to the rear of the site. The cut was aligned roughly east-west and was very deep but the only remains of the occupant were dark body-shaped stains at the bottom of the grave. The nearly total decay of the body and the bones is indicative, in Monmouth, of the age of the remains. Post-medieval bones and those of the High Middle Ages are usually well preserved although they are softer from earlier periods. Roman bones are rarely found (unless as cremated fragments) and those that are found are usually very soft and not often recoverable. The vestiges in the grave therefore appear to be more analogous with Roman rather than medieval remains. It seems certain that if the grave was not Roman it was early medieval. Some of the dark 'sludge' of the body remains was submitted for radio-carbon dating but the laboratory staff decided that there was not enough surviving carbon from which to obtain an accurate date.

However, charcoal from the grave fill has now also been submitted for radio-carbon dating.

22-24 Monnow Street. The early grave before excavation

The grave after excavation by Anne Leaver and Martin Tuck.
No human remains had survived, although the body was marked by dark stains

Monmouth's Celtic church is first mentioned around the 7th century, but it could be much earlier, for it is dedicated to one of the earliest of the Welsh saints – St Cadoc (born c.497), who is often associated with Roman settlements. If the burial at 22-24 Monnow Street were of this period there would be some five centuries or more for the bones to decay than if they were medieval. Gwethenoc, the Breton Lord of Monmouth, refers to St Cadoc's as being 'Below my castle in Monmouth' and it was where the Normans worshipped until their own church was built. Although it would be nice to think that the Celtic church lies under St Mary's Priory Church, on the site of a Roman shrine, the site at 22-24 Monnow Street is even more 'below' his castle.

Paul Courtney's significant contribution to the study – that there may have been a Saxon burgh at Monmouth – is unproven. Even so, it would be nice to know if the sherd of Chester ware found by Neil Maylan at the Kwik Save site came to Monmouth with the Normans. Although that lonely sherd hovers rather uncomfortably over the town's early history, the other pre-Norman, early English find – the 10th century hoard of Saxon coins from the Buckholt Wood – seems likely to be Welsh loot from further east.

+ ÆDELRÆD REX ANGLOɹ   + ÆLFSIGE M-O BÃRDÃ

Similar Saxon Coins (photo kindly provided by the National Museum of Wales)

Dave Streatly became fascinated with prehistoric artefacts after finding a flint arrowhead near his home in the Buckholt valley, just north of Monmouth. The story he tells is that one day in 1991 he was digging for flints in the ruins of an old cottage in woodland overlooking Monmouth when he came across a hoard of silver pennies. He showed me these coins, all of which were of the Crux type short cross pennies, and gave me a list of his own identifications. The coins were issued c.991-997 (British Museum Catalogue 3A) but before they could be examined by a specialist they were stolen. However, the late George Boon of the National Museum felt that there was little obviously wrong with the list, in fact the four Gloucester and Hereford pieces were exactly what might be expected in a small hoard just inside the Welsh border at Monmouth. A careful comparison of the indicated moneyer and mint-readings with the lists in Bror Emil Hildebrand's *Anglosachsiska Mynt* (Stockholm, 1881) and various fascicules of the *Sylloge of coins of the British Isles* makes this quite plain, and the mis-spelling GIEL for GIFEL in No 12, which corresponds with Hildebrand's No 1034 as to moneyer and type, goes far to settle any doubts as to the sole type represented: [M-O: monetarius or moneyer]. (Besley, E, 1993 and Clarke, S, 1995).

In 1056 Gruffydd ap Llywelyn came up the River Wye with a mixed army of Welsh, English and Danes to devastate Celtic Archenfield and sack the Saxon city of Hereford. Keith Kissack has commented that to the survivors (in Archenfield) there can have been little to choose between past oppressors and the advancing Normans. "Here the Wye, for so long the highway of invasion from the sea, encircled a community of warriors to whom all men were potential enemies" (Kissack, K.E., 1974).

Part Five

DEMONS IN CLAY

Potters of
The Monnow Valley

BY THE second quarter of the 13th century, Monnow Valley ware glazed jugs were dominating the finer ceramics of the Welsh borderland. It is during this fourth ceramic phase that pottery spreads outside the towns and into the countryside – obviously, some of us were now using pots made of clay.

Although cooking pots may have been made somewhere in the area since Norman times, it was not until the later 12th century that glazed wares became common. Most jugs and pitchers had been travelling long distances – from the Cotswolds, the Malverns and Bristol – but now there was an increase in the number of regionally local kilns and although distant products continued to be sold in the town the locals began to advance. The Bristol kilns kept their trade up the River Wye, holding their own throughout the century, with Redcliffe wares replacing those of Ham Green around the middle of the century. Monmouth was the limit of the effective range of the Bristol products, for both groups become rare inland and further up the Wye Valley.

The efficient Minety tripod pitcher industry of the Braydon Forest area of North Wiltshire, which was published by John Musty in 1973, exported its wares to Monmouth throughout the 13th century, presumably filling a gap in the market for large vessels. There were also other occasional imports, overland or up the Wye, including Saintonge jugs which were associated with the Bordeaux wine trade.

We have designated the local jugs and other glazed wares at this time as fabrics A5 and a more sandy local fabric as A5b. These two are sometimes mixed together on occupation sites but we have found that there is a difference in date between the two groups. The large pottery assemblages we uncovered amongst the iron forges in Goldwire Lane, Overmonnow, are almost exclusively of the sandy A5b fabric and it is apparent that this was an early phase of the Monnow Valley ware industry where the potter always added sand to his clay. This may have been in the late 12th century or the early years of the 13th century.

Decorated Monnow Valley ware

Simple rouletting on Monnow Valley ware jug handles and a body sherd

Monnow Valley ware (named by Jeremy Knight) with comb or scratch decoration, is probably dated to the later 12th or early 13th centuries while the roller or rouletting wheel is used shortly afterwards. The earliest rouletted decoration on pottery was made with simple criss-cross cuts on the (wooden?) wheel or roller and is known from Saxon times onwards. The ornamentation resulting from such a wheel being impressed onto the soft wall of a pot while it was rotating on the potter's wheel is that of small diamonds. A variety of 'simple rouletting' – herring-bone, chevron, star, rectangular and diamond motifs – occur on 13th century pots from the Gloucester-Worcester area as well as the Welsh borderland.

In 1963, John Hurst published a groundbreaking paper on *White Castle and the dating of medieval pottery*. He described and named 'complex rouletting' – a decorative technique on pottery which we had been finding on our teenage dig at Newton Mill, Dixton.

A small running leaf rouletting (the leaves are 12mm across)

Jugs bearing complex rouletting are common in the 13th century house floors, middens and the rubbish-filled pits of Monmouth. The decoration is fascinating, with a variety of running leaves and curvilinear patterns, together with fleurs de lis and other ornate designs. Artistically, our potter seems to have no real rival elsewhere in Britain. The abruptness with which pots bearing the evolved decoration appear is noticeable and shows that it was probably the work of an individual or family of potters who were travelling around the small borderland towns. Sherds bearing complex rouletting are sometimes found alongside others bearing simple rouletting or with later sherds bearing applied clay decoration which suggests that the different styles were in use over a relatively short period.

I carried out an enthusiastic study of complex rouletting many years ago and dreamed up a theory to explain how the evolved rouletting wheels were made. In a volume dedicated to John Lewis, published by the *Welsh Medieval Pottery Research Group* in 1987, I suggested that clay wheels were moulded from a flat matrix, in a similar way to that used to produce type for letterpress printing.

However, Walter Keeler, our National Eisteddfod Gold Award winning potter, showed me that the decoration could be beautifully cut (at least by him) directly into soft clay wheels which were then fired in a kiln – a salutary lesson to one whose potting career ended as a nine-year-old with a clay pig in a bonfire. Like other ceramics, the potter's roulettes might survive in the archaeological record.

200

Small running leaves

Large running leaves

Notched circles

Scroll ornament

Small fleurs-de-lis

Fleurs-de-lis

Large fleurs-de-lis

Nonsense? design

Walter Keeler's roulette

203

During the Society's excavations at 69-71 Monnow Street, complex rouletting was first found after c.1240. This dating is based on coin evidence from the earth floors of these two medieval house sites.

The fourteenth century

By the late thirteenth century, the graceful Monnow Valley ware jugs, with strap handles and evolved decoration, were replaced by more bulbous jugs, often with split round handles and a variety of applied clay decoration. This new decoration has become a marker for the disastrous first half of the 14th century *(Ominous Ceramics).*

A common use of white-firing clay was to spread it over the surface of the pot as finger smudges or to apply it in spiral strips or occasionally in more adventurous forms, as in *The Lady in the Flood.* When glazed and fired, the white clay shows through the glaze, producing an attractive light green colour. This was also sometimes further enhanced with mixtures of local iron-rich clay and the white imported clay to produce an orange colour. Darker firing clay was produced by adding iron hammer scale or crushed slag to local clay. Jugs of this period are often carinated, while others have green, copper speckled glazes, as in the case of sherds of two jugs fused together which came from Trelech Cross, in the village.

There now seems to be a wider distribution of this style of decoration compared with that of the 13th century Monnow Valley ware jugs, which became uncommon away from Monmouth. The distribution of these later fine wares extends from north Herefordshire to southern Gwent and from western Gwent eastwards to the Severn. This large area – served by more kilns – coincides with the regional Old Red Sandstone and seems to be an area where there was an increasing mobility amongst potters.

While the locally made cooking pots of this period retain their traditional in-turned rims, they are often internally glazed, usually around the base, but occasionally up to and even over the rim.

Itinerants?

Definite proof that there were itinerant potters during the Middle Ages is hard to come by. Styles of pots and decoration did spread across the country from industry to industry but this may have been the result of copying through the markets as much as through direct contact between potters. Potting may even have been a seasonal and part-time occupation, especially in remote areas. Perhaps the only way pots from different areas can be proved beyond doubt to be the work of the same potter (other than with documentary evidence) is that there be a definite difference of fabrics combined with the potter's own fingerprints. Although fingerprints are sometimes well preserved (there could be an opening here for a research student to become a 21st century Sherlock Holmes with paint brush and microscope) there are other 'fingerprints' – the roulettes – which are easier to detect.

The various wheels used in the production of Monnow Valley ware complex rouletting are as distinctive as fingerprints. Definite examples come from an area bounded by Chepstow, Caerleon, Abergavenny, Llanthony, Grosmont, and Skenfrith to Monmouth with outliers at English Bicknor and Blakeney in the Forest of Dean and Hereford. If this distribution arose from a single industry, there should be large waste heaps somewhere in or near Monmouth which appears to possess the greatest concentration and variety of pots (unless that's due to us).

If these medieval potters were travelling to different towns, it may be that they were covering similar ground to that of the post-medieval potters.

The small differences in the fabric of some pots from Abergavenny, Usk, Monmouth and the borders of the Forest of Dean is worth exploring. Other evidence comes from Hereford where complex rouletting appeared to be unknown and yet the city has produced a few sherds of kiln waste bearing curvilinear designs, which although obscured by heavy glaze look almost identical to some of the Monnow Valley ware running leaves. An interesting twist comes from Hay-on-Wye where complex rouletting similar to, but less creative than, that of Monnow Valley ware occasionally occurs on sherds of late 13th century jugs in a Hay-on-Wye fabric.

One evening in January 2005, Alf Webb, a leading light of the *Dean Archaeological Group*, brought his medieval pottery studies class to look at some of the Monmouth pottery. One of the members, Phil Riches, came along with pottery he had found in a field near his home at Ruardean. His pottery included several types of jug handles identical to those from Monmouth. However, the fabric was totally different – a mixture of sand and small pieces of concretionary limestone – Monmouth fabric A4, normally only found in cooking pots. This is the Gloucester TF110 fabric.

The most distinctive type of handle in Phil's collection was the split rod which is rare across Britain (McCarthy & Brooks, 1988) but common in the 14th century groups of the Monmouth area. The Ruardean and Monmouth jugs seem identical except for the totally different fabrics and could be the work of the same potter(s) as those at Drybridge Park. There is also a striking resemblance between the rim forms of the Monmouth A4 cooking pots and those from Ruardean fabric. This is surely further evidence for the movement of potters between settlements – even Lordships. Some of the Ruardean material may even be kiln waste, for one of the handles had sheared off the jug where it joins the rim; this is one of the common features of kiln waste at Drybridge Park.

The latest and seemingly conclusive evidence that potters were travelling between towns came from a watching brief in Hereford during the building of a new supermarket just to the south of the city. Kath Crooks discovered a dump of kiln waste which is identical to that from the Drybridge Park kiln. Although no applied clay decoration is mentioned, the wasters include split rod handles identical to those from Drybridge and, like Drybridge; the site is over the river from the main town. It is outside the King's Ditch – which enclosed a suburb on the Welsh side of the River Wye – as did the Clawdd Du on the Welsh side of the River Monnow at Monmouth (*Medieval Britain and Ireland*, 2005, M. Gaimster and K. O'Connor (Eds.), *Medieval Archaeology,* 50, 2006, 318-21).

A Monnow Valley ware complex rouletted small running leaf.
The leaf measures one centimetre across

Demons in Clay

THE thirteenth century – the High Middle Ages – was a time of success and expansion – with a population explosion that saw redevelopment in Monmouth and the establishment of settlements in the surrounding countryside.

The second half of the century, like the first, produced a flowering of ceramic art centred on Monmouth that can be compared to any in Britain and that commemorates an emancipated potter who was a fine craftsman. His (or her) work is very evocative of the Middle Ages.

This Monnow Valley ware potter depicted devils and other creatures in a manner that would probably have been unacceptable in the following century when famine and the Black Death would cast its awesome shadow across Europe. The great plague unleashed a religious paranoia that led to the horrors of witch burning when owning a model demon might have been rather risky. But now the potter's customers were happy to find room on their dinner tables for his demon jugs and, on the roof, a place for his devil's head louver.

A Demon jug spout

We found this first charming piece of this potter's art just before Christmas in 1987 during excavations at 71 Monnow Street. It is a jug spout in the form of a singing demon (or is he suffering toothache?) which, when held under a tap seemed to come alive as a medieval carol singer. This simple and superbly modelled little character has two pairs of hands with opposing thumbs under his chin and seven fingered hands above his head. The arms are modelled with applied strips while the eyes, nostrils and finger separations are made with the same round-ended tool. The jug has a green lead glaze over a generally dark reduced surface.

A Boar's Head jug spout with broken tusks

A relation of the demon jug spout is the boar's head jug spout from the rubbish which had accumulated inside 13th century iron forges at Goldwire Lane, Overmonnow, where it seems that people had taken meals for cooking. Although it has lost most of its tusks, the head is otherwise complete. Like the demon jug spout, the animal was modelled around the same 10mm thick tool, so they are likely to have been made at around the same time and certainly by the same potter. The eyes are pear-shaped pellets which have been pierced with the same tool as the nostrils, the ears, the bars on the snout and where the spout joins the pot. This was also, almost certainly, the same round ended tool the potter used to model the demon spout. The lead glaze on the boar appears a lustrous green over reduced areas of the surface and orange over oxidised ones.

A Salmon

The jug rim with a fish's head is so simple but so effective – and appropriate in Monmouth where the Wye is one of the most famous salmon rivers in the world. A blob of clay was pressed into the rim of the pot and pressed a second time to form a perfect fish mouth. Circles with central dots for eyes complete the creation.

208

The serpent-like creature on a jug handle, which also came from the Goldwire Lane iron forges, is another example of this potter's work.

Despite its snake's mouth, the creature has a hole in its neck, suggesting that it may in fact be a lamprey. Lampreys, which look like eels, are found in the Monmouth rivers, where they are often referred to as 'nine-holes' because of the line of holes below the head. These were a delicacy in the Middle Ages: for instance in a 1296-97 murage grant Monmouth was allowed to levy 'one farthing on every lamprey for sale before Easter.' This was the same as for a fresh salmon or for one thousand herrings (Keith Kissack, 1974). Another jug handle fragment from the same site has part of a second lamprey with two gill holes on it while another rim sherd has a tantalising curled tail-end (not illustrated).

209

The Devil's Head louver. From the top down: horn; nose and upper jaw with teeth; lower lip and jaw with teeth; neck with peg hole for fixing into the ridge tile; louver ridge tile

By the middle of the 13th century Monnow Valley ware potters were producing ridge tiles, louvers and finials. Roof furniture is not easily dated, for pieces could have a long life on a roof and still be re-usable on other buildings. Some pieces are, however, fairly certainly the work of an individual potter.

An ornate roof finial from Whitecross Court is a fine example of a local potter's art, and was probably made in the later 13th century. An impressive medieval finial which may have been on a house roof for centuries came from the 17th century fill of the well in Stuart Wilson's 2007 excavation along the Catbrook Road at Trelech.

However, pride of place on Monmouth's medieval roofline has to go to the louver found during the Society's rescue excavations at 71 Monnow Street which was also the home of the singing demon jug. This horned devil would have belched smoke through its gaping mouth and probably also through its eyes. Although this devil appeared to be unique in Britain, the tongue of an even bigger version – approaching twice the size – came from 61-63 Monnow Street. This was probably the home of a rich merchant.

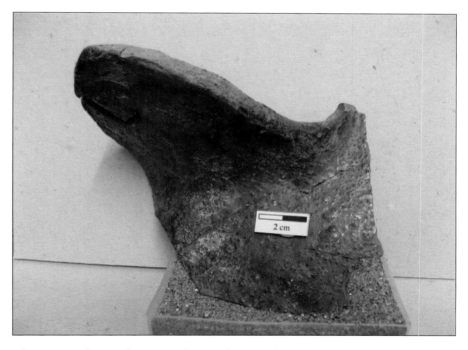

The tongue of a very large Devil's Head Louver from 61 Monnow Street

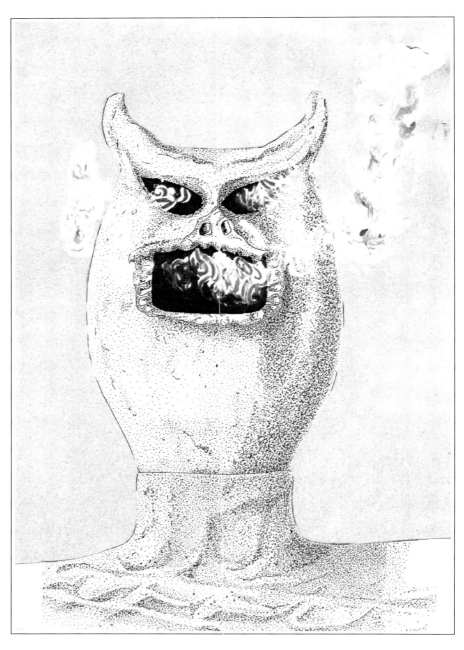

A devil on the roof: a Monnow Valley louver drawn by Clive Barrett

Ominous Ceramics

DRYBRIDGE HOUSE was the home of the Crompton Roberts family and its grounds contained one of the finest small urban parks in Wales with, so the story goes, examples of every tree that would grow in Britain.*

During Easter 2003, topsoil stripping for a new road to a new hospital being built in the Park produced 14th century pottery kiln waste and led to a rescue excavation over the Bank Holiday weekend.

This was an important and exciting discovery and Monmouthshire County Council's site supervisor kept the machines away from the area of waste and agreed that we could start a rescue excavation. But it was not long before the manager of the contractors appeared and demanded that our work stop and that we leave the site – for 'insurance reasons'. I explained to him the importance of the discovery and that as professionals we had our own insurance but he wanted no archaeologists on the site. This man did not care how rare pottery kilns were, nor did he realise the likely consequences of banning Monmouth archaeologists. However, officers of the Council were far more interested and sympathetic so the Director of Highways, Bill Parsons, intervened. After we had met with Mr Parsons and the contractor our archaeological work re-started although it was no help that more than a day had been lost.

It was this rescue excavation which resulted in a generous grant towards the publication of this book from the Robert Kiln Trust when the Society was a finalist for the 2004 Pitt Rivers Award.

The discovery of medieval kiln waste in Drybridge Park was especially surprising as watching briefs had been carried out in and around the Park for some forty years, including six building sites – all had been negative. Nearby, also outside the Overmonnow defences, neither the flood prevention scheme nor any of the numerous road works and service trenches had produced any sign of medieval activity. So when the Council's archaeological advisors enquired if we felt there should be a professional watching brief on the development we had thought that would be unjustified and said that the Society would do it voluntarily.

As the primary site cleaning progressed, it became clear that the area of wasters was very restricted and centred in the middle of the new road. The remains would have to be totally excavated and 'preserved by record'.

The kiln waste had been decorated with different coloured applied clays – the distinctive precursor of Monmouth's disastrous 14th century floods and of abandonment at the time of the Black Death.

An even bigger surprise was in store when we realised that there was no stone structure and no flues. The industry was based on a clamp – the very simplest form of pottery kiln – and had been used to produce jugs and other glazed wares and cooking pots. The kiln lay beneath a small area of waste. It was this discovery that confirmed experimental and other evidence that medieval potters could produce good quality glazed wares in clamp kilns. There were also products which had not previously been recognised in the area.

Drybridge Park, Monmouth.
The extent of the kiln waste before the clamp kiln was exposed in the middle

Drybridge Park, Monmouth.
The clamp kiln base cut into the undisturbed natural ground

214

The Kiln. The kiln was of the Musty type 5a (Musty, 1974) – a clamp consisting of a circular excavation into the natural subsoil with two rough 'floor' levels.

The kiln lay beneath the thickest part of the waste, in an area rich in charcoal and fired clay, and as this was in the centre of, and above the foundation level of, the new roadway, it was excavated and 'preserved by record'.

The original kiln base consisted of a slightly oval shaped excavation into natural, 0.60m across and 0.60m deep. The upper sides of this excavation seem to have been widened during a later phase.

There was an almost total absence of stone in and around the kiln so it is certain that there was no stone superstructure or any fireboxes. A hollow well to the north of the spread of waste was the only area where some stone was found.

Two defined, roughly levelled 'floors' in the clamp base were separated by a thin layer of charcoal. These 'floors' consisted of a flattened mixture of waste with small pebbles and little stones. There was no sign of clay lining or vitrification at any level of the kiln although there was plenty of fired clay, including some with glaze spreads.

The kiln products were lead glazed pottery and other wares, together with roof furniture, all of which is well dated to the first half of the 14th century. Internally glazed cooking pots, with coarser sand added to the fabric, were also being produced.

The limited amount of kiln waste and its isolation from another similar area of waste, with differences in decoration, just inside the medieval suburb is interesting and could be seen as supporting the theory that the potters were travelling around the region. The site lies beside the route up the Monnow Valley to the medieval towns of Skenfrith and Grosmont. This road crossed the nearby Clawdd Du ditch from Overmonnow, across a stone bridge, which presumably gave the name to Drybridge Street. The road here probably separated the medieval fields of Castlefield and Williamsfield.

The Kiln Waste

The spread of kiln waste and fired clay was limited to an area a little over 2m x 4m, with two, much smaller areas and hollows close by. It is believed that most of the kiln waste was recovered and this amounts to around 3cwt (152kg).

The remains are much the same as they were when the site was first abandoned as the wasters had not been spread beyond the immediate area around the kiln and there was no sign of the erosion of sherds which is always associated with agriculture.

Dr Vince suggests that to fire the kiln the fuel would have been heaped up in the pit and the pots arranged over it and then covered in turf or whatever was to hand (eg, a layer of wasters, especially large flat chunks of ridge tile).

The Products. Jugs, bowl, lid, money box, leg of ?tripod pitcher, small vessel (?drinking jug), cooking pots, ?curfew, ridge tiles, louvers.

Travelling Potters. Since the discovery of this kiln there has been further impressive evidence to support our suggestion that 13th and 14th century potters were travelling around the borderland – especially this potter. (*Potters of The Monnow Valley*).

Drybridge Park, Monmouth.
Kiln waste jug sherds with various applied clay and simple rouletted decoration

Drybridge Park, Monmouth.
Kiln waste fragments. Two louvers and a ridge tile

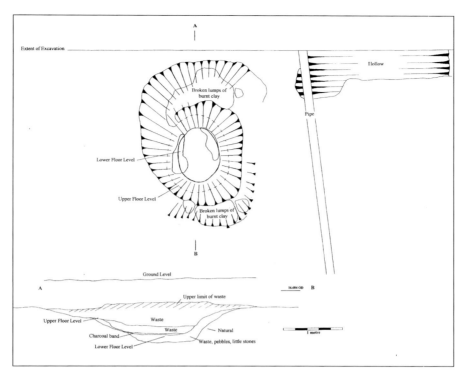

Drybridge Park, Monmouth. The clamp kiln plan and section

*DRYBRIDGE PARK has had the misfortune to be owned by successive County Councils which have seen the park as convenient building land – always, it seems, for 'good causes' which are more difficult to oppose.

Destruction of the Park has been caused by the building of old peoples' homes; an ambulance station; a home for handicapped people; sheltered housing; a fire station; more old peoples' homes; road widening which included the destruction of the charming black and white lodge; Overmonnow School access roads and a roundabout, the new hospital and the new road for the new hospital. This presumably releases other land for more profitable enterprises.

Pottery Kiln or House Fire ?

Well Farm building site, Grosmont, 1989.
We found burnt clay and charcoal on the edge of a builder's trench, with sherds
of a cooking pot that had melted.
We assumed we were close to the site of a medieval pottery kiln.

OVER the Spring Bank Holiday weekend of 1989 we carried out a rescue excavation on a Grosmont building site where we thought we had found the third medieval pottery kiln in southern Wales. The results were disappointing for the 'kiln site' consisted of an area of scorched earth without fireboxes or structures and yet there were sherds of melted and heat shattered pottery.

We decided that we had found the site of a clamp kiln – but the evidence was not impressive. We now know that this interpretation was wrong – it was not a pottery kiln at all but the discovery led to a watch for evidence of other clamp kilns which, curiously, ended in the discovery of one. But before that we had identified two other sites as possible clamp kilns, despite the apparent paucity of kilns elsewhere in the archaeological literature at that time.

One site (Pitman's Court, Monmouth) produced sherds from at least seven different pots – all of which appeared to be kiln damaged in some way or another. However, our friends outside Monmouth would have none of it – these were not kiln wasters but pots damaged in house fires or some other conflagrations. Besides that, our suggestion that clamp kilns were used to produce good quality glazed wares was also unlikely because of the problems of temperature control.

When the clamp kiln was found in Drybridge Park, the spread of waste was confined to an area of just 2m x 4m. I looked for a way to prove that other sites with just a few melted or heat-damaged pots were not kiln sites.

+   +   +

The Summer of 2003. Society excavations, led by Stuart Wilson, were centred on house sites at The Hostry, along the Catbrook Road at Trelech. The house under excavation was possibly one of those burnt during the attack in 1296 and there were cooking pot and jug sherds that had melted in the same way as the pots found at Grosmont. Pottery with similar damage to that at Trelech and Grosmont was also found in the remains of a 12th century house which had been destroyed by fire at Oldcastle, on the slopes of the Olchon Valley, to the east of Abergavenny.

However, a search for the same type of damage amongst medieval and post-medieval kiln waste from a number of local sites proved fruitless. We realised that the damage caused to pottery in burning buildings is quite different from that of kiln waste.

My study of the two types of damage – from kilns and from burnt buildings – together with other material has led to the creation of a check-list for suspected kiln sites. The check-list appears to be reliable and should prove useful for interpreting material mixed with domestic assemblages, especially in towns where there is a chance of a medieval pottery industry. On some kiln sites obvious wasters are not common – for example at St Peter's Redcliffe, Bristol (Dawson, D.P. *et al*, 1972) and a pottery kiln at St Lawrence's, Bayfield, Chepstow (Leach P., 2003).

Normal early 14th century cooking pot rim (top left) with two examples of rims of similar date 'blown' in a house fire at the Hostry, Catbrook Road, Trelech

The check-list has been used with material from local sites and shows that some from Grosmont, Trelech and Oldcastle were damaged in house fires but that the pottery from other sites may not be. At Pitman's Court, Monmouth (Clarke, 1968) for instance, at one time I accepted the conclusion of friends that the large number of damaged jugs may have come from a 13th century building fire – possibly at an inn or a shop. However, the check list indicates that this and another site in Monmouth (12-14 St Mary's Street) may after all be kiln sites. Other isolated finds of medieval pottery from Trelech may also be kiln waste.

The limited demand for pottery in Wales, as in other remote areas of Britain, could have been supplied by small production centres and this would probably have encouraged the use of clamp kilns and itinerancy. Such kilns would, of course, leave less substantial evidence. The threat to the fragile archaeological record of clamp kilns in towns would have been considerable as would have been the change from urban to agricultural land use in large decayed settlements such as Trelech or Grosmont.

The Check List – Pottery Kiln or House Fire?

Pottery that has melted in a kiln is quite different from that which has been exposed in a burning building where the temperature can exceed that of a kiln. The access to the open air in a burning house produces an aerated fabric which is quite different from the solid fabric left by a pyro-plastic melt in a kiln. There are other differences associated with the two types of site and these have been combined to create a provisional check list.

The Ceramic Check List

Kiln
Solid after melting (pyro-plastic melt).
Large laminated blisters and bubbles.
Glaze along broken edges of sherds.
Oxidation/reduction across breaks.
Glaze not flashed.
Fired clay without wattle voids.
Fired clay with glaze.
Handle cleanly sheared from body.
Sherds fused together.
Surface laminating – not common.
Hard-fired sherds – almost to stoneware.
Glaze partly/totally burned away.
Fine blistered surfaces – burned as kiln
covering – totally oxidised.
Vitrified stone (none at Drybridge).

House Fire
Light, aerated vesicular fabric when
melted (especially cooking pots).
Jugs – glaze intact, blistered breaks,
rough feel.
Small blisters and finely cratered
surfaces over vesicular fabric.
Total reduction (sometimes excluding
surface) after melt?
Fired clay with wattle voids.
Surface oxidation to purple end.
Denatured quartz – common after melt.
Surface laminating – common.
Vitrified stone (in Trelech house fire).
Non-local fire-damaged pottery.

Ceramic Check List Examples

CLAMP KILN.   Drybridge Park, Monmouth

Type of Damage	Kiln
Solid fabric after melting (Pyro-plastic melt)	X
Large laminated blisters and bubbles	X
Glazed edges of sherds	X
Oxidation/reduction across breaks	X
Glaze not flashed	X
Fired clay with no wattle voids	X
Fired clay with glaze	X
Handle bases cleanly sheared from body	X
Sherds fused together	X
Surface laminating – not common	X
Hard-fired sherds – almost to stoneware	X
Glaze partly/totally burned away	X
Fine blistered – burned as kiln cover – totally oxidised	X
Vitrified stone (not found at Drybridge clamp kiln)	
Other	
	House Fire
Light, aerated vesicular after melt (esp. cooking pots)	
Jugs – glaze intact, blistered breaks, rough feel	
Small blisters and finely cratered surfaces	
Total reduction (some excluding surface) after melt?	
Fired clay with wattle voids	X
Surface oxidation to purple end	
Denatured quartz – common after melt	
Surface laminating - common	
Vitrified stone (as in Trelech house fire)	
Other:	

HOUSE FIRE.   Well Farm, Grosmont

Type of Damage	Kiln
Solid fabric after melting (Pyro-plastic melt)	
Large laminated blisters and bubbles	
Glazed edges of sherds	
Oxidation/reduction across breaks	
Glaze not flashed	
Fired clay with no wattle voids	
Fired clay with glaze	
Handle bases cleanly sheared from body	
Sherds fused together	
Surface laminating – not common	
Hard-fired sherds – almost to stoneware	
Glaze partly/totally burned away	
Fine blistered – burned as kiln cover – totally oxidised	
Vitrified stone (not found at Drybridge clamp kiln)	
Other	
	House Fire
Light, aerated vesicular after melt (esp. cooking pots)	X
Jugs – glaze intact, blistered breaks, rough feel	X
Small blisters and finely cratered surfaces	X
Total reduction (some excluding surface) after melt?	X
Fired clay with wattle voids	
Surface oxidation to purple end	X
Denatured quartz – common after melt	X
Surface laminating - common	X
Vitrified stone (in Trelech house fire)	
Other	

Further examples of the Ceramic Check List :

12-14 St Mary's Street, Monmouth

Type of Damage	Kiln
Solid fabric after melting (Pyro-plastic melt)	X
Large laminated blisters and bubbles	X
Glazed edges of sherds	X
Oxidation/reduction across breaks	X
Glaze not flashed	X
Fired clay with no wattle voids	X
Fired clay with glaze	X
Handle bases cleanly sheared from body	X (2)
Sherds fused together	
Surface laminating – not common	X
Hard-fired sherds – almost to stoneware	
Glaze partly/totally burned away	
Fine blistered – burned as kiln cover – oxidised	
Vitrified stone (not found Drybridge clamp kiln)	
Other	
	House Fire
Light, aerated vesicular after melt (esp. c. pots)	
Jugs – glaze intact, blistered breaks, rough feel	
Small blisters and finely cratered surfaces	
Total reduction (some excl surface) after melt?	X
Fired clay with wattle voids	
Surface oxidation to purple end	
Denatured quartz – common after melt	
Surface laminating - common	X
Vitrified stone (in Trelech house fire)	
Other	

Pitman's Court, Monmouth

Type of Damage	Kiln
Solid fabric after melting (Pyro-plastic melt)	
Large laminated blisters and bubbles	
Glazed edges of sherds	
Oxidation/reduction across breaks	X
Glaze not flashed	
Fired clay with no wattle voids	
Fired clay with glaze	
Handle bases cleanly sheared from body	
Sherds fused together	
Surface laminating – not common	
Hard-fired sherds – almost to stoneware	X
Glaze partly/totally burned away	X
Fine blistered – burned as kiln cover – oxidised	X
Vitrified stone (not found Drybridge clamp kiln)	
Jug neck 2mm thick; CP neck 2.5mm thick	X
	House Fire
Light, aerated vesicular after melt (esp. c. pots)	X
Jugs – glaze intact, blistered breaks, rough feel	
Small blisters and finely cratered surfaces	X
Total reduction (some excl surface) after melt?	
Fired clay with wattle voids	
Surface oxidation to purple end	X
Denatured quartz – common after melt	
Surface laminating - common	X
Vitrified stone (in Trelech house fire)	
Other:	

Isca Grange Kiln, Caerleon

Type of Damage	Kiln
Solid fabric after melting (Pyro-plastic melt)	
Large laminated blisters and bubbles	
Glazed edges of sherds	X
Oxidation/reduction across breaks	X
Glaze not flashed	
Fired clay with no wattle voids	
Fired clay with glaze	
Handle bases cleanly sheared from body	
Sherds fused together	X
Surface laminating – not common	X
Hard-fired sherds – almost to stoneware Glaze partly/totally burned away	
Fine blistered – burned as kiln cover – oxidised	X
Vitrified stone (not found Drybridge clamp kiln)	
Other	

	House Fire
Light, aerated vesicular after melt (esp. c. pots)	
Jugs – glaze intact, blistered breaks, rough feel	
Small blisters and finely cratered surfaces	
Total reduction (some excl surface) after melt?	
Fired clay with wattle voids	
Surface oxidation to purple end	
Denatured quartz – common after melt	
Surface laminating - common	
Vitrified stone (in Trelech house fire)	
Other	

Oldcastle Churchyard. House Fire

Type of Damage	Kiln
Solid fabric after melting (Pyro-plastic melt)	
Large laminated blisters and bubbles	
Glazed edges of sherds	
Oxidation/reduction across breaks	
Glaze not flashed	
Fired clay with no wattle voids	
Fired clay with glaze	
Handle bases cleanly sheared from body	
Sherds fused together	
Surface laminating – not common	
Hard-fired sherds – almost to stoneware Glaze partly/totally burned away	
Fine blistered – burned as kiln cover – oxidised	
Vitrified stone (not found Drybridge clamp kiln)	
Other	

	House Fire
Light, aerated vesicular after melt (esp. c. pots)	X
Jugs – glaze intact, blistered breaks, rough feel	
Small blisters and finely cratered surfaces	X
Total reduction (some excl surface) after melt?	
Fired clay with wattle voids	X
Surface oxidation to purple end	
Denatured quartz – common after melt	
Surface laminating - common	
Vitrified stone (in Trelech house fire)	
Other	

St Lawrence Bayfield, Kiln, Chepstow

Type of Damage	Kiln
Solid fabric after melting (Pyro-plastic melt)	
Large laminated blisters and bubbles	X
Glazed edges of sherds	X
Oxidation/reduction across breaks	X
Glaze not flashed	
Fired clay with no wattle voids	
Fired clay with glaze	
Handle bases cleanly sheared from body	
Sherds fused together	X
Surface laminating – not common	X
Hard-fired sherds – almost to stoneware Glaze partly/totally burned away	
Fine blistered – burned as kiln cover – oxidised	X
Vitrified stone (not found Drybridge clamp kiln)	
Other	

	House Fire
Light, aerated vesicular after melt (esp. c. pots)	
Jugs – glaze intact, blistered breaks, rough feel	
Small blisters and finely cratered surfaces	
Total reduction (some excl surface) after melt?	
Fired clay with wattle voids	
Surface oxidation to purple end	
Denatured quartz – common after melt	
Surface laminating - common	
Vitrified stone (in Trelech house fire)	
Other	

Cadogan House Tile Kiln, Monmouth

Type of Damage	Kiln
Solid fabric after melting (Pyro-plastic melt)	X
Large laminated blisters and bubbles	
Glazed edges of sherds	X
Oxidation/reduction across breaks	X
Glaze not flashed	
Fired clay with no wattle voids	X
Fired clay with glaze	X
Handle bases cleanly sheared from body	
Sherds fused together	X
Surface laminating – not common	
Hard-fired sherds – almost to stoneware Glaze partly/totally burned away	X
Fine blistered – burned as kiln cover – oxidised	
Vitrified stone (not found Drybridge clamp kiln)	
Other	

	House Fire
Light, aerated vesicular after melt (esp. c. pots)	
Jugs – glaze intact, blistered breaks, rough feel	
Small blisters and finely cratered surfaces	
Total reduction (some excl surface) after melt?	
Fired clay with wattle voids	
Surface oxidation to purple end	
Denatured quartz – common after melt	
Surface laminating - common	
Vitrified stone (in Trelech house fire)	
Other	

The Hostry, Catbrook Road, Trelech.
House Fire

Type of Damage	Kiln
Solid fabric after melting (Pyro-plastic melt)	
Large laminated blisters and bubbles	
Glazed edges of sherds	
Oxidation/reduction across breaks	
Glaze not flashed	
Fired clay with no wattle voids	
Fired clay with glaze	
Handle bases cleanly sheared from body	
Sherds fused together	
Surface laminating – not common	
Hard-fired sherds – almost to stoneware	
Glaze partly/totally burned away	
Fine blistered – burned as kiln cover – oxidised	
Vitrified stone (not found Drybridge clamp kiln)	
Other	

	House Fire
Light, aerated vesicular after melt (esp. c. pots)	X
Jugs – glaze intact, blistered breaks, rough feel	X
Small blisters and finely cratered surfaces	X
Total reduction (some excl surface) after melt?	X
Fired clay with wattle voids	
Surface oxidation to purple end	X
Denatured quartz – common after melt	
Surface laminating - common	
Vitrified stone (in Trelech house fire)	X
Other	

224

A Missing Link

AN unexpected discovery at the Cadogan House floor tile kiln was that the potters had brought a wheel with them and were making 'Cistercian' style pottery. They were also producing flat and nibbed roof tiles – some two centuries earlier than any recognised in the region. There were also bricks (possibly for use in the kiln although perfectly formed and fired) which were roughly the same size as modern ones but which were better finished than Monmouth bricks of five centuries later. Tiles, bricks and flat roof tiles were found fused and scarred together – showing that they were all products of the kiln.

The End of the Middle Ages and a Missing Link

The drastic drop in the population of 14th century Europe was accompanied by a fall in the demand for ceramics and this seems to have caused the temporary demise of the local pottery industry.

From around the middle of the century wares from the Malvern Chase area filled a gap in the market. These pots are of the same fabric as the Malvernian floor and ridge tiles (Monmouth fabric B4) and came in a wide variety of forms described by Dr Vince in 1977. As earlier, Malvern wares were probably travelling overland to Monmouth but were now also reaching a large area of southern Wales.

The Malvernian industry must have remained formidable competition in the pottery market for some centuries, only failing during the 17th century. The long distance trading of the late medieval and post-medieval Malvernian industry mirrors the wide market areas of the Norman pottery industries with which we began our survey. The Cadogan House tile kiln offers the last evidence for medieval potting in the region before the appearance of the post-medieval kilns and the fine wares from that kiln constitutes a link between the two periods.

By the middle of the 15th century, the scene was set for the people of the Marches to obtain much of their pottery from small local industries which were working in the countryside, often in isolated spots.

The distinctive post-medieval wares of the rural potteries of the borderland could be seen as one industry. This pottery is sometimes referred to as 'Herefordshire Micaceous,' as 'Black wares' or as 'Cistercian type' wares. The pottery differs markedly from that of another industry which was trading around the Severn Estuary and was centred on Stroat in the southern Forest of Dean. Stroat ware has stylistic links with North Devon and has a sanded fabric which is also quite different from the Hereford and Gwent wares.

In 1985 we published the evidence that post-medieval borderland pottery falls naturally into two groups. The earlier of the two groups, Group 1, dates from sometime in the later 15th century into the 16th century while Group 2 continues until the arrival of the mass-produced wares of the Bristol and Staffordshire industries by the early 18th century.

Group 1. As the medieval potteries in the region were in or beside towns, it is not surprising that the only post-medieval kiln waste known in Monmouth is that of Group 1. This first came from Mr Sockett's excavation at St James House in the 1950s; from our work at 12-14 St Mary's Street and from Phil and Rich Grindles' dig at 20 Monnow Street. The first two of these sites, like Cadogan House, are on the north-east side of the town. An interesting and important find

225

was the discovery by Mr Sockett of a sherd of a Columbian tin glazed 'plate' amongst the wasters at St James' House. Dr Vince recognised the fabric and form and dated it to the early 16th century.

In the firebox at Cadogan House, we found a sherd of pottery which had fused to a stone bat. The sherd is thin walled and resembles small jugs or drinking vessels which are found in very early post-medieval contexts in and around Monmouth. These pots often have a copper speckled green glaze which is similar to that of Malvernian ridge tiles. The Group 1 kiln wares, that are fired to a red colour, have the same speckled glaze and it may be that the 'Black wares' amongst the waste had the same glaze but appear black through the higher firing temperature. The Cadogan House firebox also produced an unglazed (biscuit fired?) flanged bowl rim that is identical to bowls in Group 1 waste from elsewhere in the town.

It is also worth noting that the kiln waste found by Cooper Neal at Upton Bishop in 1929 was the same style as our Group 1 and included two pieces of encaustic floor tile. This, like the Cadogan House assemblage, suggests a 15th or very early 16th century starting date for this industry.

Therefore, the Cadogan House kiln appears to be Monmouth's 'missing link' between medieval and post-medieval pottery. It also provides evidence for consigning the Group 1 kilns to the middle or late 15th century.

Research into the post-medieval pottery industries of the southern Welsh borderland is continuing under Julia Wilson and Monmouth Archaeological Society has reference collections of material from sites from north Herefordshire to southern Gloucestershire. The society has substantial archives from the local sites: Cross Ash (rescue, two sites); Dixton (rescue); Grosmont (field name but only two sherds); Hazelfield, Welsh Newton (full rescue excavation); Trefaldu, Cwmcarfan (rescue excavation); Monmouth (two main sites); Ysgyryd Fawr, Abergavenny and Gwehelog, Usk.

A moulded face mask from a locally-made post-medieval pot

The remains of the post-medieval pottery kiln excavated at Hazelfield on the Welsh Newton/Garway border, by kind permission of Mr and Mrs Dave Breakwell

Post-medieval kiln waste at Hazelfield
The rule is 15cm long

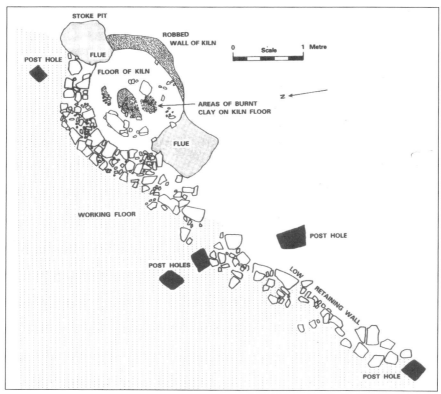

The Hazelfield kiln (Reg Jackson)

A locally made post-medieval jug rescued during the building of
Whitecross Court, Monmouth, in 1964

228

Pottery from a post-medieval cess pit at the Gloucestershire House, Monmouth in 1993

Four very large assemblages of 18th century pottery and glass have been unearthed in Monmouth – three of them in cess pits. One of these was found during rescue work at Monmouth School's development at the Gloucestershire House on the corner of St Mary's Street and Almshouse Street in 1993 and another during the Glamorgan-Gwent Archaeological Trust excavations on the Waitrose site in 1993-94. Paul Davies' 2005-06 excavations at 101 Monnow Street revealed tannery pits with another large 18th century ceramic assemblage. In November 2007, we carried out voluntary rescue work during excavations to the rear of the Baptist Chapel in Monk Street where no archaeological condition had been imposed on the development. A cess pit here produced an exceptionally large collection of material dated to the early-middle 18th century.

A fireback bearing the Royal Arms of Elizabeth I, from the cess pit at the Gloucestershire House, Monmouth

Part Six

THE SILVER TROWEL

A Million Visitors

A BARGAIN warehouse called Whoppas had closed at 22-24 Monnow Street and the premises were lying empty. The owners were Glamorgan Investments, a local firm, and so we enquired if the Society might carry out an excavation prior to any redevelopment. The response was very positive, but as we moved onto the site in 1990, we little realised that this was to be the beginning of one of the most successful archaeological projects in Wales and would attract approaching a million visitors during the last decade of the 20th century.

The building, although more than a burgage wide, is fairly narrow but very long and situated on the southern side of the street where it begins to rise towards Agincourt Square. A large sliding double door opened onto the street, allowing the light and the visitors to pour in.

22-24 Monnow Street, Monmouth. The frontage excavation from the street with Lyn Harper and Elizabeth Taylor

The excavation was to lead to the discovery of Monmouth's pre-Flavian Roman fort; to the early Norman town defences and to a large pre-Norman building. There were to be Roman wooden buildings, Roman cremations, early medieval features and a grave, forges, a well, a cesspit, 14th century flood silts and all the finds to go with them.

Digging began on the street frontage; the area was fenced so that the public could come inside and watch the work, which they did in large numbers, as this is Monmouth's main street.

Early in the excavation, below the post-medieval contexts, layers of silt were exposed and although this seemed to be very high up the street, it was likely that they had been left by flooding, so we called in the late Dr Tony Clark, one of the nicest people in archaeology. His archaeomagnetic date of 1315-1345 should have ended the argument that there were no early flood deposits in Monmouth; it did not, even though the technique would not have worked if the silts had not been dropped from muddy water.

22-24 Monnow Street. The middle part of the site

22-24 Monnow Street. The middle part of the site with Reg Jackson

During the 14th century floods, the site was industrial – the forge of metalworkers – who seem to have been caught unawares by the inundations and had to rescue their equipment from the floodwaters. The mystery of an underlying layer of coarser sands and silts has not been fully explained but it may have dropped from fast-moving water. In 1947, rapidly flowing floodwater was seen pouring out of Nailer's lane, which is almost opposite 22-24, and running down

Monnow Street. In the late 1970s a sudden rush of floodwater came through the old bus station (No 77) taking the double doors down the Street, and through the lane to what is now Chippenham Surgery and into Chippenham Mead.

22-24 Monnow Street. Part of the exhibition

22-24 Monnow Street. Visiting societies are greeted with a glass of wine and a 'lecture' at the rear of the site

The medieval floors on the frontage of the excavation were found to be sagging into earlier features which turned out to be the foundations of a large post-Roman/early medieval building. The post holes of this building had been cut through the humus which sealed the Roman levels of the site – this was one of the most noteworthy of the Society's discoveries.

On the front edge of the trench, a ditch was found which had been truncated by the tilling of the post-Roman humus and which had been filled with natural red clay during Roman times. Running in line with Monnow Street and with the pre-Norman structure, the ditch may be a drain associated with the Roman fort. Similar ditches have been found elsewhere in the town – also backfilled in military style.

Away from the frontage, but still in the first trench, sleeper beam slots of a wooden building also lay under the post-Roman topsoil. These were probably the foundations of a Roman building, post-dating the fort while the nearby cremations are most likely to be the remains of soldiers from the fort.

The second area of the excavation uncovered a post-medieval complex which included a well, a shallow cesspit and the remarkably well preserved base and parts of the sides of a wooden barrel.

The most impressive discovery of this phase of exploration was a deep ditch running at an angle across the site. When the primary fill of the ditch was reached a familiar whiff of preserved organic matter pervaded the trench. With the smell came the realisation that the line of the ditch would take it through the adjoining property to directly under Lloyds Bank.

It then dawned on us that the same smell accompanied the bones, leather and 12th century pottery that were rescued from under the bank during the installation of a new vault. This was the fill of the same ditch. As the ditch appears to have been abandoned on the street frontage in the 12th century, it must surely mean that the ditch was a part of the original Norman town defences. However, the houses of Monnow Street lay outside.

Time went on and we were allowed to cut more concrete to open new areas of the site. There was no need for a JCB while the 'heavy mob' was in action. The rewards were worth the effort and culminated in the discovery of the undated but probably post-Roman grave.

Many people took part in the decade of digging, some of the stalwarts being Sue, Ted and Melanie Chivers, Chris Cooper, Tony Dunn, Phil and Richie Grindle, Dave Hancocks, Lyn Harper, Anne Leaver, Brian Milford, Stuart and Ian Murray, John Perryman, Vic Powles, Sheila Shaw, Mr Sockett, David Stratten, Elizabeth Taylor, Martin Tuck, and Sheila and Bill Williams.

Flooding at 22-24 Monnow Street. The speed with which silts accumulate from still water inside abandoned or ruined houses close to the rivers is unknown, especially where the water flow suddenly came to a standstill *(Flooding in Medieval Monnow Street).* In March 1948, floodwater from the River Monnow was seen flowing swiftly out of Nailer's Lane to join water in lower Monnow Street. It is possible that some medieval floods were even more dramatic than this and may have deposited coarse sand. Dating of 1315-45 at 60% confidence level came from archaeomagnetic samples at 22-24 Monnow Street supported by Drybridge pottery below the silts.

Thick layers of silt containing occasional river molluscs have also been recorded on four sites beneath the road and pavements of Monnow Street. These deposits have iron slag and other detritus trodden into their surface layers and are hard to explain except as heavy flood deposits that were metalled over with new road surfacing. It seems very unlikely, in any event, that silt would be used to raise or repair a road.

22-24 Monnow Street. Anne Leaver and Martin Tuck at the rear of the site

The frontage of the ten-year dig at 22-24 Monnow Street

Death watch beetles and
a 'one-legged dog'

WITH the successful cooperation between developer and archaeologist at 61-63 Monnow Street, one might have hoped that an end to hostilities was in sight. However, another London entrepreneur appeared on the scene and displayed the same disdain for those that he clearly thought were bucolic troublemakers. His enterprise was to be recognised with a public apology from the director of his company to the Society, to the Action Group and to the newly formed conservation group, the Monmouth Association.

In 1988, Dixons Commercial Properties purchased 41 Monnow Street – on the north side of the most archaeologically sensitive part of the street. The company, through projects manager Jeff Popham, at first announced that they planned to save the 17th century half-timbered building as a feature of their development but then decided that death watch beetles were in residence. So, two planning applications were submitted to the authority – one for demolition, retaining the structure – and one for total demolition.

41 Monnow Street

We strongly objected to any demolition and an unproductive meeting was held between the District Council's Chief Technical Officer (Gareth Griffiths) and his archaeological advisors (the Glamorgan-Gwent Archaeological Trust) and the Monmouth Association and our Society.

Following later discussions with the Trust, Mr Griffiths wrote to us clarifying the Council position and maligning one of the outstanding archaeologists of the late 20th century – Ron Shoesmith of Hereford:

'The Monmouth Association and its constituent groups have no official connection with the District Council; Ron Shoesmith of the City of Hereford, referred to by a correspondent as a "recognised expert", has no professional qualifications and the council employs its own "expert" – the Heritage Officer; The Glamorgan-Gwent Archaeological Trust Ltd are the District Council's professional archaeological advisors . . . I would ask you to continue to liaise with the Trust and **not** the Monmouth Archaeological Society.'

There were other meetings and correspondence between the Trust, the District Council and the developer and Mr Popham wrote to the Town Council asking that a reply from the Trust should be treated in *'the strictest confidence in any discussions with Steve Clarke of M.A.S.'* This was rather unfortunate, as several members of the Town Council were also members of *'M.A.S.'*

The Archaeological Trust carried out trial excavations inside the building but our members we were not allowed in – for safety reasons.

A Geoff Webb cartoon during the archaeological work at 41 Monnow Street

A photograph of Mr Popham appeared in the Press pointing out a cracked beam and saying, 'It's rather like a one-legged dog' and he described other problems with the building, including the voracious beetles.

However, a survey by the historic buildings expert from the Royal Commission on the Ancient and Historical Monuments of Wales reported to Mr Popham that:

'The building proved more fascinating than I had expected: the evidence remains for most of the timber frame in three walls, so only the façade is completely uncertain.'

The shop now became a Listed Building, but Mr Popham told the Press 'The front elevation needs propping and scaffolding will be going up.'

The *South Wales Argus* commented that the conservationists were still locked in battle with Kwik Save and Monmouth District Council over the way that their Listed Building was demolished almost overnight after being declared unsafe.

Not knowing what was going on behind the scenes, I printed new leaflets and we posted pickets outside the building.

Then a rotten, worm-eaten timber appeared in the shop window with a notice:

'AN EXAMPLE OF THE TIMBERS IN THIS BUILDING'

This was an extraordinary move by Mr Popham and a notice appeared on the outside of the window pointing out that if the timber had come from the Listed Building, then a criminal offence had been committed.

On the 18th October, I received the following letter from Mr Popham:

'Dear Mr Clarke,
Monmouth – 41 Monnow Street.
It came to my notice in the middle of last week that an illegal poster had been affixed to the front of these premises, indicating that we may have carried out an illegal activity in respect of this building.

The insinuation in the Notice was completely false and has been verified (sic) by an officer of Monmouth Borough Council.

On Friday 14th October, I removed this Notice in the presence of a policeman from the local station. I advised him that the Notice was a fly poster and was illegal, as far as I was concerned, and that I would expect him to give evidence in the future against any Society responsible for these Notices.

I would also draw your attention to the Notice in the News and Weekly Argus front page, Friday 14th October, that in future Monmouth Borough Council have authorised their chief technical officer to remove any fly posters in the town and I am today writing to him indicating that such a poster existed at No. 41, and that in my opinion, either your society and another society in Monmouth was responsible.

Any further unathorised (sic) posters attached to this building will be removed and a prosecution will be brought against those responsible.

In the case of the poster recently attached and removed, I consider it to be the work of either your society or one of the other two bodies in Monmouth Town.

Yours sincerely

J H POPHAM Project Controller

Dixons Commercial Properties Ltd., 84 Grosvenor Street, London W1X 9DF'

I telephoned Reg and Philomena in Bristol: 'The Lord has delivered him into our hands!'

We instructed solicitors and prepared to take legal action. The press had a field day – except for the *Monmouthshire Beacon,* which ignored the story.

I wondered what the bemused *'policeman from the local station'* thought of headlines like 'Developer in libel row over listed building'.

The chairman of Dixons Commercial Properties withdrew the allegations and gave a full public apology to all three organisations. We did not hear again from Mr Popham and the building was saved.

+ + +

Pickets outside a shop in Monnow Street in 2006 when a developer took advantage of the planners' failure to include a condition for archaeology

Although ancient Monmouth is much safer now – with planning guidelines to protect the archaeological resource – things still go amiss. Internal excavations in Monnow Street do not need planning consent unless the building is Listed. At 36 Monnow Street, for instance, in 2007, builders' trenches which were dug into medieval house floors were covered voluntarily by our society with kind permission of the owners. The developers did not have to allow a watching brief and we had no powers.

Sometimes the council fails to include a condition for archaeology in a planning consent and again these sites are covered by our Society although developers have sometimes taken advantage of this to trench sites out of the public view. The Society cannot watch the whole of the county, so works such as the large Barratt Homes development at Gwehelog, Usk, where finds of Roman date have been made, are taking place without an archaeologist on the site.

The Silver Trowel

During the Society's rescue work at 69-71 Monnow Street, a meeting of historians and museum and local government officials was held to see if the there was a way to support the efforts of the amateurs. It was suggested that the Society apply to the Board of Celtic Studies for a grant.

An application was submitted, telling of the discoveries in the street and setting out the current rescue work. The application was accompanied by letters from a number of eminent archaeologists who felt that the work of the group was of a high standard and that the Society was capable of seeing the project through to publication.

In June, 1988, the Society was informed that its application had been unsuccessful. The reasons were twofold. Firstly, much of the application was for equipment, for which the Board did not, as a rule, provide funding. Secondly, the Board was not prepared to fund rescue excavations which they regarded as the legitimate preserve of the regional professional Trust. The Board were, however, going to write to the District Council and the Ancient Monuments Board as the site 'seems to be of some importance' . . .

+   +   +

AS the rescue excavation at 69-71 Monnow Street was drawing to a close, the archaeology of another site came under threat. Nos 61-63, two doors up the street, which had been a veterinary clinic and at one time the town bus station, came up for redevelopment. The plan was for the total demolition of the frontage and the construction of a long building that would fill much of site. The regional unit, The Glamorgan-Gwent Archaeological Trust, had negotiated with the developers and it was agreed that they would carry out an archaeological excavation of the site prior to the development.

Before any work could begin, however, there was a change of ownership and the new developers had no commitment to allow, or pay for, any archaeological work. The Trust Director, Gareth Dowdell, telephoned me to say that the excavation was off and that there was no agreement for any archaeological work with the new developers.

But there had been enough destruction in Monmouth. The Society secretary, Philomena Jackson, rang the new owners, Property Enhancements of Bristol, who agreed to a site meeting.

At the meeting, it proved that the director and his team were people that we could talk to and who were willing to listen when the importance of the archaeology was explained to them.

The outcome was that the Society was invited to tender for the groundwork contract and, if successful, take over the site, archaeologically excavating the parts that they thought necessary. We would be responsible for all the main ground works, the levelling of the site and the laying of the drains and concrete foundations, together with the later consolidation of our own archaeological excavations.

The developers supplied copies of their plans and specifications for the building and its associated works and the group approached local sub-contractors and obtained quotations for the various parts of the contract.

Philomena put the whole thing together and a quotation was submitted to the company. The following week the Society was awarded the contract and given two weeks longer than was usual for the completion of the ground-works, otherwise penalty clauses and conditions would be the same as in any other building contract. Our society committee was very cautious but after a rather ferocious pep talk from Philomena, the contract was signed. This turned out to be the first occasion that an amateur archaeological group had tendered for, and been awarded, a groundwork contract for a building development.

+   +   +

We increased our insurance and went to work, employing an experienced supervisor who had been suggested by the developers but otherwise using local sub-contractors, especially JCB owner and driver Andrew Bell. Notices were posted on the frontage hoarding – *'This is the First Groundwork Contract to be carried out by Amateur Archaeologists in Britain'* – and the development and archaeological excavations were underway.

While we began the (archaeological) excavations on half of the street frontage, the Society's sub-contractors began the levelling to the rear of the site, under our direction. Part of the frontage was temporarily required for 'ready mix' concrete deliveries and for other lorries to enter and leave the site.

Results opened impressively on the street frontage with a large medieval house with an enormous fireplace and huge pieces of cut and moulded stone. The building had been constructed on a raised ground level which was similar to that recorded at 69-71 Monnow Street. On this occasion iron forging dross sandwiched between layers of clay, was used to raise the floors. The dross had been brought from local forges in two-wheeled hand carts which left defined tracks of slag pressed into the clay.

Earlier buildings were found, together with an alleyway between the burgages with silts left by floods in the late Middle Ages. There was a large medieval grindstone and an assemblage of medieval pottery and bones. A ditch running in line with the street was found behind the burgage plot. It seems to have been quickly filled after the late 13th century and may originally have been dug for drainage or even for flood alleviation purposes.

Later, on the street frontage, a wooden house was dated by Monmouth's earliest medieval pottery. The house lay beneath other buildings with similar sequences to those at Nos 69-71. But it was to the rear of the large house that one of the real excitements occurred.

Mr Boon, of the National Museum of Wales, once said that excavation above a certain level is innate – some people are 'naturals' and we were extremely fortunate to have one of the great amateur 'naturals' in the team – Reg Jackson of Bristol. It was Reg who was the cause of one of the memorable moments of the dig.

While drawing the plan of the structures, Reg decided that there was an anomaly in the plan of the buildings and he insisted on the removal of part of the structure. When this was done, an integral stone cesspit was revealed; this had been sealed from the world in the first half of the 14th century.

Many archaeologists get very excited about cesspits as the dark, wet conditions, with little oxygen, are ideal for the preservation of organic remains. Objects of wood or leather or the remains of plants, seeds and insects, that would normally have rotted away, can be remarkably well preserved.

The excavation of this cesspit produced pottery of the 14th century and then Vic Powles, who became the Society expert on cesspits, handed up a complete comb in pristine condition. We were enthusing about this, with everyone agreeing that they had never seen a complete one before, when Vic passed up a second, perfect example. It seems that if one dropped something down the lavatory, that's where it tended to stay.

A television camera team arrived on the site to record a news item on the dig. As I had given a radio interview earlier, I asked for a volunteer but there was none, everyone had an excuse for not going before the camera. As I walked to the street frontage, I turned and shouted: 'Why do I get all the dirty jobs?' and found myself looking down the cesspit at an unbelievably filthy Vic Powles who growled: 'You've got to be joking!'

It was Reg Jackson himself, taking turns down the cesspit with Chris Cooper, who found the first medieval glass bowl fragments. The vessel was made in Italy and is rare in medieval Britain, as glass vessels were very expensive and normally handled by jewellers. The type of glass recovered from the cesspit on this dig is normally only found on royal sites or in the homes of rich merchants, in places like London and Southampton. The sight of Reg Jackson, eyes twinkling, as he displayed the find would have confirmed the suspicion of many an archaeologist's wife, that archaeologists are still, at heart, little boys.

During this dig, the writer Adam Nicholson visited the site. He was researching for the book, *Prospects of England: Two thousand years seen through twelve English towns,* that he was writing with Peter Morter. Adam was impressed with Monmouth, and although realising he had crossed the Welsh border included the town in his book. He found us busy carrying out the groundwork contract at 61-63 Monnow Street; we were just tidying up the excavations at 69-71 Monnow Street and preparing to picket an uncooperative developer over the road.

Nicholson was appalled at the Kwik Save illegal demolition, as he was with other incidents in the town. In his book, he wrote:

This kind of story, if not quite so extreme, is common enough nowadays. Throughout the country developers are moving into small towns – especially those within reach of a motorway – with an eye on the extra money that people there now have, on the poor condition of much prime-site property, and on the actual inability of local authorities to interfere very much with their commercial interests.

'What makes Monmouth different from most towns is the ferocity of the local reaction to such goings-on. In most places there is a sliding and apathetic acceptance of the decisions taken far above people's heads. Not here . . .

+   +   +

But the battle was beginning to turn in Monmouth's favour. The Society found itself amongst the finalists for the Pitt-Rivers Award, sponsored by The Robert Kiln Trust, for the best voluntary work in archaeology. Some 25 members travelled to the lecture theatre of the Royal Geographical Society in London to hear the result.

The Society won the Award outright, beating the remarkable Hasholme Boat project, led by Peter Halkon.

The television personality Magnus Magnusson presented the Society with a fine ceramic plaque, together with a British Archaeological Awards Certificate and a cheque for £2,000.

But that was not all, by a long way, for the Society was also awarded the Legal & General 'Silver Trowel', for the greatest initiative in archaeology. This Award, previously won by the Jorvik Viking Centre, York, and The Mary Rose Trust, is the highest and most coveted of all the British Archaeological Awards.

The presentation of the 'Silver Trowel' in 1988

Before we left London for home, I found a telephone kiosk and rang my old primary school teacher, Keith Kissack (our President, Sox, being with us in London) and thanked him for putting us on the road to that night, all those years ago. He was silent for several moments.

Keith Kissack
            MBE, FSA
cuts the cake at his 90th
birthday party on the
18th November 2003

    Later the Monmouth Association hosted an Awards Celebration in The King's Head – Monmouth's premier hotel – which was attended by the Mayor and Town Council together with representatives of most local organisations and amateur and professional archaeological friends of the Society from around the country. It was a memorable evening.

Four generations of amateur archaeologists celebrate the 95th birthday of their Presdent, Mr. A.L. Sockett, MA, (Oxon) on the 13th March 2008.
Photograph: Desmond Pugh

247

In 1989, the Board of Celtic Studies funded a Research Assistant in Archaeology to study Welsh Medieval pottery. The aim of the project was to produce a type-series of medieval pottery in Wales.

Monmouth, with its outstanding pottery sequences, was the key to Welsh ceramic studies and work on the Monnow Street pottery was already underway. The Society had rescued the only complete sequences from Monnow Street and the most important one to date had come from Nos 69-71. This was the site which we had been struggling to excavate the previous year when we had applied to The Board of Celtic Studies for help and been turned down partly because we were doing the work of the professionals.

As the pottery was being used in our own study, we did not allow access.

The survey went ahead without the inclusion of the Monmouth pottery and most of our earlier publications were ignored.

Our failure to cooperate and provide access to the Monmouth collection was not appreciated and was commented upon in the Board's published report: "and those from the Monmouth area in the hands of the Monmouth archaeological Society. The latter is the only substantive omission, but is an important one as the Monmouth excavations have provided a unique stratified urban sequence from the late 11th century onwards, as well as evidence of early pottery production (Clarke 1991)".

(Papazian & Campbell, 1992)

As teenagers at Welsh Newton mill

Down the Dig

The County Archaeologist for Herefordshire recently produced a draft plan for the future of archaeology of the county. In supporting the Council of Europe's Valetta Convention plan to license all archaeological excavations he said that it would not be the end of amateur archaeology but it would stop 'digging for curiosity or recreation.'

IN 1956, Mr A.L. Sockett, who was the Classics master at Monmouth School, organised an archaeological excavation in the orchard of St James' House, just inside Monmouth's eastern town wall. Before the Second World War, Mr Sockett ('Sox') had dug with Kathleen Kenyon, the discoverer of ancient Jericho, on various sites, including the Roman towns of Wroxeter (Shropshire) and Leicester and in 1939 the Iron Age Fort on the Wrekin. After his war service and after coming to teach in Monmouth, he was again working with Dr Kenyon on the Herefordshire hill fort at Sutton Walls.

Throughout the summer of 1956, several of us – thirteen and fourteen-year-olds – helped on the dig at St James' House and by the autumn we had absorbed the 'Wheeler School' of archaeology. We were made 'Junior Honorary Members' of the Society – the *Monmouth & District Field Club and Antiquarian Society*.

Sox at Leicester in 1938 and
Sox on his 90th birthday, 13th March 2003, as seen by Geoff Webb

How fortunate we were. Our town, with its three river valleys, surrounded by verdant, wooded hills, was rich in natural treasures and below ground was another mysterious and undiscovered world.

Inspired, we explored the countryside, especially the caves and limestone cliffs of the Great Doward and other hills in our part of the Wye Valley – we lived exciting and adventurous lives. Amongst our discoveries was a cache of trenching tools which had been hidden by the headmaster of Monmouth School in a cave on the Seven Sisters Rocks above the Biblins. He had been digging on a Roman settlement on the Doward but had given up, so the abandoned tools became the property of the new *Monmouth & District Junior Archaeological Society* – the result of a sort of friendly declaration of independence. Sox may not have recognised the new equipment, but if he did, he never let on. The Society duly elected him President, and now, aged 95, happily he still is.

On one expedition we came across two men digging in the entrance to King Arthur's Cave – the Palaeolithic hyena den on the side of the Great Doward. We were welcomed by the archaeologists to help in the digging and carrying buckets of breccias to the tip while their two wives avidly followed horse racing on a portable radio. It turned out that the leader of the dig was A.M. ApSimon, the famous prehistorian, who had received permission to dig in the cave some thirty years before. This caused a stir, for in the meanwhile the site had become a scheduled Ancient Monument and Sox came along with us the following weekend to explain the situation, also mentioning that the local Brigadier, who claimed to own the cave, was furious.

We also travelled by bus, with our haversacks over our shoulders to far away places like Sutton Walls where the hill fort was being quarried out and filled with rubbish and toxic waste. We ate our sandwiches on the remains of the ramparts and collected 'duck stamped' Iron Age pottery from below the quarry face.

We acquired pushbikes and joined Norman Bridgewater of the *Archenfield Archaeological Group* on his excavations in southern Herefordshire. We dug with him on the Roman Villa at Huntsham, in the great loop of the Wye, and for some years spent Sundays on the medieval moated homestead of Wallingstones near Llangarron. There, one summer's day, a visitor sat on a trench edge, apparently lost in thought, but then came over and asked if I realised that I was digging two layers at once! He gently explained where I was going wrong. Later, I learned that his name was Graham Webster.

It was through Norman Bridgewater that I joined the excavations conducted by Stan Stanford in northern Herefordshire – on the Roman fort at Leintwardine and on the Iron Age hill fort at Croft Ambrey. Most of the volunteers were students of my own age who had their summers free while I, as an apprentice printer, had but two weeks holiday a year and thereby missed the visit of Sir Mortimer Wheeler to the Ambrey. It is perhaps no surprise that many of those who dug with Stan Stanford went on to make their mark in archaeology. Of the now famous ones I remember are Professor Andrew Fleming (taught by Sox at Monmouth School), Professor Stephen Green, Doctor David Whitehouse, Doctor Ruth Whitehouse and Brian Philp (that great champion of Reculver, who gave me a lift home to Monmouth on the back of his motorbike). It is still a pleasure to recall the happy times, living in bell tents at Leintwardine and in the stables at Croft Castle and to recall the unsurpassed views from the defences of Croft Ambrey and those unforgettable barbecues in the castle grounds. I will always remember Stan Stanford and his family as some of the kindest people in archaeology.

But that was a little in the future.

One day, in the spring of 1957, three of us were exploring the Mally Brook which rises at Welsh Newton, just over the English border, and enters the Wye a few miles downstream, in Wales. Lined with alders and willows, the brook meanders through the woodlands and pastures of a beautiful little valley where the small stream, which as boys we could easily jump across, had fed at least five medieval mills.

On the land of Newton Court Farm there was a leat running beside the hedges and ending between raised banks with a drop down to a marshy area, where kingcups and wood anemones grew, overlooked by hazel trees springing from the higher ground. We had often seen this spot, where the brook tumbled over stones, and had wondered if it was the site of an ancient watermill. Armed with the plundered trenching tools, we dug a small hole into the bank above the marsh, and almost immediately turned over part of a medieval crested ridge tile. That tile, shining green and orange in the sunlight, is an enduring memory which almost brings back the smell of the soil and the thrill of the unearthing. The Valetta Convention would perhaps have robbed that boy of that experience, a moment which has lived for a lifetime and which, with the help of others, was to have a profound effect upon the heritage of our town.

We immediately walked up to the farm where we met the farmer, old Mr Price, and asked if we could dig in his field. Born in the rugged mountains of middle Wales, he simply said, 'Go on boys, that's alright'. We were there for five years. No farmer has ever refused us permission to dig on his land or to walk his ploughed fields.

Now, in another century, I look back and recall the pleasure of that excavation and how it was the foundation of my life in archaeology; how it helped to develop skills of observation and interpretation that were to be essential in the future. A boyhood expedition grew into the adventure of a lifetime.

But that is not all, for without Monmouth's amateurs, the remains beneath Monnow Street would probably have been doomed to destruction without record – they may not even have been recognised at all. I feel that digging is essential if one is to develop the skills to recognise the importance, or otherwise, of historic remains, to understand the archaeological record and to increase our knowledge of the past.

Many of us never lose the thrill of exploration, discovery, recording and interpretation while 'curiosity', apparently despised by some, has been the inspiration for many of the greatest discoveries and achievements of mankind. Surely, above all, archaeology is a sign of civilised society.

Even now, half a century on, celandines in the spring sunshine bring memories of the grassy mounds above the marsh, beside the Mally Brook. And on some summer evenings, I am again a boy, digging with a trowel in the rich, Devonian-red earth, as the sounds of the bells of St Mary's drift across the fields, down to the site of Newton Mill.

Summer 2007. Four (or five) generations of diggers at Trelech. Sox (left) and Keith, President and Vice-President, both in their 95th year, seated in the centre

ACKNOWLEDGEMENTS

Over the past fifty-odd years there have been so many people who have worked with or helped Monmouth Archaeological Society in so many ways (donations, digging, writing, picketing etc.) that it is inevitable that many will have been missed from this list. To those, I apologise, with the excuse of advancing age – and a bus pass to prove it.

Financially, the Society is greatly indebted to the Robert Kiln Trust and Monmouth Historical & Educational Trust for their generous donations towards publication. The remarkable support given to the society by local developers Glamorgan Investments introduced around a million members of the public to the archaeology of Monmouth. Also we are very grateful to the Congress of Independent Archaeologists and the organisations, businesses and hundreds of people who have made contributions during our excavations – especially those in Monnow Street. Thanks also to Mary Hughes and Bob at The Monmouthshire Beacon, Andy Sherewell at the Free Press and Bob Smyth and Ted Lamb at The Review.

It is hazardous to attempt to name names – but here goes – with grovelling apologies to those I leave out (probably some very important ones) – Jeremy Akerman, Jenny and Mrs Alderton, Stephen and Miranda Aldhouse-Green, Peter Alexander-Fitzgerald, Mike Anthony, Joan Baker, Mrs Badham and Jonathan, John and Jan Baldwin, Clive, Kim and Erys Barrett, Nick Barton, Derek Bean, Jane and John Bray, John and Jean Beare, Gerald Beaudett, Edward Besley; David Bellamy, Col Bellhouse, Billy Biggs and family, Roger Birchall, Charles and Mary Boase, George and Mrs Boon, Brian Bowen, Joy Bowen and family, Richard Brewer, Norman Bridgewater, Jenny and Ken Britnel, Ken Brown, Tim and Kirsty Buckland, Glyn Buckle, Barry Burnham, Annette Burton, Sue Byrne, Rob Campbell, Peter Carpenter, Ray Caple, Robin Caulkett, Sue, Ted and Melanie Chivers, Brian and Hilary Churches, Jonathan Clark, Elwyn Clarke, Hazel Clarke, Reg Clarke, Rhodri Clarke, Gordon Clissold, Ian Colwell, Stan and Margaret Coates, Chris Cooper, Frank and Sybil Cook, Julian Cotton, Paul Courtney, Canon James Coutts, Peter Crew, Giles Dawkes, Bobby Davies, Jeff Davies, Jerry Davies of the Gwent Detector Club, John Davies, Peter Davies, Paul and John Davies, Bob Daw, Paul Dawson, Terry and Jean Dauncey, Habib Dingle, Ian, Stuart and Ray Donald, Christina Dodwell, Gareth Dowdell, Becks Doyle, Phil and Anna Dunlop, Tony Dunn, Bev Durn, Hew Edwards, John Egan, Mike and Anne Eggleton, Dave Evans, Harry and Marion Evans and family, Hew Evans, John and Margaret Evans, Richard Evans, John Everard, Kevan Fadden, Neil Faulkner, Graham and Jenny Frecknall, Marj Feryok, Richard Fisher and family, Andrew Fleming, Bob and Joan Flynn, Sue Fox, Kath Frances, Liz Freeman, Roy and Diana Friendship-Taylor, Sue Gaylord, Doug Gentles, Ken and Mrs Gibbons, Martin and Philomena Goodall, Ken Goodwin, Tony and Frances Green and family, Charles Griffin and family, Bill and Doreen Griffiths, Phil and Richie Grindle, Neil and Anne Gunter, Bill Harris, Annette and families, Colin Harris, Dave Hancocks, Lyn Harper, David Harrison, Phil Hayter, Andrew Helme, Charles Hill, John Hines, Edward Holland, David and Mary Hopson, Ray Howell, Paul and Pat Humberstone, Tim Hunt and family, Rob Ixer, Dave and Jan Jemmett, Gareth Jenkins (Bristol), Gareth Jenkins (Monmouth), Uma Jenkins, Clive Jones, Kat King, Phil Kings, Derek and Mrs Jones, Bob Jones, Gwenllian Jones and family, Reg Jackson, Barry James, Russell James, Alan and Charlotte

Jones, Derek and Mrs Jones, T.F.R. Jones, Walter Keeler, Keith and Audrey Kissack and family, Jeremy Knight and Annie, Paul and Jane Knight, Jane Whitworth, Dominic Larkin, Martin Lawler, Anne Leaver, Karl Lee, John Lewis, Mark Lewis, Richard Liddell, Francis Lynch-Llewellyn, Bill Manning, Ian and Lyn MacFarlane, Graham Makepiece, Andy Marvell, Phil and Mrs Matthew, Neil Maylan, Geoff Mein, John Meredith, Dave, Jane and Robin Middleton, Sue Miles, Owen and Mrs Morgan, Pat Mosely, Brian Milford, Brendon Murphy, Nigel Nailing, Stuart Neal, Teddy Nicolls, Pete O'Connor, Rachael O'Shaughnessy, Frank Olding, Vernon Oxley, Canon Richard Pain, Charles Parry, Alan and Mrs Probert, Shelagh Shaw, Ken Palmer, Sue Parkinson, Barbara Parkinson, Jim Parry, Julian Parry, John Perryman, Brian Philp, Neil Phillips, Mike Ponsford, John and Mrs Porter-Davison, Richard and Esmie Philips, Alan and Mrs Poulter, Gerwyn Powell, Phil Powell, Vic and Sue Powles, Three generations of Bill Price's family from Newton Court Farm and Skenfrith, Dave and Marleen Pritchard, George Probyn, Ken and Marion Prosser, Geoff and Mrs Pugh, Pam Pugh, Brenda Purcell, Roger Pye, Annie Rainsbury, Keith Ray, Sian Rees, Mark Redknap, Sue Rice and Mrs Ruck, Mike Rumbold, George Russen, Ruth and Terry Richardson, Phil Riches, Owen and Ros Rockin-Jones, Eddy and Mrs Rogers, Lara Salha, Del Samuel, Andrew Selkirk, Arthur Selway, Andy Sherwill, Ron and Jennifer Shoesmith, Colin and Anthea Sinclair, John Sleigh, Hannah Sloman, John Smith, Charles Smart, Graham Sprackling, Anne Sterry, Don and Mrs Stroud, Sox Sockett and family, Stan and Yvonne Stanford, Richard Stone, David and Mrs Stratten, Ellie Taylor, Elizabeth Taylor, Terry and Audrey Tapper, Felicity Taylor, Brian Thomas and Joan Thomas (Joan Fleming-Yates), Geraint Thomas, Hendle Thomas, Howard Thomas, Mair Thomas, Sheila Thorneycroft, Bob and Frances Trett, Anna Tribe, Martin Tuck, Rick Turner, Mark Turner, Roy and Gwen Turner, Keith Underwood, John Van Laun, Alan Vince, Chris Waite, Richard Waller and family, Bryan and Mark Walters, Joan Ward, Jane Whitworth, Charles and Sandra Ward, Brent Watkins, Alf Webb, Geoff and Diane Webb, Peter and Janet Webster, Anne Were and family, Richard Wheelock, John and Dick Wheelock and families, Melfyn and Margaret White, Eric Wilkes, David Williams, Betty Williams, Sheila and Bill Williams, Gwyn Williams, Jan Wills, Alan and Mrs Wilson, Julia Wilson, Stuart Wilson and his family and Trelech team of diggers, Dave Wood and family. Not forgetting the diggers of the archaeological groups in Chepstow, Forest of Dean, Gloucester, Usk, Hereford and Gloucester.

Thanks also to the staff of the National Library of Wales, Aberystwyth; the County Records Office, Cwmbran; The National Museum of Wales; Abergavenny, Caldicot, Chepstow and Monmouth Museums; Hereford Museum and the staff of the Curatorial Section of the Glamorgan-Gwent Archaeological Trust.

GLOSSARY

A

Alluvium.   Silts or other material left by floods

Anaerobic.   Without oxygen

Archaeological Evaluation.   Site assessment through trial excavation and documentary research

Archaeological Resource.   Informative archaeological remains

Archaeological Watching Brief.   Archaeological cover during groundworks

Archaeomagnetic.   Remnant magnetism

Archenfield.   Originally 'Erging', the Celtic commot or kingdom of southern Herefordshire – between the Monnow and the Wye

Assarting.   Clearance of woodland for settlement or grazing

Aumoniere.   A medieval purse

B

Baulk.   Section of ground left between trenches

Berm.   A level or sloping area between a rampart and a ditch

Blestium.   The 3rd century name for Roman Monmouth

Bloomery iron furnace.   A small primitive iron smelting furnace where iron ore was mixed with charcoal and worked with a hand bellows

Bloomery iron slag.   Furnace waste

Burgage.   Medieval property within a borough usually house and land

C

Carinated.   Angled stylistic ridge dividing vessel body

CBA.   Council for British Archaeology

Chalybeate.   Iron rich water

Cinder.   Another term for iron slag

Clamp kiln.   Technique of firing pottery without a structural kiln

Complex rouletting.   Decoration impressed onto soft clay with a wheel

Concrete raft.   Base for building construction without strip foundation trenches

Conservation area.   Historically or environmentally significant area protected by planning law

Context.   Chronological position of layer or artefact

Copper-speckled.   Pottery bearing copper added to a lead glaze

Core.   The inner part of pottery fabric seen in section, also the inner stone structure of a bell mould

Cotswold Ware.   Pottery/tile with oolitic limestone inclusions

Crucible.   Vessel used in metal working

Curfew.   Pottery vessel to cover a domestic fire overnight

D

Dark Ages.   Post Roman, especially the 5th century

Dark earth.   Layer (context) separating Roman from Medieval layers

Dendrochronology.   Dating technique of studying growth rings in wood

Dross.   Waste product from iron smelting or (especially) smithing

E

Early Medieval.   From 5th century up to the Norman invasion

Encaustic floor tile.   Tile with inlaid clay decoration and glaze

Ergyn.   The Celtic kingdom of southern Herefordshire – between the Monnow and the Wye later called Archenfield

Evaluation.   Archaeological trial excavations and documentary research

F

Facade.   The exterior face of a building

Finial.   Decorative pinnacle on roof ridge

Flavian.   Dynasty of Roman emperors from AD 69-96

G

GGAT. Glamorgan-Gwent Archaeological Trust Ltd

Geophysical Survey. Data obtained by means of geophysical methods including seismic, magnetic, electromagnetic and gravity techniques

H

Ham Green Ware. Pottery produced in the Ham Green kilns at Bristol, during the mid 12th-mid 13th century

Hospice. Medieval building where religious orders took in the sick and dying

Humus. Decomposed organic matter in soil; topsoil

I

Inclusions. Temper (sand etc.) added to wet clay for making pottery

Intrusive. Artefact of later date in earlier context

Iron-enriched clay. Clay with iron added to produce dark colours when glazed

Iron-free clay. Clay without iron, producing white colour when glazed

Iron-rich clay. Clay with iron producing dark colours when glazed

K

Kiln Waster. Vessel damaged in kiln during firing

L

Laminated. Pottery separated into thin layers by heat

League. About three miles

Leat. Trench bringing water to a mill wheel

Levee. A natural riverside embankment

Louver. A pottery structure on top of the roof through which smoke escapes

M

Malvern Ware. Pottery/tile with metamorphic rock inclusions

Medieval. From the Norman invasion to 1500

Mesolithic. Middle Stone Age, 10000BC–5000BC

Metamorphic rock. Rock formed under great volcanic pressure

Microlith. Very small flint tools set into wood or bone handles to make composite tools or harpoons

Minety Ware. Medieval pottery made in North Wiltshire

Motte. Man-made earth mound for timber castle

Murage Grant. A special tax that boroughs could levy, with royal licence, on condition that the proceeds be put towards the building or repair of town walls

N

Natural. Geological deposits undisturbed by man

Neanderthal. Species of primitive man

Neolithic. New Stone Age, 5000BC–2000BC

Norman. Period after the Invasion by William, Duke of Normandy in 1066

O

Oblique arrowhead. Single barbed flint arrowhead

Oxidised. Red/orange colour pottery fabric produced through oxidising atmosphere in a kiln

P

Palaeolithic. The Old Stone Age, 50000–10000BC

Pancheon. Large shallow earthenware vessel usually associated with dairy products

Pile   A hollow column drilled into the ground and filled with steel and concrete

Pommel. Decorative knob on the handle of a sword

Post-medieval. After 1500

Post-Roman. After the 4th century

Pre-Flavian. Roman period prior to Emperor Vespasian AD69

Prehistoric. Time prior to historical records; pre-Roman

R

Rampart. Defensive embankment

Redcliffe ware. Pottery made in Redcliffe, Bristol, after mid 13th century

Reduced. Grey/black colour of pottery fabric produced by lack of oxygen in reducing atmosphere of a kiln

Residual. Material not in its original context

Ridge tile. Tiles that top the apex of the roof

Robber trench. Outline of wall where stone has been removed

Roman. Period between AD43–400

S

Saddle quern stone. Curved stone used in conjunction with a rubbing stone to grind corn into flour.

Saggar. A protective case or pot of fired clay which protects pots during firing

Samian ware. Type of Roman pottery made in Gaul

Saintonge. Pottery from South West France, 13th century and later

Saxon. Pre-Norman

Scoriae. Iron slag/dross

Sediment. Deposit settled from water

Sion Cent. Legendary Welsh wizard, also known as Jack o' Kent

Slag. Residue from iron working

Sleeper beam. Wooden beam used as foundation for a building

Slip-ware. Earthenware, where a liquid clay decorating process has been used

Spindle whorl. Weight at the end of a spindle, made from lead, bone, stone or pottery

Split-rod handle. Round sectioned jug handle slashed lengthwise

Strap handle. Flattened jug handle

Stratification. Successive layers of deposits

T

Temper. Grit etc added to clay in potter production

Tesserae. Small cubes of various coloured stones used to make Roman mosaic

Tithe barn. Type of barn used in the Middle Ages for storing the tithes – a tenth of the farm's produce

Tyg. Cup with three or more handles

U

Unslaked lime. Lime that is calcined (reduced to quicklime)

V

Vexillation fort. A military base normally between 20 and 30 acres in size, containing legionary and auxiliary battle units

W

Waster. Pottery damaged during firing in the kiln

BIBLIOGRAPHY

Bagnall-Oakeley, 1885. *Archaeologia Cambrensis.*

Bagnall-Oakeley, 1896. The Fortifications of Monmouth. *Proceedings of the Monmouthshire and Caerleon Antiquarian Association.*

Barton KJ, 1963, A Medieval Kiln at Ham Green, Bristol, *Trans. Bristol & Glos. Archaeol. Soc.* **82**, 95-126.

Barton KJ, 1964, The Excavation of a medieval bastion at St. Nicholas Almshouses, King Street, Bristol *Medieval Archaeol.* **8**, 184-212.

Besley, E 1988. Edward Besley of NMW kindly reported on 3/Find from 192: Fragment, perhaps derived from a cut halfpenny. Surface corroded away, but DII and tip of sceptre visible on obverse and arm of cross fleury on reverse: William II, cross fleury and piles type (BMC V), mint and moneyer uncertain, c.1098-1100.

Besley, E., Recent Coin Hoards from Wales 1985-1992, *The British Numismatic Journal* **63** (1993; pub. 1994) 84-85 (No. 1).

Birkeland, PW, 1984. *Soils and Geomorphology.* New York: Oxford University Press.

Bradney, JA, 1904. *A History of Monmouthshire,* Vol. **I**, pt. II: The Hundred of Abergavenny. London.

Bridgewater, NP, 1960 Ancient buried roads in South Herefordshire: Part I, *Trans. Woolhope Naturalists' Field Club,* **36** (ii), 218-27.

Casey, DA, 1931, Lydney Castle, *The Antiquaries Journal* Vol X1, No. 3, 240-261 (pottery 255-261 and plate XXXIV.

Chester Jordan, W, 1996, The Great Famine – Northern Europe in the early 14th century, Princeton University Press, Princeton, New Jersey, p24.

Clark, Dr A, Archaeomagnetic date of 1070-1130 at 60% confidence level at 69-71 Monnow Street.

Clarke, S, 1968. Pitman's Corner, Monmouth (58) in Davies, JL & Livens, RG, *Arch. in Wales,* **8,** 24-25.

Clarke, S, 1983, A Technical Note, *Medieval & Later Pottery in Wales,* **6**, 31-35.

Clarke, S, Jackson, R & P, Jemmett, D & J, 1984. Pottery from a post-medieval kiln at Dixton, Gwent, *Medieval & Later Pottery in Wales,* **7**, 9-24.

Clarke, S, Jackson, R & P, Jemmett, D & J, 1985. Post-Medieval Potteries in North Gwent, *Medieval & Later Pottery in Wales,* **8**, 1985.

Clarke, S 1986, *Monmouth Archaeology,* 18, Monmouth.

Clarke, S 1987, Decorated Monnow Valley Ware, in B. Vyner & S. Wrathmell (eds.), *Studies in Medieval & Later Pottery in Wales presented to J.M. Lewis,* Cardiff.

Clarke, S, Jackson, R & P, 1987, 75-77 Monnow Street, Monmouth, *Arch in Wales,* **27**, 29-31.

Clarke, S, Jackson, R & P, 1987, The North Gwent Potteries: An Assessment of the Evidence, in Vyner, B & Wrathmell, S, *Studies in Medieval and Later Pottery in Wales presented to J.M. Lewis,* Cardiff, 53-73.

Clarke, S, Jackson, R & P, Jemmett, D & J, 1989, Grosmont Well Farm (304), in Gaimster, DRM; Margeson, S & Barry, T, Medieval Britain & Ireland in 1988, *Med. Arch.,* **13**, 1989. Also *Archaeology in Wales,* **29**, 1989.

Clarke, S, 1990, Twelfth-Century Complex Rouletting from the Malvern Kilns, *Medieval Ceramics* **14**, 57.

Clarke, S, 1991. The Origins of Medieval Pottery in South-East Wales, *Medieval Ceramics,* **15**, 29-36.

Clarke, S, Jackson, R & P, 1992, At Goldwire Lane School, Overmonnow (425), in Nenk, BS; Margeson, S and Hurley, M, Eds.: Medieval Britain & Ireland in 1991, *Medieval Archaeol,* **36**, 303.

Clarke, S, & Jackson, R & P, 1992, The Discovery of the site of a Medieval Encaustic Floor Tile Kiln at Monmouth, Gwent, *Medieval Ceramics,* **16**, 72-76.

Clarke, S, 1995, The Monmouth Hoard of AEthelred II Coins, *Mon. Antiq.* **XI**, 1995, 55-56.

Clarke, S & Shoesmith, R, 1997, Industrial Tintern *Rescue News* **72,** 1997, 1-2.

Clarke, S & Wilson, J, *Arch. in Wales,* 37, 1997, p 107 and SM record, MAS report: The George Hotel, Brecon, 1997).

Clarke, S & Bray, J, 2002a, 43 Drybridge Street, *Arch. in Wales,* **42,** 133-4.

Clarke, S & Bray, J, 2002b, Abergavenny, Oldcastle, *Arch. in Wales,* **42,** 125.

Clarke, S & Bray, J, 2001, A Medieval Pottery Kiln at Isca Grange, Caerleon, *Arch. in Wales,* **41,** 2001, 81-83.

Clarke, S & Bray, J, 2004, *Arch. in Wales* 44, 2004, 93-95, and W.B. Report MA55.03.

Cooper Neal, S. 1929, An Ancient Cottage Pottery in Upton Bishop Parish, *Trans. Woolhope Nat. Field Club,* Vol. for 1927-29, Pt. III, 207-8.

Coxe, W, 1801. *An Historical Tour Through Monmouthshire.* London.

Darwin, C, 1881, *The Formation of Vegetable Mould, through the Action of Worms, with Observations on Their Habits.* Murray.

Dixon, P and Crowdy, A., 2001. A medieval pottery kiln, possible workshop at Eshott, Northumberland, *Med. Ceramics,* **25,** 2001, 27-44.

Dawson, DP, Jackson, RG and Ponsford, MW, 1972. Medieval Kiln Wasters from St. Peter's Church, Bristol, *Trans. Bristol & Gloucestershire Arch. Soc.,* **91**: 159-67.

Eidt, RC, 1985, Theoretical and practical considerations in the analysis of anthrosols. In *Archaeological Geology,* G. Rapp & J.A. Gifford (Eds.), 155-190. New Haven: Yale University Press.

Eginton, H. 1883, Kiln for ancient church tiles found near Malvern, *Gentleman's Magazine* **103**, 162.

Glamorgan-Gwent Archaeological Trust Ltd. (undated) *Monmouth, Gwent: Interim Report on Excavation at 83-85 Monnow Street,* Swansea, 6.

Heighway, C, 1983, The East and North Gates of Gloucester *Western Arch. Trust,* Excavation Monograph No. 4.

Hurst, JG 1962-3 White Castle and the dating of medieval pottery, *Medieval Archaeol.,* **VI-VII,** 149-55.

Kissack, KE 1974, *Medieval Monmouth,* 73-74, Monmouth Historical & Educational Trust.

Kissack, KE, 1975, 290-293, *Monmouth, The Making of a County Town,* Phillimore, 1975.

Knight, JK 1991 The pottery from Montgomery Castle, *Medieval & Later Pottery In Wales,* **12,** 1-100.

Knight J.K. The name 'Monnow Valley Ware' was originally suggested by Jeremy Knight and is now in general use.

Lewis, J, 1976. *Welsh Medieval Paving Tiles* Nat. Mus. of Wales, Cardiff.

Maylan, N, 1999. *St. John the Baptist Church, Oldcastle : Brief for an Archaeological Evaluation.* Glamorgan-Gwent Archaeological Trust.

Leach, P, 2003. Excavations at St. Lawrence's, Bayfield, Chepstow, in Burton, AM, Ed. *The Monmouthshire Antiquary,* **19,** 21-70.

Lewis, E. (ed), *Custom and ceramics: essays presented to Kenneth Barton* 81-103, Wickham.

McDonald G, 1991, The Chaxhill Chronicles–2000BC to AD1990, Private publication, The Rowans, Chaxhill, Westbury on Severn, Glos.

Mayes, P, 1967, In Selkirk, A., *Current Archaeology,* **4,** 1967, 94-97.

Moorhouse, SA, 1981, The medieval pottery industry and its markets, *CBA Research Report,* **40** : Medieval Industry : DW Crossly, DW, Ed, 96-119.

Musty J, 1968, in Talbot, EJ, *Post-Med. Arch.,* Vol. **2,** 119-139.

Musty, J, 1974, Medieval pottery Kilns in *Pottery from Excavations: Studies presented to Gerald Clough Dunning,* edited Evison, VI, Hodges, H and Hurst, JG, New York, 41-65.

Musty, J 1973, A preliminary account of a medieval pottery industry at Minety, N Wiltshire, *Wiltshire Archaeol. Natur. Hist. Mag.,* **68,** 79-88.

Orton, C, Tyers P, and Vince, A, 1993. *Pottery in Archaeology :* Cambridge Manuals in Archaeology.

Papazian, C & Campbell, E 1992, *Medieval Pottery and Roof Tiles in Wales AD1100-1600.* Medieval and Later Pottery in Wales, **13,** 3.

Ponsford, M.W. 1991 Dendrochronological dates from Dundas Wharf, Bristol, and the dating of Ham Green and other medieval pottery, in Lewis, E. (ed), *Custom and ceramics: essays presented to Kenneth Barton* 81-103, Wickham.

Rouse, D. 1999. *St. John the Baptist Church, Oldcastle, Monmouthshire : An Archaeological Watching Brief.* Hereford Archaeology Series 429. Archaeological Investigations Ltd.

Scott, A, 1959. Gislingham, Suffolk (TM 084 723) Medieval sherds from two apparent clamp-kiln floors were exposed during ploughing at Ivy House Farm. The pottery is now in Ipswich Museum (958/224) in Wilson, D.M. & Hurst, J.G., 1959. Med. Britain in 1958, *Med. Arch,* **3,** 325.

Scott-Garrett, C, 1958, Littledean Camp, *Trans. Bristol & Glos. Archaeol. Soc.* Vol. **77,** 48-60 (pottery 54-57).

Selkirk, A, *Current Archaeology,* No. **4**. 1967.

Selkirk, A 1989, 1994, *Current Archaeology,* No. **115,** 254-257 and No. **138,** 231-237.

Shoesmith, R, 1980. *Hereford City Excavations, Volume 1, Excavations at Castle Green,* Council for British Archaeology Research Report **36**. London: Council for British Archaeology.

Shoesmith, R, 1981. *Hereford City Excavations,* Volume 2, *Excavations on and close to the defences,* Council for British Archaeology Research Report **46**. London.

Shoesmith, R, 1985. *Hereford City Excavations*, Volume 3, The Finds, Council for British Archaeology Research Report **56**. London: Council for British Archaeology.

Sockett, AL, 1960, The Monmouth District in Antiquity : An Archaeological survey, *Memorials of Monmouth,* **10,** 17.

Soulsby, I, 1983, *The Towns of Medieval Wales: a study of their history, archaeology and early topography,* 1983, Chichester, Phillimore.

Swinnerton, HM, 1955, The Medieval tiles of Lenton Priory, *Trans. Thoroton Soc.* **59,** 84-97.

Talbot, EJ, unpublished M.A. thesis, Cardiff.

Talbot, EJ, 1968, Welsh Ceramics: A Documentary and Archaeological Survey, *Post-Med. Arch.* **2,** 122-127.

Taylor, E, 1991, An Early Motte and Enclosure at Upton Bishop *Trans. Woolhope Naturalists' Field Club* Vol. **XLVII,** Pt. I, 24-27).

Thomas, A & Boucher, A, (Eds.) 2002. *Hereford City Excavations,* Volume **4,** *Further Sites and Evolving Interpretations.* 65-92. Logaston Press.

Thomas, C, 1959, Imported pottery in Dark-Age Western Britain, *Medieval Archaeology,* **3,** 89-111.

Vince, AG 1977, The Medieval and Post-Medieval Ceramic Industry of the Malvern Region: The Study of a Ware and its Distribution, in D.P.S. Peacock (ed), *Pottery and Early Commerce,* 257-305.

Vince, A.G. 1983. Part 2: The Ceramic Finds, R. Shoesmith (Ed.), *Hereford City Excavations*, Volume 3, The Finds, CBA Research Report **56**: 34-83. London: Council for British Archaeology.

Vince, AG, 1980, A Monmouth-type floor tile from Llanthony Priory, Gwent, in D.H. Evans Excavations at Llanthony Priory, Gwent, *Monmouthshire Antiq.* **IV,** 20-21.

Vince, A.G., !985, Part 2: The Ceramic Finds, in R. Shoesmith, *Hereford City Excavations* Vol. 3: *The Finds,* CBA Research Report 56, 34-83.

Wrathmell, S, 1981, A medieval pottery kiln and wasters at Penhow, Gwent, *Med. & Later Pottery in Wales,* **4,** 1-7.